AF798527

School(house) Design and Curriculum in Nineteenth Century America

Joseph da Silva

School(house) Design and Curriculum in Nineteenth Century America

Historical and Theoretical Frameworks

palgrave
macmillan

Joseph da Silva
Bristol Community College
Tiverton, RI, USA

ISBN 978-3-030-08738-8 ISBN 978-3-319-78586-8 (eBook)
https://doi.org/10.1007/978-3-319-78586-8

© The Editor(s) (if applicable) and The Author(s) 2018
Softcover re-print of the Hardcover 1st edition 2018
This work is subject to copyright. All rights are solely and exclusively licensed by the Publisher, whether the whole or part of the material is concerned, specifically the rights of translation, reprinting, reuse of illustrations, recitation, broadcasting, reproduction on microfilms or in any other physical way, and transmission or information storage and retrieval, electronic adaptation, computer software, or by similar or dissimilar methodology now known or hereafter developed.
The use of general descriptive names, registered names, trademarks, service marks, etc. in this publication does not imply, even in the absence of a specific statement, that such names are exempt from the relevant protective laws and regulations and therefore free for general use.
The publisher, the authors, and the editors are safe to assume that the advice and information in this book are believed to be true and accurate at the date of publication. Neither the publisher nor the authors or the editors give a warranty, express or implied, with respect to the material contained herein or for any errors or omissions that may have been made. The publisher remains neutral with regard to jurisdictional claims in published maps and institutional affiliations.

Cover image © TimAbramowitz/ E+/ gettyimages

This Palgrave Macmillan imprint is published by the registered company Springer Nature Switzerland AG
The registered company address is: Gewerbestrasse 11, 6330 Cham, Switzerland

I am particularly indebted to my family for their sustained support and love. This book is dedicated to my daughter Shantel, son Aaron, and son-in-law Danny. Their support and inspiration have been foundational. A special dedication goes out to my wife Fatima whose commitment to this project has been unwavering and without her support this project would not have been possible. In addition, this book is dedicated to my mother Elzira and my father José for their unconditional love and care through all my life's journeys and to my sisters Filomena and Maria for believing in me and encouraging me every step of the way. Finally, this book is a tribute to my grandmother Filomena, who sacrificed much to make our family's dream possible in the United States.

Foreword

Dr. da Silva vividly illustrates why public school facility planning needs frontline educators and communities integrally engaged in the planning and design of public schools. Dr. da Silva explains how the dominant and competing educational ideologies, philosophies, and culture drive key aspects of the design of school buildings.

The tensions of state, economy, and culture that he cites are no less in play now than they were in the nineteenth century and so his exploration and study are strongly relevant today. The innovation that is the foundation of this country is not that Americans do not have within us a nature different than those described in a Hobbesian society—nasty, brutish, and short—but that democratic rights of free expression, assembly, due process, and elective government would give Americans a better way to navigate the tensions of power, money, and human nature which are embedded in the state, economy, and culture.

The design arts and building sciences and trades are at the essence of school facilities design and construction. However, the decisions about the location, design, care, and utilization of our built environment for public school spaces requires the application of our democratic tools and innovations. When there is respect for the perspectives, aspirations, and input from traditionally disenfranchised communities—low income, non-English speaking, female, and minority—the educational facility planning and design processes will build social capital and facilitate a shared educational mission and objectives.

School(house) Design and Curriculum in Nineteenth Century America: Historical and Theoretical Frameworks is a must read for educators, designers, and civic leaders, alike, who work in the nexus space around education, community, and equity. The complexity of planning and designing school places, most of which have endured major governmental, economic, educational, and cultural movements and reforms, requires our collective intelligence and humility. This book is a framework that will help.

Washington, DC, USA Mary Filardo

Preface

My personal and professional life has long been predicated on the politics of "dwelling" in American schools. As a young student—a working-class immigrant to Massachusetts in the 1960s—my schooling refused to let me think and act in particular ways. Abjecting my academic interests and Portuguese tongue, my education quickly silenced my sense of self. Today, this history ignites my professional practice as a school architect and policy-maker; daily, my work is fraught with questions about what ways of thinking and being a school might nurture or foreclose. What curricula might a particular kind of architecture support? Which ones might it thwart? What kind of citizens might a certain curriculum, delivered in a specific spatiality, rear? In taking up these questions, I have to consider the context in which a school will be built; the history and norms of the culture in which it will inevitably intervene. To figure out what it will mean to dwell in a school design that has yet to be built, I always have to first consider what, exactly, it means for students to dwell in American schools today.

Surely, whatever "dwelling" in our schools means today is deeply tied to what it has meant to do so historically. Centuries of theory about what exactly "education" and "educational" spaces are, together with the construction and standardizing of schools and the pedagogies carried out within them contour our senses of what the school is and what it can be in the twenty-first century. And so, I dove into the history of American school design. As I combed through the past centuries, I found one period particularly important: the nineteenth century defined American education like no other. Enlightenment legacies. A burgeoning American identity, independent from its British roots. Industrialization. During these years, America's sense of schooling underwent meaningful changes. From education predicated on humanist ideals to scientific management, nineteenth century pedagogy and architecture were deeply debated and fiercely fought over. The impact of these complex struggles on America's historic approaches to school design remains the foundations of education in the nation today. *School(house) Design and Curriculum in Nineteenth Century America* carefully unfurls this history, all the while curious about what the politics of dwelling in nineteenth century schools says about how students are and are not allowed to dwell today, and the ways in which builders, policymakers, and teachers—all those stakeholders in our children's education—might best respond to the historicized politics of the present schooling to hold the institution to its founding democratic commitments.

Tracing the history of American school design through individual experiences gives an opportunity to unpack the intricacies of its formative impact. The theories I develop in this book offer important frameworks to query the ways in which school design shapes students, to be sure. But the ideas these frameworks can yield are so much more when they engage with experience. My own history stands as an entry point; a way to locate the limits and stakes of the study by humanizing it (while also doing the double duty of establishing my positionality as a researcher): my original "classroom" was a far cry from the ones I design today, both geographically and politically. Growing up in Portugal, at six years old, my most formative environment was a narrow, cobbled street in the island region of the Azores. Whenever the oxen-pulled carts gave the street over to us, my friends and I transformed these roads into sites of discovery and play, colonizing the cobblestones with conversations, experiments, jacks, hide-and-seek, and marbles. But as the Apollo missions kissed the moon, my family left Portugal for Boston, taken by the promises of the American Dream. Stepping foot on the Promised Land's gilded soil, we realized my uncle wasn't waiting for us as agreed. Unable to speak English, my family was disheartened and quite literally disoriented. The stress mounted as my mother's high heel caught in an escalator—a cruel metaphor for how stuck and powerless we were already feeling.

The anguish I felt that day at the airport didn't let go: it followed me to Fall River, Massachusetts, where my family settled on the third floor of a six-tenement house on the city's main street. (Ironically, Fall River is where the *Dollars for Scholars* program was founded in 1958; a program that earned Fall River the nickname of "Scholarship City" despite the fact that the city has historically underperformed compared to the majority of other Massachusetts communities). It followed me to my first school, an uptown bilingual school for immigrants. Realizing that I was unable to negotiate the English public transportation system, the school administration quickly transferred me out of my bilingual school and into an English school in my neighborhood, Laurel Lake Elementary. But Laurel Lake only intensified my anxiety. There was no cafeteria or gymnasium, and certainly no spaces for art or music. Laurel Lake had only classrooms, an administration office, corridors, stairs, and a large boiler room. Dishearteningly, the staff filled these spaces with repressive pedagogies. Take for example, Laurel Lake's rule that—rain or shine—the school day began with students lining up in the outside courtyard before parading to class in military-style. Arrive late and miss the line up? Principal's office. Mess up the line? Reprimand. Fail to walk as instructed? Shamed. Bare, militaristic, and unforgiving, Laurel Lake tolerated no "disruption". Education was predicated on obedience; discipline, staff believed, made learning possible. "Play"—my first pedagogy—was banned.

At Laurel Lake, my kindergarten classroom was square, spacious, south-facing, approximately 900 square feet, and—intentionally or not—determinedly committed to assimilating children into the nation's white, Anglo-Saxon Protestant culture. More specifically, miniature tables and chairs made for six-year-olds sat in the center of the room, oriented toward a chalkboard on the north teaching wall. The room's south side offered a storytelling greenhouse-like nook with soft perimeter seating and flooring surrounding a rocking chair and books. On the window sill, seedlings planted by students sprouted, nurtured by the bright rays of the sun, which filled the room with a soft, radiant, and soothing glow. The classroom's entrance was bookended by a long, narrow closet in which we hung our coats. But despite these welcoming signposts, the classroom remained a painful site for many of its students: the coatroom doubled as an area where doctors and nurses would vaccinate students—immigrants given many more vaccines than other children. The scars from these extra shots stood for me as permanent marks of my outsider status. Meanwhile, it was between the hopeful plants and the gentle rocking chair that I found myself, again, completely disoriented in an English world—unable to understand what I was being asked to learn and given no support, I was sidelined academically and often ignored. Though an upright piano diagonally positioned in the room gave some relief when played by my kindergarten teacher, Ms. Bernstein, it produced a glorious and unfamiliar sound, this experience was dampened when the first grade class would join us for a group sing-a-long. The first grade teacher, an immigrant to Fall River, was French-Canadian preferred we sing in French. Already lost in English, French only deepened my despair. Equally unsettling were the strict, disciplinary pedagogies with which my teachers carried out these activities and the school's stark environment, so disarming after my free and unregulated island life. Quick and dirty assimilation techniques, Laurel Lake's harsh stance against self-expression and its inability (or refusal) to engage my language and, with it, all my senses of self beholden to Portuguese, systematically pathologized everything I thought I was. Caught in a new geography, a new culture, a new language, a new community, and a new time zone with no support, my confidence plummeted. In this new world, esteem and agency became freshly predicated upon silencing any desired expressions and movements other than those licensed by the teacher. Coming of age in America, this system suggests, meant obeying authority. I struggled with the transition, but had no choice other than to adapt and assimilate as best I could.

My anguish followed me to junior high. The school segregated students within their grade levels based on their academic performance, making clear to everyone which students the school considered "successes" or "failures". This silent labeling, which likely influenced the teacher's instructional pace and so too their students' expectations, did not escape us and many students reiterated this hierarchal system, using its labels to bully each other. This sense of "sorting" continued into high school at BMC Durfee. I vividly remember telling my high school counselor that I wanted to become an architect. I had grown up watching the *Brady Bunch*, enthralled by Mr. Brady, an accomplished architect who lived in a modernist mansion with a family of six children—a lifestyle to which I aspired. Later in life, I would come to recognize the show's economic, racial, and gendered stereotypes and realize how starkly different my own experiences were from those it depicted. Few people in my neighborhood owned a single-family home and no one had an "Alice". Every male adult I knew was consumed by working extended hours at jobs that involved physically exhaustive labor, trying to make enough of a living to support their families, with little extra time to devote to their loved ones. In my world, young adults were encouraged to work full-time, as soon as possible. Many teenagers accordingly dropped out of school to help their families pay the bills. I myself, at the age of 13, started working on a farm alongside seasonal migrant workers to help my family buy a house (albeit in one of Fall River's lowest-income zip codes).

In this environment, the *Brady Bunch* represented a kind of American Dream, portraying the architectural profession as a viable path to success by suggesting it could support a gorgeous house and family. The luxury of Brady's modern mansion stood in stark contrast to my six tenement apartment or my one-room island home with a half-story bedroom loft. Recalling the promises of the Promised Land that brought us to America, I believed that if I worked hard, I could be like Mr. Brady. And so, I told my counselor I wanted to be an architect. His reply was, to say the least, discouraging: he advised me that architecture was a "gentleman's profession", work suited for middle- and upper-class (read: white, Anglo) males like Mike Brady whose families could afford a five-year private education and who, upon graduation, would have access to networks of wealthy patrons through their social circles. What he meant was that I did not fit into America's particular "architectural subjectivity". Class distanced me from my dream and I knew, once again, that due to my background I simply didn't fit into the mold America wanted me to; that despite my best attempts, I still wasn't part of the dreams my nation had for its children.

To his credit, my counselor wasn't wrong: in my senior year of high school there were no affordable public institutions of higher education in New England that offered a degree in Architecture, and all the nearby institutions (Harvard, MIT, Yale, and the RISD) offering such a program were financially and academically out of reach. I knew I couldn't stray far from my family who felt more alone than I did in our new world, and so further but more inexpensive institutions weren't an option for me. My plans to move beyond my neighborhood, beyond physical labor; to own my own home and enjoy my profession; to achieve, as my family sought to in leaving Portugal, the American Dream, felt impossible. At 18, I didn't understand that the Dream was really an ideological illusion rarely realized in practice and blamed myself for my inability to climb the "ladder". And so my anguish deepened. The realistic post-secondary solution for me was to enroll in an engineering technology program, which was, disappointingly, a program that would not lead to my becoming registered as a professional architect. After applying to and getting accepted by three local colleges for engineering, I ultimately enrolled in the Associates Engineering Transfer Program at Bristol Community College, working full-time to support my education.

But I knew I wanted something more than my Associates Degree would offer. After graduating, I transferred to the University of Massachusetts in Amherst, where I earned a Bachelor of Science degree. BSc in hand, I went to work for an architecture firm and there, finally, was able to become a registered professional architect. Yet my anguish stayed with me. I knew I wasn't the only student whose subjectivity couldn't meet my schools' expectations. Driven by this concern, I wanted to transform educational spaces, to make them more compassionate, responsible, and caring environments. To understand how best to do this, I went on to complete an MSc in environmental science, MA in education, and a PhD in educational leadership. In the fall of 2011, at my PhD cohort's first colloquium, I engaged in a discussion prompted by a speaker's evaluation of English as a Second Language programs against more inclusionary alternatives. Openly, I communicated what I believed at the time was my successful experience as a first-generation immigrant dropped into a classroom at an English-only school by an administration with a sink-or-swim attitude. I recounted how I had learned to speak English through immersion, and questioned the focus on separate programming for English language learners. The colloquium scholars, well versed in critical theory, deconstructed the assumptions of my narrative, gently suggesting that I might more carefully consider how my journey spoke not just to a personal success but, more broadly, to the failure of America's education system to meet its democratic (or, at least meritocratic) promises. I am forever indebted to these scholars for helping me to understand myself and my work in such an empowering new light.

Personally, critical theory gave me a new sense of agency: the inverse of my K-12 education, agency in critical theory emerges with self-determination, not obedience. The field taught me to systematically dissect my identity and rework it anew. Professionally, critical theory helped me define and focus my research. It gave me a new language and method with which to recognize the common sense of schoolhouse design and curricula and to situate such norms as part of broader arrangements of power. Moreover, critical theory inspired me to develop my work into a social critique always concerned with emancipation, justice, and equity. By introducing me to and helping me navigate such a meaningful discipline, my professors and peers in the educational leadership program at the University of Massachusetts have shaped this research more than they know. Without the tutelage of such distinguished scholars and the support of my fellow students, I would not only have been unable to complete this research, but also unable to so deeply understand my positionality and potential.

Today, I'm a nationally recognized school architect and public educational administrator (now, somehow, part of that "gentleman's club" that rightly plagued my counselor's imaginary). As a school construction coordinator and architectural design reviewer for the Rhode Island Department of Education (RIDE), I had unusual access to the detailed historical data necessary to complete this project. More specifically, I obtained data through the libraries, resources, and archives of the Rhode Island State Capital Library, Rhode Island Board of Education, Rhode Island Department of Elementary and Secondary Education, Rhode Island Historical Archives, University of Massachusetts, University of Rhode Island, Rhode Island College, Bristol Community College, Brown University, Rhode Island School of Design, Roger Williams University, University of Vermont, Yale University, Tiverton Public Library, Bristol Public Library, Bristol Preservation Society, Providence Preservation Society, Newport Historical Society, and Newport Public Library. I am deeply grateful for these opportunities and to these institutions for their support. In addition to my position at RIDE, I also have the privilege of being an instructor to a diverse group of students at Bristol Community College, whose ingenuity inspires me every day. And yet, my anguish remains. Today, our education systems continue to silence, marginalize, give up on, and push out otherwise gifted learners simply because they struggle to locate themselves in an institution that refuses them from day one. Of late, with the run up to and aftermath of the 2016 Presidential election, such attitudes towards immigrants and other non-normative ways of thinking and being have only grown more hostile. If something doesn't change, our children and our children's children will have to reckon with the assimilative modus operandi of the nation and its schools; will have to learn, from day one, that who they are just doesn't make the grade.

Tiverton, RI, USA Joseph da Silva

Acknowledgments

I extend my gratitude to my friends and colleagues who supported me throughout the writing of this manuscript. To the distinguished University of Massachusetts scholars, Dr. Donaldo Macedo, Dr. Joao M. Paraskeva, Dr. Ricardo Rosa, Dr. Ken Saltman, and to my Educational Leadership doctoral cohort, thank you for your guided research advise for the manuscripts initial iterations. I would like to express my appreciation to Dr. George Willis from the University of Rhode Island for helping to craft this manuscript and encouraging its publication, Eileen Botelho colleague at the Rhode Island Department of Education for critiquing countless earlier versions, and Dr. Jeffery Vincent the University of California for feedback on the final manuscript. A very special tribute goes out to my Rhode Island School Building Authority colleagues, Mario Carreno and Manuel Cordero, for their long term contributions in venting, editing, and critiquing countless versions through the seven-year tenure of this manuscript. To Brian Agular, Kevin Dore, and Daniel Quaile go out special thanks for assistance with graphics. I want to especially thank Danielle Matark who helped copy edit the manuscript from dissertation to final manuscript. I am sincerely indebt to countless others whom I have neglected in mentioning but who helped shape this manuscript. Thank you.

Finally, I want to honor my late Rhode Island Department of Education colleague Forrest Avilla, who generously handed down to my custody his exhaustive historical legal collection of the Rhode Island Board of Education official publications from the late nineteenth to early twentieth century. These precious archives are the very foundation of this historical research, without these volumes this work would not be possible.

Contents

1 Introduction 1

2 From Origin to Modernity: A Brief History of American School Design 17

3 Hotspot of Change: Case Studies in Nineteenth Century Rhode Island 75

4 Structuring Sociality: School Design as Social (Re)Production 117

5 Conclusion 167

Appendix: Chronological Inventory Chart of Public Schoolhouses in RI from 1870s to 1920s 191

Index 209

List of Figures

Fig. 2.1 Exterior façade photo of replica *wetu* from the Wampanoag Homesite at Plymouth Plantation highlighting the central roof venting mechanism. *Wetu* is a bark-covered domed hut dwelling that provided shelter for families wandering the wooded coast hunting and fishing. These dwellings were made with sticks of red cedar and grass and had a deerskin door. (da Silva Photographer, 2015) 19

Fig. 2.2 Illustrates an extent exemplar of the timber frame design typical in New England in the seventeenth century. The existing Wanton-Lyman-Hazard House built in 1670 in Newport, Rhode Island is characteristics of this popular seventeenth century architecture in the US. It includes a robust timber frame, brick or stone foundation, high pitch roof, medieval techniques, low ceilings, an exposed wood structure, relatively spacious rooms, two and a half stories, wide vertical siding boards, large central hearth opening, small windows, plaster brick chimney, small ornamental jett, and wide floor planks. The house has undergone many renovations in the last centuries, particularly noteworthy is the main entry and multiple expansions to the original modest dwelling. (da Silva Photographer, 2015) 23

Fig. 2.3 Colony House, 1739. (da Silva Photographer, 2015) 28

Fig. 2.4 Redwood Library, 1748–50. (da Silva Photographer, 2015) 29

Fig. 2.5 Touro Synagogue, 1759–61. (da Silva Photographer, 2015) 30

Fig. 2.6 Henry Barnard's architectural plans for a graded school. (da Silva, 2018) 38

Fig. 2.7 Plan for a one-room schoolhouse recommended by Horace Mann. (McClintock & McClintock, 1970, p. 118) 39
Fig. 2.8 Typical 'Quincy Plan' floor plate incorporating four classrooms. (da Silva, 2015) 40
Fig. 2.9 'Philadelphia Plan' floor plans designed by Sloan. (Cooledge, 1964) 42
Fig. 2.10 Photograph and typical floor Plan of historically preserved Nathan Bishop Middle School in Providence, RI. (da Silva Photographer, 2013) 64
Fig. 2.11 Photograph and site plan of the restored Central High School (built circa 1931) in Providence, RI. (da Silva Photographer, 2006) 65
Fig. 3.1 A school room for young children. (Board of Education, 1898) 79
Fig. 3.2 A rendering and floor plans of the Rogers High School in Newport (1875). The building is of Venetian Gothic architectural styling and measures 53 by 60 feet. (Board of Education, 1875) 85
Fig. 3.3 Stone foundation, Gargoyle, and Windows at Rogers High School. (da Silva Photographer, 2014) 86
Fig. 3.4 Photos of the Thayer School built in 1873, now a Boys and Girls Club. In this recent photo, the mansard and turret roofs have been demolished and the building now supports a flat roof. (da Silva Photographer, 2014) 88
Fig. 3.5 Photograph of the Townsend Industrial School in Newport, RI (circa, 1894). (RI Board of Education, 1894) 89
Fig. 3.6 Floor plans of the Basement, First, Second, and Third of the Townsend Industrial School in Newport, RI. (Board of Education, 1894) 90
Fig. 3.7 The Thompson Middle School addition to the existing historic Townsend Historic School in Newport, RI. (da Silva Photographer, 2015) 91
Fig. 3.8 An aerial site plan of the Bristol Town Common. (da Silva & Cordero, 2013) 93
Fig. 3.9 The front façade of the Byfield School in Bristol. (da Silva Photographer, 2003) 94
Fig. 3.10 Photos (front and rear) of the Walley School in Bristol, RI. (da Silva Photographer, 2014) 96
Fig. 3.11 A photo of the Walley School in Bristol. (RI Board of Education, 1895) 97
Fig. 3.12 The typical floorplan of the Walley School in Bristol. (RI Board of Education, 1895) 98

Fig. 3.13	A photo of the Oliver Memorial School in Bristol, RI. (da Silva Photographer, 2003)	100
Fig. 3.14	A photograph of the Oliver Memorial School in Bristol. (RI Board of Education, 1903)	101
Fig. 3.15	The floor plans of the basement level, main level, and upper level of the Oliver Memorial School in Bristol. (RI Board of Education, 1903)	102
Fig. 3.16	A rendering of the Point Street Grammar School in Providence RI (1874). The building of French Gothic styling is located on Plane Street. (RI Board of Education, 1876)	105
Fig. 3.17	The floor plan of the Point Street Grammar School in Providence RI (1874). The building is 131 feet by 86 feet. The school rooms are relatively square, measuring about 32 feet by 33 feet with gendered split wardrobe rooms. Each room has a raised platform for the teacher and sits 49 students at fixed desks. (RI Board of Education, 1876)	106
Fig. 3.18	A rendering of the third floor of the state Normal School in Providence. (RI Board of Education, 1879)	109
Fig. 3.19	Floor plans of the first floor, second floor, and third floor of the state Normal School in Providence. (RI Board of Education, 1879)	110
Fig. 3.20	A rendering of the Providence Manual Training School in Providence, RI (circa 1892–1894). (Board of Education, 1894)	112
Fig. 3.21	Floor plans of the Providence Manual Training School in Providence, RI (circa 1892–1894). (Board of Education, 1894)	113
Fig. 4.1	Floor plans of the Rhode Island Normal School in Providence. (RI Board of Education 1899)	146
Fig. 4.2	A rendering of the Rhode Island Normal School in Providence. (RI Board of Education, 1899)	148
Fig. 5.1	Photograph of the Paul Crowley East Bay MET School in Newport, RI. (William Marchetti Photographer, 2014)	188

List of Tables

Table 2.1	*The Yale Report*: Pedagogy and Spatial Forms	34
Table 2.2	Translating the scientific management curriculum to spatial forms	62
Table 3.1	Efficiency factor analysis of Bristol Memorial Schools	104
Table 5.1	An overview of the history of US culture, architecture, and curricula from 1760 to 1950	169

CHAPTER 1

Introduction

This book explores the relationship between American curricula and school architecture in the nineteenth century. The need for a more nuanced history of schooling in the US is all too apparent given today's pedagogical landscape. Over the last few decades, American education has increasingly moved away from its founding democratic commitments of introducing students to a vast range of scholarly traditions in ways that nurture curiosity, critical capacities, and confidence. Instead, our children spend their days learning that success means getting the right answers on a standardized test—any other intellectual pursuit is a waste of their already limited time (Saltman & Gabbard, 2010). Security guards and police patrol our schools' already prison-like learning environments, their presence telling our kids that they're not to be trusted from day one, reminding them that stepping a toe out of line is not youthful experimentation, but criminal behavior deserving of zero-tolerance and, in some cases, strong-armed arrests (Giroux, 2009). We're fining children for being too poor to afford a healthy lunch (Siegel, 2013). And we're sorting students by class and competency, the pressure of state standards leaving little room for teachers to consider the complexities and undoubtable potential of young life beyond background. In short, for our kids, coming of age in America means surviving—not thriving in—school (Saltman & Gabbard, 2010). I want to know where we went wrong.

© The Author(s) 2018

J. da Silva, *School(house) Design and Curriculum in Nineteenth Century America*, https://doi.org/10.1007/978-3-319-78586-8_1

To be sure, the answer to such a question reaches far beyond this study. But what I hope to do here by unpacking nineteenth century schoolhouse[1] design and curriculum[2] is offer a history with which we might better understand the issues in American education today. The nineteenth century was a deeply influential time for American education: it saw the concretization of the earliest forms and aims of the nation's schooling and the development and standardization of the curricula and school architecture from which our current system emerges—in short, growing in this period like no other in American history, nineteenth century schooling firmly established the nation's pedagogical norms. This history thus exposes certain assumptions about what education should be from this period that, though they might have been forgotten over time, nevertheless continue to shape contemporary schooling. By making the nineteenth century nuances of American education clear, I hope to offer a site of inquiry for exploring the power structures of contemporary American education, an institution in desperate need of change. Though schoolhouses stand as complex and immensely formative sites, though they hold such transformative potential for the students who dwell within them, we relegate them too often to the backdrop of educational and architectural tapestries. Very often their conditions—however poor—are naturalized and ignored in public discourse. *School(house) Design and Curriculum in Nineteenth Century America* stands as a reminder that schoolhouses are critical sites of interrogation and intervention in education.

Certainly, I am not the first to have these concerns. Many scholars have already exposed the formative impact of architecture and curricula in nineteenth century America and beyond.

There is a common sense that school facilities matter; that their architecture does indeed impact learning. This sense is captured in a speech delivered by Churchill to the House of Commons in October of 1944 in which he articulates that "[t]here is no doubt whatever about the influence of

[1] As prescribed by the Rhode Island Department of Education's (RIDE) *Public Schoolhouse Assessment* (2013) and *State of Rhode Island Schoolhouses* (2017), I use the term "schoolhouse" to denote educational architecture, by which I mean any space created to deliver schooling.

[2] After William Schubert, I use "curriculum" to signify any and all directives advocated for teaching and learning. For Schubert, a curriculum is made up of internal and external school environments and explicit and implicit as well as general and detailed notions of subject matter and its development, attainment, and consequences (Schubert, 1984).

architecture and structure upon human character and action. We make our buildings and afterwards they make us. They regulate the course of our lives" (Churchill, 1994). Similarly concerned about architecture's formative power, thinkers such as D. Vitiello, M. Clapper, G. E. Thomas, and A. S. Weisser have carefully documented developments in US schoolhouse forms, which focus on school design, siting, planning, and administration.

In a 2006 article published in the *Journal of Planning History* titled "Re-Forming Schools and Cities: Placing Education on the Landscape of Planning History", Vitiello introduces the integration of education with its corresponding schoolhouse history. He acknowledges that there has historically been a lack of discussion around their integration and opens avenues to explore the role of education in planning history. According to Vitiello (2006), the collaborations produced a number of related questions that the authors attempted to answer, which are worth quoting at length here:

- How have school design and planning shaped the physical and social fabric of city and suburban neighborhoods?
- How does public school planning tell us about citizenship, power, and the state in neighborhoods, cities, and regions? What have been the meanings of "public" in public school design and development? What does the history of education suggest about the relationship between church and state in planning and policy?
- How have race, class, and gender shaped the politics of education reform and school development? (Since women have made up the vast bulk of the educational workforce in the United States since the nineteenth century, the history of schools represents an especially promising area for exploring the roles of women in planning.)
- How have students, teachers, neighborhood residents, and architects shaped education-together or in competition with district administrators and educational pundits and reformers, the typical protagonists of educational histories?
- How have the public and private economies of school building been organized in divergent contexts of urban growth and decline?
- What challenges and opportunities face planners engaged in school reform, and how can planning historians contribute to current and future debates about school reform? (p. 186)

These questions have helped to inform and shape the question of how race, class, and gender shaped the politics of education in the nineteenth century. In the volumes of published reports of the Rhode Island Board of Education in the nineteenth century, the silence concerning women governance is deafening, which is second only to the screams in the deliberate omission of education of persons of color.

In Clapper's 2006 article, "School Design, Site Selection, and Political Geography of Race in Postwar Philadelphia", he reveals the ways in which the school siting and design process in post-World War II Philadelphia escalated racial inequities in the city and suburban school system despite the 1954 *Brown v. Board of Education* decision to prohibit segregation. He documents how schools built in urban African-American communities demonstrate catastrophic disparities when compared to their suburban counterparts, and in doing so, shines a light on the ways in which school design can function as a racist mechanism of social control. He draws attention to the centralized educational and architectural professionals responsible for the inequities, as well as the financial failure of the state and federal governments to remedy these inequities.

In a 2006 article, "From Our House to the Big House", George Thomas brilliantly posits that Philadelphia public schools are products of the dominant ideologies of their time, supporting his claim by analyzing *The Public School Buildings of the City of Philadelphia*, seven volumes that document the development of the city's schools from 1745 to the early 1800s. Thomas claims that

> When education was embedded in the home, schools looked like houses; when education became civic, schools took on a civic character; when Philadelphia gave itself to the forces of industry, schools were derived from industry. In the twentieth century, as schools became places of conflict, they took on the character of the architecture of reform-prisons. (p. 218)

Finding that Philadelphia school designs mimic familiar architectural prototypes, such as the house, mansion, church, mill, factory, prison, fortress, and office park, Thomas argues that these prototypes reflect the values of the culture that were popular at the time they were built. More recently, Gyure examines the high school schoolhouse over the course of 150 years in his 2011 book, *The Chicago Schoolhouse*, taking us from the schoolhouse's beginnings in the 1820s through its transformative period from the 1880s to the 1920s and into its current form. Throughout, Gyure sheds light on the histories that underpin today's educational architecture and argues that schoolhouses reflect curricular improvements and inventions.

Weisser, in her 2006 article titled "Little Red School House, What now? Two Centuries of American Public School Architecture", briefly articulates the relationships between educational philosophy and schoolhouse shapes. Weisser (2006) describes the 200-year history she traces as "a typical American story of call and response: reformers consistently demand greater clarity and amenity in the face of perceived unhealthy disarray, and communities regularly soldier on with inherited structures that have proven suitable for generations" (p. 214). This *residual pastness* tension between extant structures and desired transformations speaks to a universal struggle between theory and design, between practice and building, and between functional goals and available forms. It plays out in the landscape of Rhode Island schoolhouses in the nineteenth century and its lag time can be as long as a half of a century.

Meanwhile, educational theorists, such as Pinar, Schubert, Watkins, and Kliebard, have succinctly theorized the history of American curricula. Each theorist compartmentalizes and expands ideologies within diverse theoretical frameworks fashioned to specific curriculum orientations. In many instances, these groupings shared similarities across theoretical orientations. Predominantly these orientations (according to Kliebard [1986]) include four basic ideologies: the ***humanists***, the ***developmentalists***, the ***social meliorists*** (***social reconstructionists***), and the ***social efficiency educators***. Humanism (an ideology based in the ancient tradition of western cultural heritage) was led in this period by Elliot and Harris; developmentalism (an ideology based on the natural order of child development in alignment with the child's interests) was led by Hall; social meliorism (an ideology focused on social change and justice and the opportunity of schools to create a new social vision) was led by Ward; and social efficiency (an ideology based on specialized skills necessitated by technological advantage) was led by Rice (Kliebard, 1986). These philosophies were later exemplified by Bobbitt's (1918) *Curriculum;* solidified by Tyler's *Basic Principles of Curriculum and Instruction* (1949); and countered, manipulated, and refined by Dewey's *School and Society* (1900), *Child and the Curriculum* (1902), *Democracy and Education* (1916), and *Experience and Education* (1938).

These struggles over the US curriculum involve continuous reinterpretations of the basic building blocks, which are grounded in questions about *what* knowledge and *whose* knowledge society should impart to its inheriting generations. Important to note is that the prevailing humanistic aspirations and imaginings in the nineteenth century were void of non-western epistemological possibilities and therefore work to reproduce a *western hegemony*. Out of these humanistic quasi-belligerent struggles of the nineteenth century was produced two crucial moments, namely: that period in which the famous *Yale Report* was released and remained popular and the heyday of scientific management, a period in which the work of intellectuals and educators such as Eliot (1893–1984) and Bobbitt (1876–1956) was highly influential.

To be sure, school architecture has a long and circuitous relationship with curricula. As far back as nineteenth century educational reformer Henry Barnard's day, curriculum and supportive schoolhouses were fundamentally related and both documented as requisites to a sound and fully functional educational system (Barnard, 1860). However, the reverse is also true that curriculum history is intertwined in a multiplicity of ideologies, grounded in (though not *bounded* to) specific groups many of which have failed to take up the formative relationship between curricula and schoolhouse architecture. This tapestry of curricula, silent with regard to its schoolhouse architecture is grounded in humanistic origins. This silence extends beyond the place of schooling to extant social constructions of the human subject, such as race, class, and gender. These silences of subjects (how) and schoolhouses (where), according to Gert Biesta (2006), are a byproduct of modernity's Kantian humanism of the person considered as "subject", which ignores the essential ontology of Martin Heidegger's (1996) "dwelling".

More recently, school architects have been working to improve best practices for using curricula to incorporate into schoolhouse design. Certainly, the profession has long considered various methodologies to translate curricular expectations into spatial forms. In 1969, the Council of Educational Facility Planners International (CEFPI) wrote the "Guide for Planning Education Facilities," a document that made clear that determining the spatial forms that might follow a particular curriculum is a *multistage* process. Today, as a long-standing Recognized Educational Facility Planner (REFP), I have the privilege of expanding and developing these ideas. Putting these ideas into practice as an architect and educational planner, I have had the opportunity to conduct this multistage process over the years for many school districts. In my current capacity as a School Construction Coordinator for Rhode Island School Building

Authority at the Rhode Island Department of Education, I serve as the lead architect and educational planner for the state, a role in which I am responsible for the oversight of the state's school construction program under the leadership of the Office of the Commissioner of Education. In this capacity, I review, reject, and approve educational facility plans from local educational agencies and make preliminary recommendations to the State Board of Education for approval and eligibility of these plans for state housing aid reimbursement, which ranges from 30% to 95% of the cost for design and construction. More specifically, the multistage process of determining spatial needs for schoolhouses involves converting educational objectives into architectural floor plans as well as identifying the types, quantities, sizes, and adjacencies that primary and secondary educational program spaces will require (Myers & Robertson, 2004). This process begins with a survey that helps planners identify program needs embedded in ideologies, philosophies, and policies based on approved curriculums adopted by the local school boards or educational agencies (Castaldi, 1987). More specifically, these surveys collect information such as: the school's vision, mission, goals, learning objectives, activities, number of students and staff, necessary spatial relationships (i.e. who needs to be close to who or what), necessary accessories and equipment (e.g. learning technologies), furnishing and fixtures, and special environmental treatments. As educational planners, we then translate these preferred purposes, policies, and practices into spatial recommendations to make sure a building facilitates those things educators find central to the learning experience (Myers & Robertson, 2004). From this process an educational specification can be outlined that translates the educational vision to spatial forms in detailed qualitative and quantitative tabulations (Castaldi, 1987). These spatial requirements then inform the design, organization, and formation of the schoolhouse (Myers & Robertson, 2004). In 2006, the *Journal of Planning History* published a group of articles—inspired by a conference in St. Louis by the University of Pennsylvania's Urban Studies Program—that brought a number of new considerations to bear on planning educational facilities. Namely, these articles asked educators to consider: the ways in which school design might shape a neighborhood's social fabric; what planning conveys about the relationship between a site and citizenship, power, and the state; the racial, classed, and gendered dynamics of school development; the roles of students, teachers, neighborhood residents, district administrators, and educational pundits in school planning; how the public and private economies of school building have been organized in divergent contexts of urban growth and decline; and the challenges that planners have historically faced.

But while such work has been done on how curriculum inspires school architecture and on the formative power of schoolhouse form and curriculum as separate forces, only a small number of scholars consider the ways in which curricula and architecture have historically worked together to shape teaching and learning and what we understand it to be. Notably, John Dewey, the acclaimed early twentieth century educational philosopher, most powerfully emphasized the need to study how different types of space would impact teaching and learning (1938). Dewey believed that pedagogy should consider what he called the student's "experience". Two coordinates define this experience: (1) *continuity*—the notion that one's past experiences contour one's present, and (2) *interaction*—the idea that one's experience is shaped by an interplay between the nuances of the current moment and one's formative past (1938). Dewey asks educators to take into account his philosophy that *continuity* and *interaction* were central to experience when considering how to best encourage students to engage the school setting and the knowledge unpacked within it. More specifically, he advises teachers to teach material by rooting it in their learners' everyday experiences, knowing that such everyday experiences are informed by their individual and shared pasts and that drawing on these only enlivens the experience they have in the classroom. Trying to implement such an experientially based pedagogy himself, Dewey became "acutely aware" that the educative environment needed "distinctive facilitates compatible with [this] educational vision" (Wirth & Bewig, 1986) to be able to meaningfully support every student's experience—their requirements, requests, resolves, and aptitudes. As I discuss in more detail in Chap. 2, when designing his own school (the Laboratory School), Dewey considered aspects room size, adjacencies, lighting, ventilation, furniture, fixtures, and equipment (Wirth & Bewig, 1986). Years later, acclaimed French philosopher Michel Foucault located space as a key site of power. For Foucault, a physical space, the operations carried out within it, and the discourses informing what it means to dwell in that space together define the workings of power within that site (1977). Thinking Foucault's theory of space together with Dewey's argument that the form of a schoolhouse impacts teaching and learning, this book brings seminal studies in architecture and curriculum into conversation to fill in the blanks in the history of US schooling about the combined impact of schoolhouse design and curriculum in the educational relation. To better articulate this formative relationship, I want to suggest that the physical environment of the school and the ideas taught within it intersect to create what I term an *ideo-spatial nexus of school design*. Crucially, this nexus always forecasts a particular kind of student; a learning subject whose ways of thinking and being a school design limits.

To make legible the norms of nineteenth century American schooling, Chap. 2, "From Origin to Modernity: A Brief History of American School Design", outlines the history of the school design nexus, carefully locating its nineteenth century politics and considering the kind of student its different configurations anticipate. Methodologically, Chap. 2 employs a historical qualitative strategy of inquiry by exploring curricular trends, architectural design sensibilities, and socio-cultural movements to shed light on the type of students schoolhouses serve. I unpack this history across four sections: "Pre-history of 19th Century School Design", "19th Century School Design", "Legacies and Complications of 19th Century School Design", and "The American Student". "Pre-history of 19th Century School Design" explores the *wetu*, the first known structure used for knowledge transfer in America, the theological school design of early Puritan settlers and their demonization of Indigenous forms of education, and colonial America's first public schools and universities. Next, "19th Century School Design" surveys the traditionalist (Enlightenment-inspired) school design running up to, during, and in the wake of the American revolution. The year 1828 saw a paradigm shift in American education with the writing of *The Yale Report*. Inspired by the liberalist ideals of the European Enlightenment, a committee at Yale College wrote a traditionalist curriculum—calling for students to be taught classical languages, the arts, and science with rote, disciplinary pedagogies—that would come to define nineteenth century school design and, eventually, American education. The years following *The Yale Report* were defined by the complex impact of the gold rush, the civil war, mass immigration, and the Industrial Revolution. By mid-century, a new ideological hegemony emerged that developed Enlightenment ideals with the needs and insights of a rapidly industrializing sociality. This was the era of scientific management. In this period, school design became increasingly inspired by advances in science, mathematics, and technology, and increasingly predicated upon efficiency and vocational training. Throughout the nineteenth century, the role of the architect varied. Early on in the 1800s, few architects collaborated on schoolhouse designs because much of education took place in homes and churches. As education evolved from subscription schools to centralized administrative controlled schools, schoolmasters and architects began to collaborate in the design of the school's built environment. After unpacking the nuances of nineteenth century school design, I trace its legacies in school architecture and curriculum up to the early twentieth century. Here, I explore the many developments in school design that occurred as the US became a military, technological, and economic powerhouse, specifically highlighting education's increasing attention to classroom architecture and the rise of a new pedagogy—life adjustment education—and take to task the assertedly democratic designs of post-war schooling.

Throughout Chap. 2, I draw attention to the fact that, as Amy Weisser (2006) details in "Little Red Schoolhouse, what now?", the last two centuries have seen many schools built with particular pedagogies in mind used to carry out different curricula for years after those educational ideologies that inspired their designs fell out of popularity. For Weisser, the history of American schooling is thus "a typical American story of call and response: reformers consistently demand greater clarity and amenity in the face of perceived unhealthy disarray, and communities regularly soldier on with inherited structures that have proven suitable for generations" (214). Undeniably, such tensions between architecture and curricula deeply complicate their shared impact. To highlight this nuance of school design throughout this book, I term this trend of anachronistic architecture ***residual pastness.*** Considering this history, Chap. 2 establishes that nineteenth century American schoolhouse design and curriculum are both predicated upon two of the era's most popular ideological trends: (1) the classically inspired trend of traditionalism (outlined in *The Yale Report*) and (2) the empirically predicated trend of scientific management (championed by developmentalists, social meliorists, and social efficiency educators alike). In conclusion, Chap. 2 considers the politics of these two competing ideologies as they emerge in nineteenth century school design. I argue that the norms of *The Yale Report* and scientific management respectively normalize the ideals of (1) European colonialism, the Enlightenment, and American independence and (2) the Industrial Revolution in school design, orienting early American education to anticipate a white, rational, liberatory, productive, and obedient student—an orientation that would powerfully inspire school design over the century to come.

Chapter 3, "Hotspot of Change: Case Studies in Nineteenth Century Rhode Island", delves more deeply into the nuances of nineteenth century American school design by performing case studies in Rhode Island, a "hotspot" or charged site of this dynamic history. With an extraordinarily rich and well-preserved heritage deeply expressive of broader American norms, Rhode Island stands as an exemplary site of study. This chapter takes up nineteenth and early twentieth century Rhode Island schools in Newport, Bristol, and Providence to consider how they support, complicate, or trouble the aims of traditionalism and scientific management. Each case study includes annotated images of site plans, floor plans, facades, and other architectural features. The *Newport Case Studies* include the Rogers High School (1873), and the Townsend Industrial School (1894). The *Bristol Case Studies* survey those schools situated on the "Bristol Commons": the Byfield Memorial School (1872), the Walley Memorial School (1896), and the Oliver Memorial School (1901). Lastly, the *Providence Case Studies* include the Point Street Grammar School (1874), the State Normal School (1879), and the Providence Manual Training School (1894).

Chapter 4, "Structuring Sociality: School Design as Social (Re)Production", locates schools as powerful formative sites for youth. Engaging the work of seminal theorists such as Louis Althusser who explore schools as sites of power that regulate the limits of thinking and being, this chapter considers curricula as ideological constructs that define epistemological fields or ways of knowing. But to be sure, as Dewey et al. emphasize, a curriculum is always complicated by the space in which it is taught. Applying this theoretical framework to the history of school design I unpack in my earlier chapters, I consider what kinds of knowledge nineteenth century school design prioritizes—what ways of thinking and being its norms suggest are most worthwhile. Taking seriously Althusser's argument that schooling can stabilize (reproduce) a normative cultural formation (e.g. class structures) by affirming existing ideologies and destabilize that same formation by deviating from the existing ideologies that support it, I explore the ways in which nineteenth century schoolhouse design nurtures and represses different modes of sociality. For example, the State Normal School in Providence (1879) displays recitation rooms in step with the rote pedagogies of *The Yale Report*. Nineteenth century methodologies of recitation worked to first reveal what the student already knew or did not yet know, giving the teacher an opportunity to then celebrate or pathologize a given epistemology, controlling the student's sense of "truth" ("truth" for Althusser is a culturally constructed "ideology" promoted by the teacher). Crucially, the Normal School's recitation rooms compelled a traditional curriculum, defined in this period primarily by the (Eurocentric) Enlightenment ideals of *The Yale*

Report and the (not unrelated) liberatory dreams of an independent America. Prioritizing the teacher's "truth" in her or his intelligibility, the ideal student comes (at least within the classroom) to engage the world within the limits of this traditionalist way of thinking; an intelligibility of Eurocentric, Enlightenment, and patriarchal ideals that reproduces the white male-dominated middle- and upper-class hegemony defining America in the nineteenth century. *Othering* and *Resistant* deepens my study of the regulatory work of nineteenth century school designs. Spurred by Chap. 2's conclusion that the century's popular design nexuses nurture a subjectivity that is white, reasonable, liberatory, productive, and obedient; plus the ways in which Rhode Island schools differentially reproduce or destabilize the cultural norms supporting this ideal "student", this section asks (after the epistemologies and ontologies that nineteenth century school designs silence), what has been done to counter that silencing? To uncover these silenced ways of thinking and being in nineteenth century American life, I engage the prevailing curricular ideologies that directly impact students whose perspectives did not make the grade—of school-age children excluded from schooling, of youth living alternatively—to bring their voices back into discourses of schoolhouse design. Excavating these silenced voices with the help of resistant pedagogues, this chapter seeks to hold American education to its democratic promise by writing a more participatory history of its work that takes into account those children its designs have left behind.

In closing, I return to the regulatory work of late modern American education with which the book opens. As I've suggested, my schooling's silencing of my initial sense of self is not a unique experience: in writing a history of nineteenth century American school design, this work makes clear that American education has long marginalized non-normative ways of life. Putting this study to work on the present, I end by considering the legacy of nineteenth century school design in twenty-first century American education. Today, rote learning, Eurocentrism, and inequity—those norms of nineteenth century education—continue to plague schooling in the US. Standardized testing reduces pedagogy to "skill-and-drill"—educators, whose jobs depend on their students' scores, are pressed to teach only to the test. Notably, this test-related curriculum remains primarily concerned with Western epistemologies—slanted versions of history, literature, the arts, and science that silence non-Western ways of thinking and being within the school. Under these conditions, traditional public and charter schools (their curriculum and architecture constricted by standardized testing, calls for heightened security measures, and the cost-cutting imperatives of a recessionary market) struggle to support the voices and agency of already under-served youth, orienting American education to support, as scholars like Diane Ravitch argue, only *middle-class* students. Rife with gaps in opportunity and achievement between well-to-do communities and those marked by poverty—dynamics that remain, as in the nineteenth century, racially predicated—formal education continues to deepen pre-existing inequities in American life. With school-age children spending more time in schools than any other buildings other than their homes, it is clear that the ways in which schoolhouses are designed and built matter. These constructed spaces affect the ways in which students move, work, learn, and interact. Therefore, by studying the epistemological and ontological influences that gave birth to their form, space, and order, it may be possible to better understand the historic norms that continue to shape our learners. This book offers an opening into the broader project of making current schoolhouse spatiality more conducive for pedagogies that, true to the nation's democratic assertions, help youth to grow and build fulfilling and productive lives as active participants in our society. Ultimately, *School(house) Design and Curriculum in Nineteenth Century America* contributes to today's conversations about school reform and responds to a more diverse student body in common cause and common good.

While this book focuses on the ways in which school design constrains subjectivity, it is important to remember that a schoolhouse's form and prescribed curriculum can never absolutely determine the movements of those who dwell within it. I close with this sense of possibility, encouraging school architects and educators to open schooling up—against the marginalizing legacy of nineteenth century school design—to more diverse student bodies, giving previously silenced subjects a voice in American education. In short, I conclude by compelling a consideration of how school design—far from its oppressive history—might work to *decenter* the still-present white and patriarchal hegemonies it stabilized in the nineteenth century; might be reoriented to meet its democratic promise.

References

Barnard, H. (1860). *School Architecture or, Contributions to the Improvement of School-Houses in the United States*. New York: Barnes & Burr.

Biesta, G. J. J. (2006). *Beyond Learning: Democratic Education for the Human Future*. Boulder, CO: Paradigm Publishers.

Bobbitt, J. F. (1918). *The Curriculum*. Boston: Houghton Mifflin.
Brown v. Board of Education. (1954). 347 U.S. 483.
Castaldi, B. (1987). *Educational Facilities, Planning Modernization, and Management*. Boston: Allyn and Bacon.
Churchill, W. (1994). October 28, 1944 House of Commons Speech.
Clapper, M. (2006). School Design, Site Selection, and the Political Geography of Race in Postwar Philadelphia. *Journal of Planning History, 5*(3), 241–263.
Council of Educational Facility Planners International CEFP. (1969). *Guide for Planning Educational Facilities*. Ohio: CEFP.
Dewey, J. (1900). *The School and Society*. Chicago: University of Chicago Press.
Dewey, J. (1902). *The Child and the Curriculum*. Chicago: University of Chicago Press.
Dewey, J. (1916). *Democracy and Education*. New York: Macmillan.
Dewey, J. (1938). *Experience and Education*. New York: Macmillan.
Foucault, M. (1977). *Discipline and Punishment: Birth of the Prison* (A. Sheridan, Trans.). London: Allen Lane.
Giroux, H. A. (2009). *Youth in a Suspect Society: Democracy or Disposability*. New York: Palgrave.
Gyure, D. A. (2011). *The Chicago Schoolhouse: High School Architecture and Educational Reform 1856–2006*. Chicago: University of Chicago Press.
Heidegger, M. (1996). *Being and Time*. New York: State of New York Press.
Kliebard, H. (1986). *The Struggle for the American Curriculum: 1893–1958*. New York: Routledge.
Myers, N., & Robertson, S. (2004). *Creating Connections – The CEFPI Guide for Educational Facility Planning*. Phoenix, AZ: Council of Education Facility Planners International.
Rhode Island Department of Education. (2013). Public Schoolhouse Assessment. *Rhode Island Department of Education*. Retrieved from http://www.ride.ri.gov/
Rhode Island Department of Education. (2017). State of Rhode Island Schoolhouses Assessment. *Rhode Island Department of Education*. Retrieved from http://www.ride.ri.gov/
Saltman, K. J., & Gabbard, D. A. (2010). *Education as Enforcement: The Militarization and Corporation of Schools*. New York: Taylor & Francis Group.
Schubert, W. H. (1984). *Curriculum Books*. Lanham, MD: University Press of America.
Siegel, B. E. (2013). *The Lunch Tray*. Retrieved from http://www.thelunchtray.com/schools-interfere-with-home-packed-lunches-and-my-surprising-reaction/. Accessed 20 Dec 2017.
Thomas, G. E. (2006). From Our House to the "Big House": Architectural Design as Visible Metaphor in the School Buildings of Philadelphia. *Journal of Planning History, 5*(3), 218–240.

Tyler, R. W. (1949). *Basic Principles of Curriculum and Instruction.* Chicago: University of Chicago Press.

Vitiello, D. (2006). Re-Forming Schools and Cities. *Journal of Planning History,* *5*(3), 183–195.

Weisser, A. S. (2006). Little Red School House, What Now? Two Centuries of American Public School Architecture. *Journal of Planning History,* *5*(3), 196–217.

Wirth A. G., & Bewig C. (1986). John Dewey on School Architecture. *Journal of Aesthetic Education*, – JSTOR.

CHAPTER 2

From Origin to Modernity: A Brief History of American School Design

Scholars from Cicero to Derrida have long celebrated the study of history as a "life teacher". By unpacking the past, historical research presents an opportunity to analyze the consequences of various ways of thinking and being in different contexts and, as such, helps us to read the present more critically and capaciously. Capturing this concept most succinctly is Orwell's classic novel, *Nineteen Eighty Four* (1949). Asserting that the one "[w]ho controls the past controls the future" and that the one "[w]ho controls the present controls the past" (35), Orwell underscores history's transformative power. And ultimately, it is this Orwellian premise that inspires this chapter: here, I unravel the history of American school design to shed light on how various combinations of school architecture and curriculum differently impact the educational relation. Though this book is primarily concerned with the politics of nineteenth century school design, it is important, Orwell reminds, to contextualize this period within the eras that precede and necessarily shape it as well as those histories the period went on to shape as well. In doing such work, I take up some of American history's major cultural, philosophical, architectural, and educational trends and turning points (paying special attention to Rhode Island where the next chapter's case studies take place), knowing well every one of these domains deeply influences what it means and has meant to dwell in American schools.

© The Author(s) 2018

J. da Silva, *School(house) Design and Curriculum in Nineteenth Century America*, https://doi.org/10.1007/978-3-319-78586-8_2

Certainly, these trends and turning points are greatly defined by the American ideal of freedom, evident in the wars for independence, land acquisition, self-determination, and national self-interest surging throughout this chapter. But while "freedom" defines American history in so many ways, it also fails to exhaust it. Taking this prevailing signifier of American history to task, this chapter—and this book more broadly—attempts to approach the nineteenth century (as well as its pre-history and its legacies) in a way that makes room for more pluralist understandings of American history.[1] For precisely this reason, this chapter begins by remembering the architecture of Indigenous cultures of the US and not, like many other historical narratives, that of early European colonists. Such normative histories cement a Western bias in historical epistemologies, one rooted in the Enlightenment's linear notions of "progress" and "freedom" and Humanism's ethos of person as "subject". Against such deterministic linearities, Indigenous epistemes emerge as more circular—concepts are interconnected and related. For example, some Native Americans have no noun that describes the environment as a subject; their vocabulary frames it as a relation. Though such a sharp divide between Indigenous and Western epistemologies are admittedly reductive, I articulate them to expose the epistemological undercurrents that pervade my research. Ultimately, by unsettling the traditional historical narrative and giving space to non-western epistemologies or what Bonaventura De Sousa Santos calls "southern" epistemologies, I hope to expose the colonial hegemony still naturalized in and by the US today.

Pre-History

12,000BC—1500AD: Indigenous Education

It was in the Neolithic period, commonly known as the "New Stone Age", that the first human populations flourished. During the period, small bands of nomadic hunter-gatherers, "the Paleo-Native Americans", left Asia and traveled to North America, including the area now known as Rhode Island. On the East Coast, these groups formed agricultural villages, effectively becoming the area's first known settlers. A primary interior space of education in these communities was the *wetu* (see Fig. 2.1).

[1] Important to note is that I am not attempting to reconcile the epistemological perspective, but rather, I seek to acknowledge its existence.

Fig. 2.1 Exterior façade photo of replica *wetu* from the Wampanoag Homesite at Plymouth Plantation highlighting the central roof venting mechanism. *Wetu* is a bark-covered domed hut dwelling that provided shelter for families wandering the wooded coast hunting and fishing. These dwellings were made with sticks of red cedar and grass and had a deerskin door. (da Silva Photographer, 2015)

An archetype of Indigenous educational architecture, the *wetu* provides a space for a community to gather; its u-shaped layout conducive to communal participatory exchanges centralized around a fire.

Brilliantly, the *wetu* provides space for a fire to be placed directly under an opening that allows smoke exhaust to escape, aided by sailed directed pole flues that harness wind to help move exhaust away from the tent, but maximize the heat flow through the perimeter interior dome structure. Moreover, the *wetu*'s flexible stick-framed perimeter seating, cushioned with several layers of animal skin, creates a flexible and comfortable space in which to hold group assemblies. This spatial organization seems at first glance to equitably position participants. Though the u-shaped layout, which faces the dwelling entrance, may indeed have supported hierarchal relationships, its organization does seem to inhibit it because there is no elevated station or platform within the space that would draw the focus to one individual. More specifically, the *wetu*'s architecture seems more likely to facilitate democratic decision-making, knowledge transfers, and governance. To be sure, this is *not* to say that actual practices in these communities were not hierarchal but, rather, that the *wetu*'s form was conducive to a more egalitarian politics. For our purposes, the *wetu*'s simple and highly functional layout supported many kinds of educational activities. For example, the *wetu* facilitated storytelling, a pedagogical method many Indigenous cultures used to pass down language, knowledge, and heritage to inheriting generations.

Tragically, by the early sixteenth century, European explorers killed and assimilated many Native Americans, effectively destroying much of their culture and certainly their architecture. Columbus' log of his initial meeting with the Indigenous people of the US, quoted in Howard Zinn's *A People's History of the United States* (1980), speaks to the brutality of this history:

> They…brought us parrots and balls of cotton and spears and many other things, which they exchanged for the glass beads and hawks' bells. They willingly traded everything they owned.…They were well-built, with good bodies and handsome features.…They do not bear arms, and do not know them, for I showed them a sword, they took it by the edge and cut themselves out of ignorance. They have no iron. Their spears are made of cane.… They would make fine servants.… *With fifty men we could subjugate them all and make them do whatever we want.* (1, my emphasis)

After this unfortunate meeting, Native American civilizations would be routed by way of genocidal conquest at the hands of Columbus, Cortes, Pizarro, and the Puritans (Zinn, 1980). In the Rhode Island region more specifically, the Puritans solidified their conquest of the Pequot Natives in 1676. This conquest was marked by the end of the King Philip War that was fought in the south shore region of the Massachusetts Bay Colony, which included parts of Rhode Island that were occupied by the Wampanoags who were assumed to be led by Chief Massasoit and his sons Wamsutta and Metacom (known as King Philip) (Zinn, 1980). Before European colonization, the Wampanoag and Narragansett Natives populated what is known as Aquidneck Island for at least eight centuries (Yarnall, 2005). During colonization, many of them were killed.[2]

1500–1650: Cultures Transformed and Transplanted

The story of the American Colonies is one of European cultural transplantation to a new world. Early European settlers struggled tumultuously to adapt to their new American environment. Their hardship was, in large part, due to their view that they were superior to Native Americans, who they viewed as less than human. Accordingly, early settlers were determined not to follow the clever local Native American customs for shelters and food harvesting that offered quick construction using only local, easily harvested materials. Consequently, the settlers' early shelters were not well suited to the environment. Disregarding and in some cases demonizing Indigenous knowledge and architecture, early American settlers instead understood themselves and their world within a long history of Western thought, formally beginning with the Classical period's elevation of the individual and establishment of Western philosophy, natural science, and representative art (crucial to note for our purposes is that these traditions stimulated the American ideal of individual freedoms). Notably, these classical ideological dispositions were also home to sensibilities about dwellings: they split the creation of a space into multiple

[2] It is important to point out that this history is a Western account, a subjective narration of the past. This is evident in that Native American Indian Nations were, in many respects, matriarchal societies, and, as such, Metacom would not likely have been known as "King" Philip to its people. If this history had been written from a southern epistemological perspective, perhaps it would have portrayed the matriarch (the female elder) as the central figure of power, rendering the alleged "King Philip" secondary in the historical narrative.

responsibilities, differentiating between a master builder (i.e. architect) who would determine a design and a builder who would do the hard labor of constructing said design. Later, the fall of the Roman Empire and the dawn of the Middle Ages—an era of chiefdoms, shared values, and religious and political demands for guidance—saw a shift in architectural style from Classical to Gothic. While, Classical architecture emphasized the individual as a "subject" with certain rights and rational, intellectual, and sensory relationships with the physical world, Medieval culture celebrated hierarchical social relations and spiritual and emotional interests in the divine. These sensibilities would go on to inform colonial architecture and education.

More specifically, the early Puritan settlers of New England— who were primarily from East Anglia (East England)—brought with them the architecture of their homeland so informed by Classical and Gothic traditions (Gelernter, 1999). Accordingly, many of the early Puritan buildings in New England were made of wood and demonstrated Gothic styling; for example, high-pitched roofs (see Fig. 2.2).

Moreover, Puritans also transplanted their educational traditions—informed by Classical and Medieval ideals—from England. Much of Puritan education was founded on medieval theological norms that prioritized the literacy of clergy members who would then communicate the teachings of religious texts to a larger group. To be sure, Puritans did not believe that all group members needed to be educated; rather they believed only a few, like those in the clergy, required formal training. What formal training did exist was primarily concerned with the surrounding world and the laws of nature. It organized inherited logic in five key categories: chronological (history), quantitative (math), analytical (studies of cause and effect, e.g. science), linguistic (grammar), and aesthetic (arts) (Willis et al., 1993). Architecture, education, and religion were very much intertwined in this period, in part because of the convergence of numerous religious movements, such as Jewish, Catholic, Roman Catholic, and Protestant, in Rhode Island in the 1600s. For example, in 1635, Roger Williams, the founder of Rhode Island, escaped the religious intolerance of the Massachusetts Bay Colony and declared a new colony in Rhode Island founded upon religious freedom. A few years later, in 1638, Ann Hutchinson, who had been banished from the Massachusetts Bay Colony for religious intolerance, purchased land from the Narragansett Native Americans in what is now Portsmouth, Rhode Island and an area also known as Common Fence Point (Yarnall, 2005). Soon after, in 1639,

Fig. 2.2 Illustrates an extent exemplar of the timber frame design typical in New England in the seventeenth century. The existing Wanton-Lyman-Hazard House built in 1670 in Newport, Rhode Island is characteristics of this popular seventeenth century architecture in the US. It includes a robust timber frame, brick or stone foundation, high pitch roof, medieval techniques, low ceilings, an exposed wood structure, relatively spacious rooms, two and a half stories, wide vertical siding boards, large central hearth opening, small windows, plaster brick chimney, small ornamental jett, and wide floor planks. The house has undergone many renovations in the last centuries, particularly noteworthy is the main entry and multiple expansions to the original modest dwelling. (da Silva Photographer, 2015)

Easton, Coddington, and Clarke led a group to form Newport, Rhode Island in a quest to substantiate their religious freedom through the Newport Compact (Yarnall, 2005).[3] In short, this period saw Rhode Island become the epicenter of religious freedom in the early America, a

[3] This compact can be said to have led to the incorporation of chapel space in extant public schoolhouses into the early nineteenth century, as I will discuss in more detail in the chapter here.

site that countered the political actions of the Church of England. The nation's first institution of higher learning, Harvard College, opened in Massachusetts in 1638, designed in the Gothic style. Founded on the seventeenth century developments of the Classical ideals (complicated by Gothic norms) described above, Harvard echoed the sensibilities of the American settlers' English education. Such pedagogical commitments are evident in documents from the period such as the "Rules and Course of Study at Harvard College" (1642). Eventually, Harvard's guidelines came to inform the period's elementary, secondary, and post-secondary education of the period (Morrison, 1936).[4]

1650–1760: Colonial Culture

In the century running up to the American Revolution, European settlers violently transformed America into an amalgam of diverse populations by colonizing the lands of Native Americans and bringing enslaved Africans to the soil. During these years, the Crown tried to unite these populations in its service by emphasizing that they were all indeed answerable to Great Britain. Colonial America's first official schoolhouses were part of this imperial effort: in the 1650s, the English House of Burgesses passed laws mandating that colonial towns establish and build elementary schools (Button & Provenzo, 1989). Crucially, this particular law sparked the building of one-room schoolhouses. In these schools, students of all ages were under the control of one teacher in one dedicated room. While this might seem like a simplistic (and perhaps poor) design compared to today's schools, the schoolhouse as dwelling was initially only built with the objective of giving both schoolmaster and students *basic shelter* during lessons. As Kowalski (2002) details:

> Americans believed the setting was of little consequence. Schools were plain, wooden and meant for protection from the elements. The school site was usually on wasteland, not suitable for farming. The ceilings were low, ventilation bad, lighting unsatisfactory, heating uneven and sanitary arrangements often unmentionable. (p. 4)

To be sure, this early view of schoolhouses as simply needing to provide basic shelter suggests that they were not thought of as meant to respond

[4]As I detail in subsequent sections, in 1828, *The Yale Report* would popularize some aspects of the Puritan educational model.

to other educational or, more broadly, human needs (such as those articulated by Abraham Maslow (1943) in his hierarchy of needs that more recent educational architecture and curricula take into account). These early one-room schoolhouses were typically rectangular in design and had gable-roofs "reflect[ive]...of domestic building[s]" (Thomas, 2006, p. 219). Many were built and fueled from local wood. Sticks were commonly driven into the log walls of the schoolhouse to create shelves for desks, while dirt floors were used as blackboards, upon which lessons would be presented (Monk, 2006). In colder temperatures, students and teachers would have to use foot-warmers to prevent frostbite and children were encouraged to bring firewood to school, with preferential treatment given to the student who brought the most wood and boys being responsible for keeping the wood burning stoves lit (Sloane, 1972).

But schoolhouse architecture developed during the early eighteenth century. This period saw schoolhouses created more frequently *in* villages, out of the way of Native Americans and animals (Monk, 2006). Within their walls, schoolhouses began to sometimes serve as living spaces for schoolmasters, an architectural design that, Thomas (2006) asserts, positioned the schoolmaster as a kind of "parental mentor" (p. 219).[5] Still other schoolhouses took on the elite shape of mansions or exhibited center-hall plans that echoed the style of the Quaker meetinghouse (Thomas, 2006). Thomas (2006) claims that "[t]hese early buildings provide insights into the nature of schooling and the values behind it": even "their name, *schoolhouse*, correlates with their architectural typology", signaling the growing consensus in the eighteenth century that schools might be places of nurturing, similar to a "home" (p. 219).

Pedagogically, early eighteenth century curriculum was taught by lecturing and recitation and the subject matter emerged from "whatever textbook lay at hand. Often these books wedded the dream of worldly success to an absolute morality; cultivation meant proper diction and polite accomplishment" (Tyack & Cuban, 1995, p. 19). By mid-century, some reformers began to query this curriculum and the way it was taught. Notably, Benjamin Franklin charged these "traditionalist" pedagogies as limiting: in his *Proposals Relating to the Education of Youth in Pennsylvania* (1749), Franklin advocated for "education [to] become closer in touch with the practical pursuits

[5] This "parent-mentor" posturing enabled schoolmasters to enact "corporal punishment [on students, an act] that was part of the craft of the culture of the eighteenth century" (p. 219). This norm of discipline and control in the schoolhouse would remain hegemonic for centuries.

of colonial life". He argued that curriculum should be expanded to include physical education, drawing, the mechanical arts, civics, and horticulture. Franklin's idea was significantly progressive in that it expanded the curriculum beyond religion to the practical arts. Though it would take almost 150 years for Franklin's proposed developments to take full root (in part because the one-room school limited the kind of pedagogies that could be carried out within it), his calls to expand education and make it more socially useful would eventually become primary pedagogical considerations in American education (Willis et al., 1993). This period also saw the creation of Rhode Island's first institution of higher education: the College of Rhode Island (now Brown University). Founded in 1764, the College of Rhode Island was the nation's third college. Notably, today's Brown University demonstrates some similarities to Harvard College: both reflect early architectural styles in the US, such as the Gothic multi-storied style,[6] and incorporate similar construction techniques, such as high-pitched roofs (see Fig. 2.2).

Ultimately, despite the Crown's attempts, seventeenth and eighteenth century education and culture was already well on its way to Independence. Settlers saw schoolhouses as vehicles of change: early schools "drew on and appealed to a pervasive Protestant-republican ideology that held that proper education could bring about a secular millennium and could make the United States quite literally God's country" (Tyack & Cuban, 1995, p. 16). Accordingly, with the burgeoning of US schoolhouses, colleges, and curricular debates, this colonial period set the stage for the birth of America as a new, independent nation and democratic experiment; a politics the nation believed schooling—properly designed—could support.

Nineteenth Century School Design

1760–1830: The Age of Revolution

In 1776, European colonists combined to secede from England. The American Revolution was constitutionally framed within doctrines of freedom, liberty, equality, and a representative government, ideals that emerged

[6] As I state above, the American settlers and colonialists' aesthetic cultural sensibilities reflected a medieval (gothic) sensibility, unlike their European counterparts who were already committed to a Renaissance aesthetic, and as a result, they did not produce internationally notable works of ornamental architecture during this period (perhaps because these settlers celebrated functionality, often only had enough to subsist on, and were still in the process of solidifying their socio-cultural apparatuses). Instead, in this period, the American architectural landscape was filled with predominately medieval gothic styling. Any echoing of the European stone renaissance styling was primarily derived in wood.

from the scholarship of the European Enlightenment, an intellectual movement that was in full swing by the end of the eighteenth century. More specifically, the Enlightenment was an intense period of scholarship that dramatically transformed philosophy, religion, science, economics, art, culture, and education by emphasizing critical inquiry and reason. Emerging from the Renaissance, with its roots in humanism and reliance on reason borrowed from classical Rome and Greece, the Enlightenment created an arguably unprecedented momentum in scientific discovery that practically dismantled medieval Aristotelian epistemology, which was predicated on the notion of a fixed universe (Urban & Wagner, 2014). This universe was replaced by one defined by physical laws, based in mathematical principles that were inspired by Descartes, Kepler, Galileo, and Newton. Coupled with the social scientific revelations of Bacon, Hobbes, and Locke, this turn to science transformed humanity's sense of the universe and its place within it (Urban & Wagner, 2014). For Enlightenment scholars, approaching the world "reasonably" would ensure that society was always progressing, moving forward. For Foucault, the Enlightenment's faith in progress and linear construction of the past (see, e.g. Hegel's *Philosophy of History*) were best characterized as metanarratives of aspirational perfection, creating a spark of optimism in the belief that the future will be ever so better than the past. Ultimately, these Enlightenment ideals of reason and progress would come to define modernity. In America, this "modern" sensibility emerged as *freedom* from the familiar (notably British colonial) past, sparking the evolution and the building of the US (Urban & Wagner, 2014). These Enlightenment norms, transcribed during Independence into American ideals, would come to characterize a new age of US school design.

Though Independence emerged from such progressive ideals, during the Revolutionary period many American schools were closed and fell into disrepair. Where schooling still existed, the educational climate was deeply moralistic. While in some cases the church took on educational responsibilities (especially in less affluent communities), private, for-profit schools were also common. Taking up these conditions in the late 1770s, many political leaders—such as Thomas Jefferson and Benjamin Rush—argued for America to establish a *publicly* supported school system to make education available to its general population. While it would take over 50 years for their visions to really come to fruition (with the common schools movement I will discuss below), the Age of Revolution did see some early attempts at mass education with schoolhouse designs inspired by the Industrial Revolution. To be sure, America's Industrial Revolution sparked a paradigm shift in art and architecture, giving birth to remarkable works in many new styles (Gelernter, 1999). Some Revolutionary architecture emerged from the styles of the earlier colonial period. Jefferson, for example, was credited with developing colonial architectural styles into the notable reductive and cubic style (Jefferson favored the Italian classical style—especially the Roman style—for public structures and the Palladian style [as well as that of the French Revolutionary architects] for private residences). Meanwhile, Asher Benjamin (1773–1845), who opposed the invention of new architectural orders, is credited with devising a second key style of post-Revolutionary architecture, known as the Greek revivalist style (Kruft, 1994). Rhode Island's exemplars of this architectural heritage is most evident in Newport's Colony House (see Fig. 2.3), Redwood Library (see Fig. 2.4), and Touro Synagogue (see Fig. 2.5). But broadly, architecture in the post-revolutionary period reflected the emerging ideals of the Enlightenment, the acceleration of the industrial complex, and America's rising nationalism, grounded in commitments to political liberalism (Gelernter, 1999).

Fig. 2.3 Colony House, 1739. (da Silva Photographer, 2015)

Fig. 2.4 Redwood Library, 1748–50. (da Silva Photographer, 2015)

In school architecture, the Industrial Revolution inspired the development of the Puritans' utilitarian approach to schoolhouses. The pedagogical goal at this time was to teach an ever-growing student population as efficiently and economically as possible. One winning "flash in the pan" school concept was the Lancaster system (also known as "monitorial school[ing]" [Tanner & Lackney, 2006, p. 5]). Originating in England, the Lancastrian learning environment's original objective "was to lower the cost of educating poor children who were forced into labor under harsh conditions in England" (Tanner & Lackney, 2006, p. 5). The system involves one teacher and approximately 50 student monitors who each, in turn, teach 10 students. Teaching takes place in clusters around the perimeter of the classroom. These giant one-room schoolhouses, designed to house 500 children were common in cities and were typically 50 feet by 100 feet in size, with rows of benches for students (Upton, 1996). This type of schooling, which "emphasiz[es] group instruction over costly, time consuming individualized instruction[,] was successful in convincing

Fig. 2.5 Touro Synagogue, 1759–61. (da Silva Photographer, 2015)

some people that the cost of universal education did not have to be prohibitive" (Tanner & Lackney, 2006, p. 5). The Lancaster system caught on briefly in Rhode Island: in 1826, the town of Bristol established a private school on its Common using the Lancastrian system. Before the Lancastrian model came on to the scene, education was usually delivered only to small groups and accordingly, was often expensive and exclusive. In step with the traditions of industrial mass production, the Lancaster model helped to establish small group instruction at a low cost and thus paved the way for free, compulsory public education (Graves, 1993). With Lancaster School Houses, American education began to take seriously the idea that the *form* of a schoolhouse could support its *function*. Important to note is that while the Lancaster model was popular, the post-revolutionary period also saw the growth of many other kinds of school designs. For example, in 1821, America's first public high school, the English Classical School, opened its doors in Boston (Tanner & Lackney,

2006). Though the English Classical School was public, its enrollment was limited to students of privileged families who did not need the additional income of their children's labor.

But perhaps the most meaningful event in nineteenth century school design took place at the end of this period, in 1827. On September 11 of that year, the Yale College Committee of the Corporation (made up of "His Excellency Governor Tomlinson, Rev. President Day, Rev. Dr. Chaplin, Hon. Noyes Darling, and Rev. Abel McEwen" [Yale Report, 1828, p. 1]) gathered to consider the college's curriculum. The question at hand was whether the.

> regular course of instruction [at Yale should be] to leave out of said course the study of the dead languages, substituting other studies therefor; and either requiring a competent knowledge of said languages, as a condition of admittance into college, or providing instruction in the same, for such as shall choose to study them after admittance. (Yale Report, 1828, p. 3)

In April, the Committee turned to Yale's faculty for an answer.[7] They expediently detailed their response in the *Reports of the Course of Instruction in Yale College by a Committee of the Corporation, and Academic Faculty* (1828), now commonly referred to as *The Yale Report*. As the *Report* details, the faculty could not bear to part with the college's traditional curriculum—for them, "[t]he expediency of retaining the ancient languages, as an essential part of our course of instruction, [was] so obviously connected with the object and plan of education in the college that justice could not be done to the particular subject of inquiry" (Yale Report, 1828, p. 3). They made their case in "two parts: one containing a summary view of the plan of education in the college and the other an inquiry into the expediency of insisting on the study of the ancient languages" (Yale Report, 1828, p. 3). The faculty argued that if Yale was to indeed do its duty to America's emerging ideals, its education needed to foster wise and critical citizens committed to improving society. To offer such a superior liberal education, the committee contended, Yale must deliver "a course of discipline in the arts and sciences" (31) that was resolutely "thorough" or, as the *Report* declares, "*broad, deep, and solid*" (1828, p. 6, my emphasis)—designed to "strengthen and enlarge the faculties of the mind and...familiarize it with the leading principles of the great objects of human investigation and knowledge" (31). More specifically, the *Report* argues that.

[7] Notably, these faculty members were all male.

> The two great points to be gained in intellectual culture, are the discipline and the furniture of the mind; expanding its powers, and storing it with knowledge. The former of these is, perhaps, the more important of the two. A commanding object, therefore, in a collegiate course, should be, to call into daily and vigorous exercise the faculties of the student. Those branches of study should be prescribed, and those modes of instruction adopted, which are best calculated to teach the art of fixing the attention, directing the train of thought, analyzing a subject proposed for investigation; following, with accurate discrimination, the course of argument; balancing nicely the evidence presented to the judgement; awakening, elevating, and controlling the imagination; arranging, with skill, the treasures which memory gathers; rousing and guiding the powers of genius. All this is not to be effected by the light and hasty course of study; by reading a few books, hearing a few lectures, and spending some months at a literary institution. The habits of thinking are to be formed, by long continued and close application. The mines of science must be penetrated far below the surface, before they disclose their treasures. If a dexterous performance of the manual operations, in many of the mechanical arts, requires an apprenticeship, with diligent attention for years; much more does the training of the powers of the mind demand vigorous, and steady, and systematic effort. (Yale Report, 1828, p. 7)

In short, the *Report* advises Yale to encourage its students to develop a balanced (*broad and solid*) character, nurtured by the equal but *deep* development of a range of intellectual disciplines (from Latin to Science) and mental faculties (e.g. critical reasoning, taste, decision-making, memory, imagination, and inventiveness). Founded on the popular nineteenth century theory that the mind was a "muscle" that could be strengthened with focused, frequent, and sustained "training", the *Report*'s course of instruction embraces lectures, recitations, and debates. To be sure, such a general liberal education was not geared, as the *Report* states, "to teach that which is peculiar to any one of the professions" (14), but rather to lay the foundation which is common to them all" (14). Negating education that seeks to professionalize students for specific kinds of work (e.g. mercantilist, mechanical, or agricultural work), the faculty argued that the broad education it was proposing would most powerfully prepare students not only for a variety of professions,[8] but also for civic duty. In a country

[8] And yet, those "professions" that didn't require more specific hands-on training in this period were those most often enjoyed by members of the upper- and middle-class for whom Yale was an affordable rite of passage.

that assertedly "gives full liberty to the human intellect to expand and operate", *The Yale Report* declared, "education should be proportionally liberal and ample" (p. 30), because "a mind richly stored with general knowledge, has an elevation and dignity of character, which gives him commanding influence in society, and a widely extended sphere of usefulness" (p. 15).

Turning back to the committee's original question, the faculty reasoned that these pedagogies the *Report* argued defined a strong liberal education *demanded the study of ancient languages.* First: such an education surveyed "the principle branches of [Western] knowledge" (31). Because these branches derived from Greek and Roman classics, the faculty argued that such texts and ideas were central to Yale's curriculum. Arguing that the classics were best learnt in their original forms, the *Report* called for Yale to continue to teach its students classical languages to optimize their studies of such texts. Second, the *Report* presented the classical curriculum as effectively "working out" the mind (as muscle): "the study of classics is useful," the faculty claimed,

> not only as it lays the foundations of correct taste, and furnishes the student with those elementary ideas which are found in the literature of modern times, and which he nowhere so well acquires as in their original sources, – but also as the study itself forms the most effectual discipline of the mental faculties... The range of classical study extends from the elements of language, to the most difficult questions arising from literary research and criticism. *Every faculty of the mind is employed; not only the memory, judgment, and reasoning powers, but the taste and fancy are occupied and improved.* (p. 36, my emphasis)

Taking their defense of the classics a step further, the faculty also recommended "that [Yale's] terms of admission may very properly, be gradually raised so as ultimately to render necessary, as a condition of admission, much greater acquirements, especially in the classics, than the laws of the college at present prescribe" (Yale Report, 1828, p. 56). But though Yale's faculty defended their extant curriculum, prescribing some development in the *Report*, they also allowed that moving forward, "changes may, from time to time be made with advantage [to the *Report*'s curriculum], to meet the varying demands of the community, to accommodate the course of instruction to the rapid advance of the country, in population, refinement, and opulence" (Yale Report, 1828, p. 5). Satisfied with the *Report* and its caveat, the Committee passed the faculty's resolution in September 1828, almost a year to the day Yale first began to consider the value of the traditional curriculum. Yale's formal sanctioning of this developed traditional curriculum kicked off a new era in American school design.[9] The following sections will explore the *Report*'s legacies in more detail, but before unpacking them more closely, I want to first establish a sense of how the *Report*'s pedagogical directives translate into spatial forms to make more evident the ways in which the *Report*'s curriculum would influence school architecture in the 1830s and beyond.

See Table 2.1, which translates the *Report*'s directives first into pedagogical approaches and activities and then into spatial requirements, namely: a lecture hall, a classroom, a recitation room, a debate room, a laboratory, a studio, and a library. Though some aspects of the Report's curriculum might warrant more customized spaces, they would have been more or less considered accessories to the primary spaces listed below. And so generally for our purposes, a schoolhouse that exhibits those spaces listed in Table 2.1 is a model "*Yale Report*" school.

1830–1865: Expansion and Realignment

In the wake of *The Yale Report*, the third decade of the nineteenth century was home to another sea change in American approaches to primary education. At the time, the country's early Puritan and Protestant tuition-

Table 2.1 *The Yale Report*: Pedagogy and Spatial Forms

Pedagogical directive	*Pedagogical activity*	*Spatial form*
Listening	Fixing attention	Lecture hall
Decision-making	Balancing evidence and judgment	Debate hall
Memorization	Directing thought, analyzing	Classroom
Reasoning	Accurate discrimination of argument	Laboratory
Taste	Reading classics	Library
Fancy, imagination, invention	Awakening imagination	Studio
Knowledge acquisition	Evaluation	Recitation room

[9] Though the *Report* pays no attention to school architecture, many schoolhouse designs in the years to come were deeply inspired by its pedagogies. The absence of spatial requirements of *The Yale Report* is consistent with the historic (up to this point) lack of attention to the material conditions of the classroom.

based schools still dominated the educational landscape, teaching relatively small numbers of local youth (many of whom paid to attend school) literacy, numeracy, and other basic knowledge. But as agricultural activity declined on the East Coast with the rise of industrialization and growing numbers of immigrants arrived in the nation, many argued that this extant system of education just wasn't making the grade. Rapid industrialization and immigration had intensified racial, social, and economic disparities (especially visible between locals and new Irish immigrants) in the still-young nation and—influenced by the progressive ideals of the Enlightenment and the dreams of Jefferson and Rush—a growing number of Americans believed that education could be the great equalizer for the new republic; a force that, by empowering the common man, could stabilize the nation's increasingly diverse and economically polarized population. This burgeoning belief sparked calls for education that could foster a new, assertedly more opportunistic social order (this emerging common sense, just before the civil war was perhaps best captured in the Republican Party's then-platform/ideology of "free soil, free labor, free men" and free schools (Foner, 1995, my emphasis]). Taking these emerging (notably nationalist) calls to heart, a group of educational reformers led by politicians Horace Mann and Henry Barnard advocated for the creation of a "*common school*" system. In brief, these reformers called for high quality, free, and universal[10] public education, believing that providing schooling to those who formerly would not be able to afford it would lessen the era's unsettling socio-economic tensions (by reversing the extant societal stratification) and foster more harmonious socialities (Willis et al., 1993). Around the same time, the American Institute of Instructors held a contest for the best schoolhouse designs. This contest made clear that school architecture and the curricula it could support were matters the nation now took seriously: school architects and educators were professionals in their own right (up until this point, schools had been designed and operated by local community representatives [Krugg, 1969; Tyack, 1990]). The common schools movement, by locating primary education as a public good, and the school design content of 1830, by taking seriously the schoolhouse itself, together stimulated a national desire to standardize school design (Button and Provenzo).

Heading this new attitude to school design, Mann and Barnard both echoed the Institute's interest in school architecture. Speaking to the burgeoning national interest in school architecture, in 1838 Barnard wrote a

[10] This "all", in this period, signifying white youth.

bill—“An Act to provide for the better supervision of the common schools”—to establish a national board of commissioners to oversee public education. More specifically, insisting that poor physical conditions inhibited wholehearted learning, the “Act” mandated that.

> [e]very village, town and school in Connecticut would have at least one edifice in good taste, in a conspicuous and agreeable situation, a correct model of architecture pleasing to the eye of every spectator and agreeable to those for whom the school house was designed. (Button & Provenzo, 1989, p. 114)

Putting the “Act” into practice, in 1839, Barnard became the Secretary of that very Board of Commissioners of Common Schools (of Connecticut). In this role, he evaluated schoolhouses through the lens of an implied comprehensive educational philosophy, which would later be known as curriculum, and in doing so became the nation’s first professional educational facility planner (Nye MacMullen, 1991) (unsurprisingly, his pioneering school inspections found that many schools were in absolutely miserable physical condition). A few years later in 1845, he became the first Superintendent of Schools and in this position went on to implement similar reforms (Steiner & Camp, 1919). While Barnard’s “Act” and tenure as Common School Secretary affirm his early commitment to considering school architecture, it was his 1860 book *School Architecture: Or a Contribution to the Improvement of Schoolhouses in the US* that paradigmatically established a “proper” schoolhouse form as a prerequisite to a sound common school education (Cutler, 1989). Supporting Barnard’s argument that good school architecture deeply impacted learning and so the success of both school and society, Mann helped to emphasize the need for well-built schools during his time as Secretary for the Board of Education of Massachusetts (Hansen, 2002, p. 1).

But Mann and Barnard were not content to focus only on school architecture: the two also sought to establish a suitable curriculum for common schools. As Barnard details in *School Architecture* (1848), schools at that time were broadly organized around five systems of instructional arrangement or “didactic designs”: *individual* (each age group requires individual scholarly recitation and instruction); *simultaneous* (intellectually proficient groupings receive whole group instruction, thought to make classroom sizes more manageable); *monitorial* (i.e. the Lancastrian system, designed to facilitate large class sizes by employing advanced students to assist in supervision and instruction); *mixed* (combines the simultaneous and monitorial system and uses assistants for support and standard procedures); and *facher* (different teachers teach different subjects, all under the supervision of a principal). These designs emerged across a range of schools, from the ungraded and unclassified *district* schools (serving all white boys and girls, taught by one teacher in one room) to *primary* schools (for students from 5 to 8 years of age, taught by women), *secondary* schools (for students from 8 to 12 years of age, taught by women [for the younger grades] and men [for the older grades]), *public high* schools (for students age 12 and above, taught by men), *intermediate schools* (serving young adults who were unable to attend consistently), *supplementary* schools (evening, training, industry, and reform-type schools serving mainly adult students), and *normal* schools (training young men and women to become teachers). Considering these didactic designs, Mann and Barnard believed common schools should focus on fostering an adept citizenry by strengthening students' characters, morals, and minds—in other words, they imagined common schools as founded on the pedagogical directives of *The Yale Report*.[11] With these goals in mind, they favored the *facher* design (McClintock & McClintock, 1970, p. 199). Barnard in particular advocated for developing the *facher* design into a *graded* school configuration that covered a range of different subjects—taught in age-appropriate ways by the most experienced teachers. Located within this broader concept of graded *facher* schools, Barnard pressed a curriculum that covered spelling, reading, writing, arithmetic, natural philosophy, vocal music, religion, and physical education. Thus empowered by the common schools movement, *The Yale Report*'s traditional pedagogical directives remained the prevailing curricula throughout the rest of the first half of the nineteenth century.

Firmly believing that school architecture was necessary for instructors to properly carry out his traditional pedagogies, Barnard's school designs (see Fig. 2.6) called for schools to include a hallway dividing a library and a lecture hall and separate spaces for girls, boys, and teachers. Moreover, Barnard imagined common school classrooms as self-contained, graded by

[11] Barnard, who was attending Yale when the *Report* was written, explicitly develops his own pedagogical commitments from the *Report*, Mann's *Selection Among Studies* (1842), and the work of Pestalozzi whose educational theories encouraged **harmonious intelligence**, ethics, and physical growth taught with active sensory pedagogies (eventually, Pestalozzi's work received so much acclaim it became synonymous with the common schools movement) (Nye MacMullen, 1991).

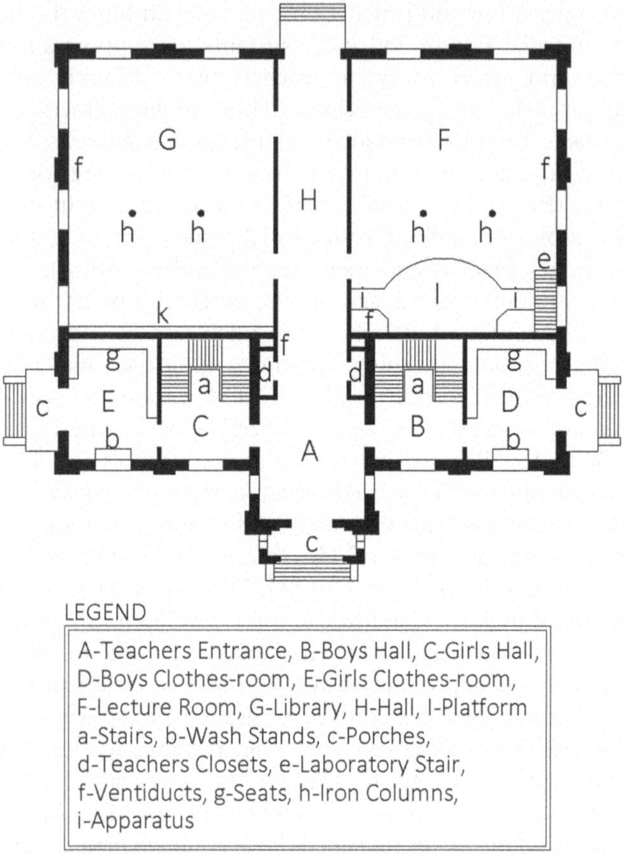

Fig. 2.6 Henry Barnard's architectural plans for a graded school. (da Silva, 2018)

age, and taught by women.[12] Meanwhile, Mann proposed a one-room schoolhouse (see Fig. 2.7), crediting his design to Dr. Alcott of Hartford, CT (McClintock & McClintock, 1970) and accordingly naming it the "Alcott Plan".

[12] Women were thought to be the best teachers because popular ideology at the time framed them as having given those innate caring characteristics associated with motherhood. Pulling from this assumption, the hope was that women would be the best at delivering a curriculum of play, cleanliness, obedience, mutual kindness, piety, and other virtues.

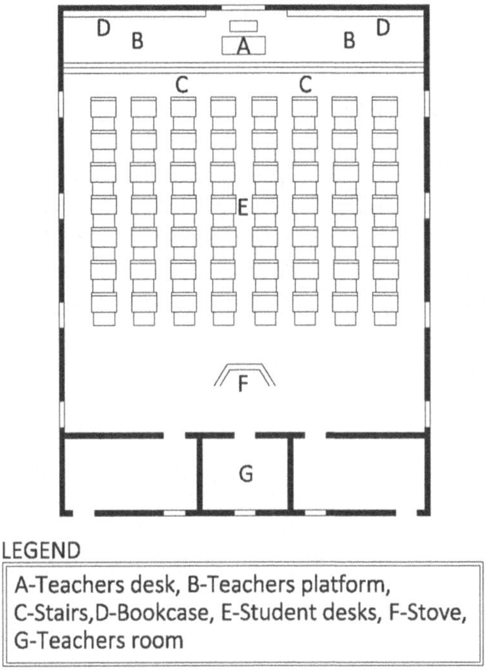

Fig. 2.7 Plan for a one-room schoolhouse recommended by Horace Mann. (McClintock & McClintock, 1970, p. 118)

More specifically, the Alcott plan accommodates 56 students in fixed seating. It measures approximately 30 feet wide by 40 feet long. There is minimal space in the aisles between student desks to discourage student movement. The teacher is positioned front and center on an elevated (three steps high) platform that runs the total width of the room, a design that locates her as a kind of "gatekeeper" of the required knowledge. Meanwhile, a bookcase to be filled with the texts of the appropriate knowledge symmetrically flanks the teacher's desk. Notably, much attention and purpose in the Alcott plan has gone to separating entries and alcoves by gender. In addition, prominently stationed and centralized at the entrance of the class is the recitation room which, as its name suggests, was used to evaluate what students had learned through recitation in addition to being used as a small multipurpose group room for meeting with parents and as a private space where one might recover from a minor ailment. In such schools, heating was still an optional amenity—something that might speak more to the seasonal period of schooling than a dedication to economy.

Ultimately, Barnard's and Mann's emphases on traditional liberal curricula and the kinds of school architecture that would support it kicked off an era of collaboration between architects and educators in the 1840s that would yield many beautiful and innovative schoolhouse designs,[13] such as octagonal and diamond-shaped plans and gingerbread facades (Wriston, 1963). For our purposes, one of the most telling schools of this movement is Boston's Quincy Grammar School. The very first graded school, Quincy Grammar began construction in 1847 (Graves, 1993), its plan was borrowed from a Prussian example (Graves, 1993). Quincy Grammar was a four-story structure, designed to house 660 students in 16 classrooms separated by grade levels. Innovations in stairs and the introduction of the stair tower allowed for the building of such multi-leveled facilities, for the "stacking" of floor plans on top of one another to maximize space in small sites. The school's first three floors housed classrooms that were sized for 55 students (see Fig. 2.8). Inside the classrooms, the seating layout was characterized by seven rows of eight desks bolted to the floor (most schools built before Quincy Grammar gave rise to what would be called the "Quincy Plan" had double-loaded hallways with student seating on each side) (Cutler, 1989).

Fig. 2.8 Typical 'Quincy Plan' floor plate incorporating four classrooms. (da Silva, 2015)

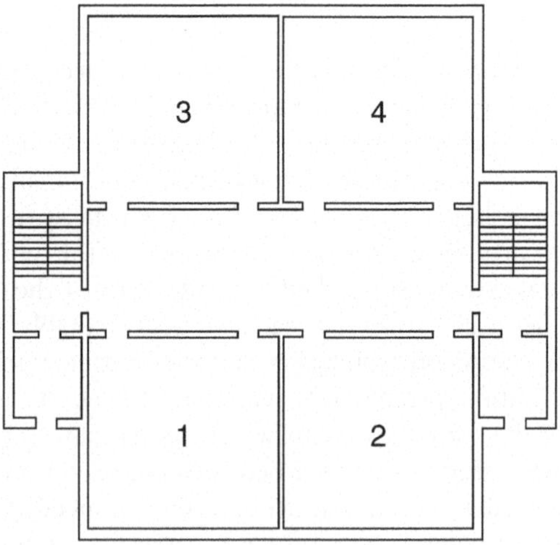

[13] Some notable architects of this time include Town, Davis, and Dwyer (Heath, 1982).

The Quincy plan was deeply influential for US educational architecture, in part because so many influential American educators of the time visited the school. Accordingly, soon after Quincy Grammar opened its doors, stunning numbers of common schools inspired by its plan began to pop up in major cities across the country (Graves, 1993). In the 1850s, for example, the Norwich Free Academy School (see Fig. 2.6) was built, designed to support Barnard's desire to further refine school architecture in the ambitions of *The Yale Report*. More specifically, the Norwich Free Academy's plan exhibits a dedication to pedagogies founded on the *Report*'s belief that the "mind is a muscle": the lecture hall serves as the place for the teacher oratorical role, set up on the hierarchical platform, as the expert imparting knowledge. Meanwhile, the library is located as the sacred space of knowledge, offering lots of room for displaying books as testaments to the opportunity for the kind of broad, deep, and solid education such a school sought to provide. In addition, like other schools of the period, the Norwich Academy demonstrated a desire to separate gender with different entries for boys and girls on either side. Predominately positioned at the main façade was the teacher's entry (with closets). Another popular national schoolhouse plan in the common schools period was the "Philadelphia" plan,[14] designed by Samuel Sloan. Notable for its concept of flexible (but still instructor-focused) classrooms, glazed movable walls, and amble circulation, the Philadelphia plan was ahead of its time (see Fig. 2.9). Moreover, Sloan's plan advanced school design by introducing innovative lighting techniques and multipurpose spaces (Cooledge, 1964). Though traditional humanistic "mind as a muscle" educational philosophy was still the prevailing ideology at this time, the Philadelphia Plan did embody some of the progressive sensibilities more aligned with the student-centered learning directive of the child psychology movement that would gain momentum in the 1890s (Cremin, 1970; Krugg, 1969; Tyack, 1990). Ultimately, these "common school" plans all advanced American school design and brought home the notion that properly planned schoolhouses would optimize learning, though the progression of school design along these lines was admittedly slow. Over a half a century later, one-room schoolhouses still numbered in the hundreds of thousands and many rural and urban schools continued—as they do even today—to suffer from inadequate light, heat, and sanitation, flaws that certainly hinder the effectiveness of instruction and learning (Cutler, 1989).

In addition to the common schools movement, the years between 1830 and 1865 were also home to a number of other important developments

[14] Interestingly, no plans of this type were discovered in Rhode Island.

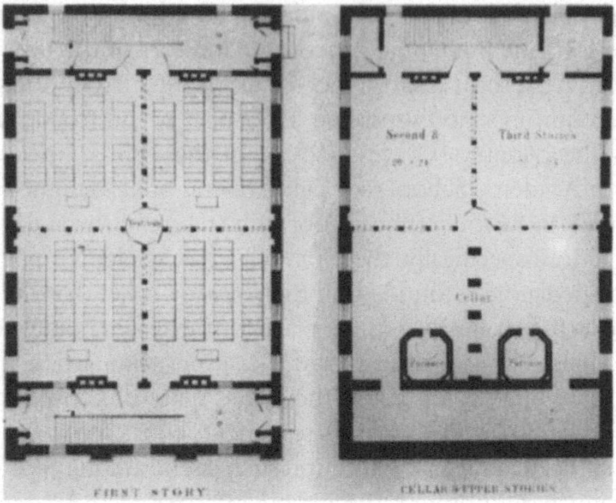

Fig. 2.9 'Philadelphia Plan' floor plans designed by Sloan. (Cooledge, 1964)

in the fields of architecture and education that would inform American school design over the coming century: in architecture, the oppositional Greek Revival theories of Greenough (1805–1852), published in 1843 in the *United States Magazine and Democratic Review*, gave rise to functionalist architecture, based on the Transcendental Organic-Functionalist Aesthetic of Nature (Kruft, 1994).[15] Moreover, the Gothic architectural theory of John Ruskin, expressed in *The Seven Lamps of Architecture* (1849) and inspired by the rational and functional work of Welby, Purgin (Hearn, 2003), and Lacygarbett (Kruft, 1994), brought to light honest and principled expressions of the Gothic, its structural nature, and its directives of social improvement (Hearn, 2003). Not since Viollet-le-Duc (who is credited with establishing the theory of modern architecture in *Discourses on Architecture* (1863)), and Alberti (of the fifteenth century) had there been as comprehensive and as systematic an architectural theory as Ruskin's (Hearn, 2003). This period also saw the emergence of transcendentalist sensibilities in architecture with the Shakers, stemming from the deeply religious and philosophical tenets they expressed in their practi-

[15] This organic architectural theory—based on an organic skeleton covered with a skin, prioritized room layouts and the structure's ability to link to the outside environment—would come to inspire modern architecture like that popularized by Wright's architectural designs (Kruft, 1994).

cal ways of living and knowing. A commitment to simplicity, a focus on economy, and a reduction of the ornament went hand in hand with Shaker philosophies (Kruft, 1994). But despite these emerging styles, American architecture in the expansion and alignment period was still predominantly influenced by the European traditions of Sloan (1815–84), Downing (1815–52), and Vaux (1824–95) and by the Victorian pattern books produced by Bicknell that offered architectural style choices (such as Queen Anne and Shingle Style) (Kruft, 1994). Meanwhile, in education, the common schools movement inspired two major events: (1) the founding of the National Teachers Association in 1857[16]; and (2) the 1862 the Morrill Land Grant, which provided land for states to establish colleges (this seemingly humble step in our nation's history is highly responsible for making the US the epicenter of higher education internationally).

1865–1900: Industry and Turmoil

Although many years had passed since 1828, the traditionalist ideologies of *The Yale Report* remained popular throughout the 1800s, their emphasis on pedagogy propelling curricula into a more popular object of study—by mid-century, curricula was seen as the "heart of education" (Schubert, 1986). But in the second half of the nineteenth century, the bloody toll of the Civil War, the Reconstruction, and the still-burgeoning industrial complex prompted new modalities that changed the face of American education. The Reconstruction, with the internal migration of African Americans northward, shifted national identity and culture—a change that variously stimulated hostility and democratic activism. Meanwhile, many people driven by the further development of the robust industrial complex that required an immense industrial labor force, moved from rural to urban areas. To be sure, the impact urbanization had on schooling in this period cannot be overstated: in 40 years, the number of high schools in the country increased 20-fold to 6000 in 1900 (Graves, 1993). By the turn of the century, approximately 80% of school age children (school age, by this time, extending from 5 to 17 years old) were attending school due to the newly implemented child labor laws and advances in manufacturing (Button & Provenzo, 1989). As the nation shifted it began to feel overwhelming to some, sparking prominent thinkers to consider new methods of social control. Many scholars turned to education as a way to manage

[16] Renamed the National Educational Association in 1870.

the country's new demographics, their methods inspired by a burgeoning commitment to science as *the* path to progress that encouraged calls—especially by a group named the Herbartians (Schubert, 1986)—for educational reformers to develop and reconfigure education as social control around more pragmatic, empirical principles. Many combined this empiricism with the management principles of the Industrial Revolution (Schubert, 1986, p. 70) that emerged as thinkers tried to determine how to make production as efficient and profitable as possible: together, scientific and industrial ideologies merged to usher in a new social control methodology that mechanical engineer Fredrick Taylor would call "*scientific management*". Based on scientific evaluations, economics, and workplace structures, scientific management used specialization, routines, strong supervision, and control to facilitate efficient mass production (Pinar, Slattery, & Taubman, 1995). Predicting scientific management's influence on school design in the late nineteenth and early twentieth centuries, in 1885, E.T. Tomlinson, the Headmaster of Rutgers College Grammar School, declared that "an era of new things is seemingly upon us" (Krugg, 1969, p. 400). Considering this period in pedagogical history, Kliebard argues that American school design during the second half of nineteenth century (and well into the twentieth century) is most accurately characterized by four different groups: first, the *traditional humanists* (who echoed and/or developed the directives of *The Yale Report*). And second, three groups who worked to reform education by developing pedagogies under the rubric of scientific management: *developmentalists*, *social meliorists* (also known as social reconstructionists), and *social efficiency* (discussed below in "1900–1920") *educators*.

The traditional tilt of nineteenth century pedagogy was most visibly upheld by two famous educators: William Harris, a superintendent and philosopher who would become the US Commissioner of Education, and Charles Eliot, the then President of Harvard University. Harris championed a humanist idealism that stemmed from the philosophies of Immanuel Kant (1742–1804) and Georg Wilhelm Friedrich Hegel (1770–1831), who both saw education as central to human progress (Schubert, 1984). Accordingly, Harris promoted a humanist curriculum that nurtured what he liked to call the "five 'windows of the soul'": grammar, English literature, arithmetic and math, history, and geography (Kliebard, 1986, p. 15). In 1876, Harris penned a Hegelian synthesis titled the *Report of a Committee on a Course of Study from Primary School to University*. The report argued for a universal curriculum that combined the traditional pedagogies of *The Yale Report* with more practical studies that he believed would best prepare students for modern life (Cremin, 1970; Kliebard, 1986; Krugg, 1969; Tyack, 1990; Willis et al., 1993). Meanwhile, Eliot argued for "systematic development of reasoning power as the central function of schools" (Kliebard, 1986, p. 9). Though Eliot held steadfast to the human capabilities of "power of reason, sensitivity to beauty, and high moral character", he did not support the social reform elements of education (Kliebard, 1986, p. 10). As a scientist, Eliot envisioned the process of reason as "observing accurately, making correct records of the observations, classification, and categorization, and finally, making correct inferences from these mental operations" (Kliebard, 1986, p. 9). Moreover, unlike other mental disciplinarians (e.g. Harris), Eliot supported electives in the curriculum even in the elementary grades (Kliebard, 1986).

In 1893, Eliot chaired a committee (of which Harris was a part) for the National Education Association that sought to determine the pedagogical directives of American high schools. The committee's conclusions, published in the *Report of the Committee of Ten on Secondary School Studies*, held that high school curricula should primarily seek to prepare students for college by building their capacities in those traditionalist areas of learning recommended by *The Yale Report* (the committee maintained the assumption of mind as muscle (Kliebard, 1986)). But while the Committee of Ten defended traditional education, it also advocated for an expansion of program offerings in higher education by relieving its emphasis on the classics (Willis et al., 1993). That same year, Eliot appointed Harris as chairman of a committee charged with studying elementary curriculum (the "Committee of Fifteen on Elementary Education") (Kleibard, 1986). Harris was a practical and credible choice for the task, given that he had been the Superintendent of Schools in St. Louis for over a decade and that he was also the editor of a Hegelian journal (Kliebard, 1986). As chair, Harris divided the committee into three sub-committees of five members each to focus respectively on: teacher training, correlation of studies, and school organization (Paraskeva, 2011). Harris argued that the curriculum should have two functions: subjective training and the objective representation of the world (Paraskeva, 2011). However, he was suspicious of the growth of the natural sciences. For Harris it was the subject's content, rather than its form, that mattered; he felt that content could foster humanist values (Paraskeva, 2011). In the end, the committee's report solidified the status quo of curricula in elementary education by reinforcing that classical subject matter should remain central to American pedagogy.

America's growing scientific community responded to the *Committee of Ten* and the *Committee of Fifteen* reports with severe criticism.[17] The first group to speak out against the committees' defense of the traditional curriculum was called the *developmentalists*; its most notable scholars included G. Stanley Hall, Charles Francis Adams, Colonel Francis Parker, and John Dewey (Kliebard, 1986). In general, the fundamental difference between the humanists and the developmentalists was one of content: while humanists were primarily concerned with *what* was taught, developmentalists argued that more attention needed to be paid to *how* teachers taught said content (Krugg, 1969). Believing that "the natural order of development in the child was the most significant and scientifically defensible basis for determining what should be taught" (Kliebard, 1986, p. 11), developmentalists studied children's growth to determine what ways of teaching would work best for different types of students (hence why the progressive "developmentalist" movement is sometimes also referred to as the "child study" movement) (Kliebard, 1986).

Hall was considered the leader of the child study group, having published the seminal *The Contents of the Mind of Children* (1883), a text hugely influenced by Adams' and Parker's work. But early on, Adams drew scientific attention to the mental habits of children in 1879 and helped catapult Parker's child-centered work in Quincy, Massachusetts into national prominence (Kliebard, 1986). More specifically, Parker introduced greater freedom into the drudgery of schooling of the period by discarding the traditional course of study for one that was more in line with children's tendencies for play and activity (Kliebard, 1986). It was Parker's instinctive reforms that helped thrust Hall into the spotlight as the leader of the developmentalist movement (rather ironically, Hall's *The Contents of Children's Minds* emerged from a lecture that *Eliot* of all people had invited him to deliver at Harvard over a decade earlier [Kliebard, 1986]). As the title of his book suggests, Hall was searching for what the "child" might already know, concluding that teachers often overestimate children's knowledge (Kliebard, 1986). Hall was headquartered at Clark University, where the periodical circulation the *Pedagogical Seminary*, together with the help of the women's club network in the collection of data, enabled him to execute national scientifically-grounded research in

[17] For Kliebard (1986), the *Committee of Ten Report*'s initial incitation of this traditional/ humanist vs. scientific/practical debate located the report as the main event in late nineteenth century educational reform.

child study and to develop it into a movement (Cremin, 1988). Influenced by Adams (1879), Parker (1875), and Burnham (1883), Hall believed that child-centered curriculum had the opportunity to stimulate teachers by helping them to best adapt their instructional methods to meet the actual needs of their students. For Hall, who rejected the notion "that all students should learn the same way and for the same period of time" (Paraskeva, 2011, p. 35), the recommendations of the committees of ten and fifteen—which he saw as pressing for the "college [to dominate] the high school curriculum" (Kliebard, 1986, p. 13)—were unresponsive to the vast intellectual diversity of children who came into the classroom. Disregarding the faculty psychology notion of "furniture", Hall was strongly against the proposition that teaching the same subject matter in the same way would have equal educational value for all students (Kliebard, 1986).[18] Accordingly, iterating what would come, the defining concern of the developmentalists, Hall advocated for educators and educational researchers to use child development science to create methods of instruction that would make assigned materials more meaningful for students (Schubert, 1984). Notably, the creation of the National Learning Lab in 1894 made clear the growing popularity of the developmentalists' determinedly scientific approach to education: designed to study the ways in which a child's behavior was related to his/her learning environment, the lab effectively located pedagogy as a science.

But of all the developmentalists the most famous was arguably John Dewey, a philosopher and psychologist who applied his scholarly training to questions of school design. Ultimately, Dewey would come to develop a revolutionary curriculum at the turn of the century, formulated out of his conflict between Hall's atheoretical developmentalist notions of the science of child study and Harris' humanistic but fragmentized approach to knowledge (Paraskeva, 2011). More specifically, believing that pedagogy should center around a learner's experience, Dewey advocated for teaching methods based on self-expression, discussion, analysis, and investigation and thus, in step with Froebel and Montessori, called for new pedagogies and new subject matter (such as geography and science) that would more effectively meet the needs of students for "free play, creative self-activity, and motor expression" (Tanner & Lackney, 2006, p. 9).

[18] Though Hall critiqued the one-size-fits-all tone of the curriculum, he did not apply this same logic to interrogate the replication of prototypical schoolhouse forms, which embodied the same premise.

Accordingly focusing on the student, Dewey's (1902) *The Child and Curriculum*, "helped set new conditions for the twentieth century debate about curriculum" (Willis et al., 1993, p. 123), by suggesting that a curriculum should respond to the interests and developmental needs of the youth it engages to optimize educational outcomes and benefits—a framework that increased the momentum of the child-study movement (Willis et al., 1993). To be sure, Dewey's pragmatic educational philosophy deviated from the humanistic tradition that had prevailed through much the nineteenth century in the wake of *The Yale Report* and that had remained front and center in the debates surrounding the reports of the committees of ten and fifteen, in which subject matter was fixed and prêt-à-porter (Willis et al., 1993). Moreover, Dewey's educational philosophy also deviated from the Herbartian cultural epoch theory: he insisted that subject matter and the learner's experience make up one centralized reality or *process* (1938). To understand this process, Dewey (1902) continues, one must:

> abandon the notion of subject-matter as something fixed and ready-made in itself, outside the child's experience; cease thinking of the child's experience as also something hard and fast; see it as something fluent, embryonic, vital; and we realize that the child and the curriculum are simply two limits which define a single process. Just as two points define a straight line, so the present standpoint of the child and the facts of truths of studies define instruction. It is a continuous reconstruction, moving from the child's present experience out into that represented by the organized bodies of truth that we call studies. (p. 11)

As the above quote details, in his mapping of this process, Dewey articulates two coordinates: the first, the learner's present experience in a continuity of circumstances and the second, the cumulative generation of realizations methodologically organized into *studies* or *facts* (Dewey, 1902). Dewey equates the translation between these coordinates to a map of a past journey, but the map is just a set of directions describing how to get from point A to point B, with established common principles to help direct the future journey. It is not the educational journey itself, which is based on a growth process filled with ideas, concepts, perceptions, intellections, simplifications, and organizations (Dewey, 1902). According to Dewey, unlike the archetypal scientist whose interest is in subject matter (as a body of knowledge to be explored), the teacher creates interest and relevance through a psychological process of impartial settings. The teacher nurtures such an interest by providing the opportunity for the subject matter to be satisfying, motivating, and accepted by the student. This psychology-based educative process is centralized in concert with the student's present continuity of situations, the engagement of which Dewey argues makes subject matter relevant and worthwhile. Through this process, the learning activity is contextualized—that is, it takes place in a medium or situation with reference to impartial conditions created by the teacher, the school, and the environment. Here, the subject matter becomes primary to the teacher as a facilitator of learning but, in true developmentalist style, it matters only insofar as it is taught with the right, experientially-predicated *method* (Dewey, 1902).

Slowly, Dewey's philosophies would come to shape schoolhouse design (Graves, 1993), most obvious in the kinds of school architecture that followed his own "Laboratory" school. More specifically, in 1896, Dewey designed and built what he called a "Laboratory" school to test his pedagogical theories. Based on his experiential educational philosophies, Dewey's Laboratory School was "a small cooperative society in which children gain[ed] social experience and insight as well as intellectual and manual skills" (Tanner & Lackney, 2006, p. 9). In contrast to the directives of the traditional curriculum, the school's "objective was rather to create a new curriculum in which developmental, intellectual, and social goals were integrated" (Tanner & Lackney, 2006, p. 9). Accordingly, the school worked at "relating the curriculum to children's experiences, integrating the curriculum, teaching critical thinking and problem-solving skills, stimulating creative thinking, supporting cooperative learning, providing hand-on activities, and supporting collaborative decision making by the teachers and staff" (Tanner & Lackney, 2006, p. 9). The physical structure was supportive of this development philosophy in that students:

> would work in the garden in the school yard, apply principles learned in their classes as they cooperated in building and furnishing a clubhouse,... make articles in a shop for use in connection with their other work, eat a gourmet lunch they planned and prepared in their French class,...study industrial history by working out the entire process of making cloth, study the nature of community life with the help of model houses brought into the classroom,...and use technologies of early peoples to turn grain into food. (Tanner & Lackney, 2006, p. 9)

In addition to his concerns with student experience and schoolhouse architecture, Dewey was also deeply captivated by schooling's political potential. Among many other core values of education, Dewey held democratic philosophy as paramount. For Dewey, the school was the practical space for democracy's social and individual interplay. As Paraskeva (2011) details:

> In essence, rather than proposing the school as the basis of democracy, rather than a democracy with a powerful social and political significance, rather than a democracy born out of mind, Dewey defended democracy as the method and the means by which the school proceeds with the transformation of society. (p. 120)

In advocating this pedagogical turn, Dewey criticized popular curricula that sought to teach students only simple concepts, maintaining that the lack of methodological democracy in schools—which he believed his experiential pedagogies would enact—was one of the primary causes of educational waste (Paraskeva, 2011). For Dewey (1916), education that responded to students' diverse experiences and interests *was* democratic education. And so, instead of approaching education as preparation for later vocations (a trend that was beginning at this time and that I explore below), Dewey's progressive social democratic approach advocated for education through occupation, which is analogous to a comprehensive education system (Dewey, 1916, p. 309). This comprehensive education system promoted reflective thinking through a process of student choices that facilitated student confidence, which Dewey believed was fundamental for participating in a democracy, versus simply training students for a specific job. To be sure, Dewey's work had a massive impact on the next group of "scientific management" pedagogues, the social meliorists (or social reconstructionists)—a movement that sought to put education to work to create more equitable societies.

The most notable figure of the social meliorist movement was arguably Lester F. Ward, a botanist and geologist who, in his 1883 *Dynamic Sociology* strongly rejected Spencer (1864) and Sumner's (1872) message of Social Darwinism, an ideology that celebrated "survival of the fittest" logic. More specifically, Ward condemned their laissez-faire position as a corruption of Darwinian theory. Drawing from his strong scholarly background and extensive observation of natural evolutionary phenomena, Ward argued that there was more to adaptations to environmental conditions than Spencer and Sumner wagered (Cremin, 1988). He postulated that Spencer had ignored the development of "the office of the mind," its purposes and ability to plan, and so too the mind's power (Cremin, 1988, p. 394). Instead, Ward argued that the mind.

> is to direct society into unobstructed channels, to enable these forces to continue in free play, to prevent them from being neutralized by collision with obstacles in their path. In a word, mind has for its function in civilization to preserve the dynamic and prevent the static condition of the social forces, to prevent the restoration of equilibrium between social forces and the natural forces operating outside them. (Ward, 1883, p. 689)

Ward believed that humanity had developed the power to intervene intelligently in order to counter the blind forces of nature—this capacity being, for Ward, the seed for social progress (Kliebard, 1986). Ward reasoned that dynamic social progress rested on "the great social duty[:]...the universal diffusion of all the most important knowledge now extant in the world," a task perhaps possible through a proper education (Cremin, 1988, p. 373). Accordingly, Ward advocated for an educational system that intentionally transmitted the most important existing world knowledge to all of its members (Cremin, 1988). Unlike education derived from experience and discipline, character and mental power, for Ward, came from the ownership of knowledge rather than the reverse (Cremin, 1988). He thus argued that educational systems should be governed by three "cardinal principles"; that schooling should be public, universal, and designed to increase the content of all minds (Cremin, 1988). Recalling the efforts of the common schools movement in *Dynamic Sociology*, Ward insisted on an equitable society in which no differences of race, gender, or class could hinder the development of one's intellect, envisioning a public education system as the life blood of social progress—an argument that placed his pedagogical theory at the core of a new scientific review of society and established Ward as the "father of American Sociology" (Cremin, 1988, p. 396). Ward affirms his egalitarian commitments in *Psychic Factors*,[19] writing that "the denizens of slums are not inferior in talent to

[19] Reviewing *Psychic Factors*, Dewey makes clear that he also believed that education was critical to correcting social ills and promoting social justice and progress. Important to note is that during the twentieth century Dewey engaged many different educational reform groups in his own work, a practice that would make him a central figure in the history of educational philosophy.

the graduates of Harvard College" and, moreover, that "criminals are the genius of the slums. Society has forced them into this field, and they are making the best use they can of their native abilities" (Ward, 1893, p. 290). Seeing social divisions as structurally or socially produced (rather than as stemming from an individual's strengths or weaknesses), Ward argued that education could equally redistribute cultural capital and its inherent power. In so doing, he positioned himself as the "prophet of the welfare state in the twentieth century" and the leader of the social meliorists (Kliebard, 1986, p. 23). While social meliorism, under Ward, certainly enjoyed its time in the sun, with the turn of the century would come the rise of a new form of scientific management school design called social efficiency that would soon dominate the educational landscape.

Legacies and Complications

1900–1920: Modernity, Diversity

In this episode of the nation's history, the US established itself as a military powerhouse backed by rapidly advancing technology and fueled by a robust economy. The turn of the twentieth century also saw significant changes in Western culture, curriculum, and architecture. The tensions of the Enlightenment age had stretched to the breaking point. The First World War was erupting in Europe. Meanwhile, at home, the stress around the historical stratification of US society came to a head in this period, with much violence breaking out as the working-class tried to establish a strong solidarity in reaction to long-extant inequities (Gelernter, 1999). In architecture, similar tensions existed between many diverse revival approaches with complex combinations. At the time, new, traditionally-based trends were emerging, such as Arts and Crafts, Craftsman, Prairie Styles, and Modernism.

Emerging amidst these transformations was the last of the scientifically-inspired pedagogies Kliebard (1986) locates: "social efficiency". The social efficiency movement started as an interest group worried about the common schools movement's fixation on humanistic theories (Kliebard, 1986) and was led by a young pediatrician turned educational reformer named John Mayer Rice who was deeply critical of Harris' report. Rice studied pedagogy in the university centers of Germany in Jena and Leipzig, between 1888 and 1890 (Cremin, 1988). Like other loosely affiliated

American Herbartians, such as Hall, Parker, and Dewey, Rice was influenced by the experiential pedagogical laboratories that Wilhelm Wundt had established in Germany (Kliebard, 1986). After observing several schools in Europe, Rice returned with reform plans grounded in the "science of education". Taking these theories to task in a tour sponsored by the prominent journal *The Forum* between January and June of 1892, Rice visited 36 American cities and surveyed elementary education; documenting his observations of those schools and classrooms he visited (Kliebard, 1986). During these surveys, Rice spoke with teachers and students, interviewed parents, and attended school board meetings (Cremin, 1988).[20] This scientifically-based, comparative study (synthesized into nine *Forum* articles) was published as a book titled *The Public School System of the United States* (Kliebard, 1986). In this research, Rice argues that he found many issues within the educational systems he studied, including: "rote learning, mindless teaching, administrative ineptitude, political chicanery, and public apathy" (Rice, 1912, p. 20). Based on these findings, he charged the public school system with incompetence, inadequate pedagogical knowledge, and, moreover, as having low-quality teachers (Schubert, 1984).[21] (However, Rice also observed exemplary progressive schools in Minneapolis, where he found teachers dealing reasonably and compassionately with disadvantaged students; Indianapolis, where he found that teachers were encouraging students to perceive relationships between subjects; and in Laporte [in Indiana], where students were working collaboratively rather than competitively (Cremin, 1988). Notably, Rice found that teachers at Cook County Normal School in Illinois [then under the leadership of a Principal Parker] used maps, drawings, models, and stuffed animals to teach students literature, sciences, and the arts [Cremin, 1988].)

Against unrelenting opposition from professional educators, Rice conducted a second survey in 1893 in which he focused on collecting data related to the success of third graders in English and math (Kliebard, 1986). Despite being recognized as the father of comparative methodology by Ayres, Rice was unable to discover superior techniques of teaching and only concluded that instruction on spelling appeared unrelated to

[20] Despite this exhaustive approach to school evaluations, facility matters were essentially trivialized in this discourse.

[21] Again, these critiques came with little regard for the condition of the facilities that were built to support these processes.

student spelling achievement (Kliebard, 1986). In 1912, as a social behaviorist who believed that poor teaching and poor leadership existed, Rice called for schools divorced of politics and a "scientific system of pedagogical management [that] would demand fundamentally the measurement of results in the light of fixed standards" (Rice, 1912, p. xiv). He believed the nation needed professional teacher training that would direct educators to teach children to observe, to reason, to be manually dexterous, and to memorize facts with the aim of fostering their intellectual, moral, and physical faculties (Paraskeva, 2011). Slowly, Rice's position changed from that of an outraged educational researcher to that of an advocate for the elimination of waste in curricula through the application of Taylor's scientific management methodology. The social efficiency movement thus emerged with the directive of determining the most efficient uses of time, money, and human resources in education. What social efficiency educators celebrated, in short, was discipline and hard work (Pinar, Slattery, & Taubman, 1995). Accordingly, social efficiency experts were task-driven: rather than viewing curricula as a "mental discipline", as the "window of the soul", or as "child centered", these experts advocated for curricula that worked as a kind of assembly line—in other words, curricula that worked toward the economic imperative of mass-producing socially appropriate citizens committed to generating profit (Kliebard, 1986).

Crucial to note is that the social efficiency movement was firmly grounded in the period's new emphasis on social control ("the art of combining social forces so as to give society at least a trend toward an ideal" [Vincent, 1896, p. 490]), a directive perhaps best captured in the works of sociologist Edward Alsworth Ross. More specifically, Ross' *Social Control* (1901) highlighted, at a macro level, the role of social order in quashing deviance and bringing about non-violent social associations and collective accords to create a "harmonious society". The book also outlined his ideas for different means of control, the importance of cohesive social structures, and the impact of social hierarchies in reinforcing and legitimizing social control. He believed social order and control were best established by accordingly orienting social institutions; he pinpointed the school as a key site (1901). Notably, many critics charged Ross' theories as conservative and as encouraging a racist white Anglo-Saxon superiority complex (from which he would later attempt to distance himself). The following quote from *Social Control* (1901) best exemplifies this tone:

> Now, it is the purpose of this inquiry to ascertain how men of the West-European breed are brought to live closely together, and to associate their efforts with that degree of harmony we see about us. Social order, even among the passive, unambitious Hindoos, presents a problem for solution. But it is a much more serious problem among the dolichocephalic blonds of the West. The restless, striving, doing Aryan, with his personal ambition, his lust for power, his longing to wreak himself, his willingness to turn the world upside down to get fame, or the fortune, or the woman, he wants, is under no easy discipline. The existence of order among men of this daring and disobedient breed challenges explanation. Especially is this true of the European man in America or Australia. The same selective migrations that made the Teuton more self-assertive than the docile Slav or the quiescent Hindoo, have made the American more strong-willed and unmanageable than even the West-European. (Ross, 1901, p. 3)

To be sure, Ross' hierarchializing of elite institutions and subordination of less powerful citizens speaks to ways in which society presses its citizens to conform through a multitude of processes. These conformist pressures work to produce assertedly "responsible" citizens and to Americanize immigrants. In no place is this hierarchical power of social control more prevalent and naturalized than in the turn-of-the-century US school, where scientific management pedagogies work to regulate impressionable pupils and socialize them in particular ways. This pedagogical focus on social order stands in contrast to the traditional emphasis on the individual in the pedagogies espoused by *The Yale Report*, the common schools movement, and the reports of the committees of ten and fifteen in the nineteenth century. Despite (or perhaps because of) its racist underpinnings, Ross' social control theory gathered a number of followers (such as Parsons [1951], Lapiere [1954], and Landis [1956]) and remained popular up to the Second World War (Janowitz, 1975).

Driving the social efficiency movement alongside Rice and Ross was John Franklin Bobbitt, a Professor at the University of Chicago (also inspired by Wundt) who believed that the best curricula taught practical skills that prepared students for life (Willis et al., 1993). Bobbitt (1918) (and later Tyler [1949]), defined social efficiency by a scientific behavioral process in which educational directives and experiences were effectively organized and evaluated to determine the level of student achievement. For Bobbitt, education and educational achievement was not about measuring progress in childhood, but about preparing youth for adulthood

(Dewey, in contrast, insisted that education was actually life and not a preparation for it). In his work, Bobbitt focused on controlling efficiency and standards and prescribing a formulaic approach to guiding practice. In *The Elimination of Waste in Education* (1912) and *The Curriculum* (1918), Bobbitt famously argues for a scientific curriculum-making process based on the student's future role in an industrialized society and that favored a utilitarian occupational efficiency. Bobbitt believed that gearing education to prepare the student for adulthood would optimize the learner's participation in the activities of the future (Bobbitt, 1918). In general, his curriculum—which he understood as a "series of things which children and youth must do and experience by way of developing abilities to do the things well that make up the affairs of adult life; and to be in all aspects what adults should be" (Bobbitt, 1918, p. 42), or, more broadly, as capturing "the entire range of human experiences, both undirected and directed, concerned in unfolding the abilities of the individual" (1918, p. 41)—emphasized student aptitude and aimed to prepare children for a healthy life that involved an appropriate vocation, civic duty, health, and leisure. True to Taylor, Bobbitt's approach really did resemble that of a product-driven assembly line with particular fabricated ends in mind that required technical management. To develop such a pedagogy, Bobbitt advised breaking down life into the numerous and diverse "abilities, attitudes, habits, appreciations, and forms of knowledge that men need" and the tasks that they must perform in the "real world" and then building a curriculum around them accordingly (Bobbitt, 1918, p. 42) (his *The Curriculum* (1918) argues for education "to develop a type of wisdom that can grow only out of participation in the living experiences of men, and never out of mere memorization of verbal statements of facts" (Bobbitt, 1918, p. iv)). Though Bobbitt did advocate for a general education that included some traditional subject matters, he primarily insisted on specialized occupational training based on scientific testing that paralleled societal needs, a pedagogy that would come to replace many traditional subjects. Ultimately, Bobbitt believed such an approach would be the best way to maximize educational services, staff, and infrastructure at the lowest possible cost at a time when growing populations were still putting a strain on the school system (Bobbitt, 1912).

Bobbitt's ambitions echoed those of scientific management educators more broadly, who sought at large to transform schools with the lessons of profitable and efficient factories. Translating scientific management into schooling in this way begins with a number of associations or allegories:

first, the concepts of learning are established as a process by which student behavior is changed through a scientific method toward the desired outcomes. Second, the roles of schooling must be translated in terms of the employer (management-principal or teacher) and employee (worker-teacher or student). The manager would conduct behavioral engineering by identifying the objectives and creating the proper sequencing of tasks or learning experiences, to produce the desired outcomes. In this way, the teacher was regarded as an educational manager or engineer who scientifically designed and implemented the curriculum to achieve specific pedagogical goals. The learner in this case becomes the employee that fulfills the standard outcome. The teacher as manager was there to scientifically guide the worker (learner), evaluate his or her outcomes, and make adjustments accordingly. Through this reductive approach, schooling became a kind of assembly line. In addition, the overall performance of the school "plant" was to be supervised by another layer of management, the principal, who became the manager of the teacher-leaders. This scientific management scenario positioned teachers as "workers". The principal, responsible for breaking down the necessary teaching tasks, provides the teachers with necessary professional development, equally distributes the work, and finally evaluates the teacher's mastery of the scientific tasks, while discouraging their application of rules of thumb in fashioning the desired learning outcomes (the manufactured products). These two-tiered hierarchal scientific management techniques were progressive and rooted in professionalism and specialization.

Thinking through the city of Gary, Indiana school system, Bobbitt applied the principles of scientific management to schooling and advised four according transformations in school design (Bobbitt, 1912, pp. 260–271). First: *the optimization of school infrastructure* (1912, pp. 260–264). Finding that as much as half of many school facilities stood idle and unoccupied at any given school period, Bobbitt argued that school spaces were usually only in use 50% of the time. In *The Elimination of Waste in Education*, Bobbitt provides an example of an elementary school demonstrating such waste in which students occupied eight classrooms for primary studies (which consisted of 90-minute blocks of studies in arithmetic, history, geography, and formal languages), while the spaces for special studies/activities (which consisted of 90-minute blocks of studies in nature, manual activities, drawing, literature, music, and play) remained underutilized. Bobbitt's coursework spaces included the customary classrooms as well as playgrounds, laboratories, specialized science rooms, vocational workshops, assembly halls, gymnasiums, bathing areas, and swimming pools. By incorporating dual use of both primary and special activity spaces, the enrollment of the school could be doubled or the number of required classrooms cut in half (provided the program durations were also accordingly redistributed). Moreover, he called for the school day to be extended by three hours to make use of facilities before school, during lunch, and after school. In addition, he proposed the use of the facilities on Saturdays and Sundays and over the summer. Bobbitt claimed that these extended uses would optimize the utilization of schoolhouses as a way of maximizing their efficiency, allowing them to serve greater populations in an era of increased enrollments. Second: *the reduction of employees and the maximization of the employees' time* (pp. 264–66). Employees in Gary primarily included teachers who were supervised by school principals and the city superintendent. The principals and superintendent worked together to maximize the efficiency with which teachers worked by delineating divisions of labor—assigning specific teachers to special populations (e.g. assigning teachers for play, shop, music, science, gardening, and civic activities)—and adjusting the work load of teachers to strengthen and normalize their performance. Third: *eliminate waste in the school system* (pp. 266–269). This sense of "waste" applies to the pupils themselves, in the case of ill-health and depressed exuberance. In these cases, Bobbitt argues, pupils need to be given more individual attention (a move possibly facilitated by extended day, weekend, and summer programs) to help reinforce students in any areas of deficiency and to combat the negative external influences of street cultures. And fourth: *a flexible curriculum* (pp. 269–271). This principle is best described in Bobbitt's own words as follows: "[w]ork up the raw material into that finished product which is best adapted". Applied to education this means: "educat[ing] the individual according to his capabilities" (p. 269). In short, Bobbitt's fourth principle calls for curriculum that can be personalized to suit a student's and a community's needs. At first glance, this principle seems fairly developmentalist. But Bobbitt's fourth principle deviates in a significant way from the views of the child-centered educators: Bobbitt's emphasis on personalizing the curriculum focus is *economically* driven; his primary concern was harnessing aptitude to improve Gross National Product (GNP) growth, rather than nurturing the student's personal and natural development for its own sake. As such, Bobbitt's flexibility principle is concerned with orienting students to fill particular societal roles based on their cognitive ability rather than with providing students with more opportunities from which they might choose. In this way, the fourth principle effectively emphasizes a differentiated curriculum based on established social science norms of what is considered intelligence, a concept defined in this ideology largely through the measure of IQ.[22] Briefly: students were tested on their abilities to perform certain tasks robotically. The ability to perform these tasks was commonly translated into a student's IQ, a scaled descriptor that assertedly marked low and high levels of intelligence. Students who merely copied patterns were considered differently than those students who could design patterns. Students on the low end of the IQ spectrum would be directed toward the motor skills-related vocational curriculums and careers (e.g. mechanical drawing, woodwork, electrical, plumbing, sewing), while students on the high level were directed to studies geared to fostering abstract skills, such as academic and college preparatory course offerings that would set them up to become managers later on in life. Crucially, this differentiated school approach fostered the creation of two high school tracks in the early twentieth century: academic and vocational. Moreover, Bobbitt also takes his fourth principle up with a consideration for gender: at the fifth grade level, girls and boys were segregated by gender in courses on physical education, swimming, manual activities, applied science, math, and personal hygiene. This gender bias is based on the prevailing notion that girls required feminine leadership and boys required masculine leadership. Eventually, Bobbitt's emphasis on sorting students based on intelligence and ability (and, to be sure, as I will discuss in Chap. 4, cultural capital) gave rise to a new sense of schooling as based in *merit*, overwriting contemporary attempts to ground education in the constitutional assertion that all are equal (with the consequence that, accordingly, schooling should focus on leveling the playing field for all students). Against such egalitarian or democratic directives, **"merit"** pedagogies necessarily segregated and stratified students. While this increasingly meritocratic sense of school was brewing with Bobbitt and others in the early twentieth century, it wasn't until mid-century, with the work of sociologist Michael Young, that merit schooling became a formal concept in and of itself.

[22]These methods of testing were based in the study of child psychology, physical assessments, and phrenology and craniometrics, fields that were believed to be able to determine mental capacities. Later research produced by Gould (1996) strongly argued against these methods.

Together, developmentalist, social meliorist, and social efficiency educators gave rise to a new pedagogical paradigm in the late nineteenth and early twentieth centuries that, as I suggest above, is described as "scientific management". Below, I translate the directives of scientific management as a broader educational movement into spatial forms just as I do above with *The Yale Report* (however, this particular chart also offers a "program offerings" column to make clear what subject-driven programs reflect specific scientific management principles). But first, I want to quickly recap the nuances of the marked change in school design from the era of *The Yale Report* to that of scientific management. In brief, scientific management educators gave rise to pedagogies that involved deeper studies of science, more time to study what they called "leisure" (e.g. music and art), and vocational training. They also called for educators and scientists to more frequently test student capacities and evaluate their growth. At the same time, the burgeoning and rapidly transforming populations of the late nineteenth and early twentieth centuries compelled educational reformers—many of whom were inspired by the calls of the common schools movement to make education more widely available—to devise ways to educate (and manage) unprecedented numbers of students, a task that led to the proliferation of educational administrators (e.g. principals).

Architecturally, such transformations inspired the creation of new school designs that devoted more space than ever before to laboratories (customized for different kinds of life sciences and social sciences) and that also allocated space for practicing "leisure" activities. Exceptionally seminal was the introduction of spaces to study vocational activities, a design that was especially popular at the high school level. Architects worked to create environments similar to those in which students would later dwell as industrial workers to prepare them for an adult life of work, which at the time included draughting, carpentry, fabrication shops for metal forming, and milling. Moreover, architects strove to accommodate the developmentalists' and social efficiency educators' obsession with empirically assessing student aptitude and knowledge acquisition. Sometimes these tests were done in the classroom and sometimes architects designed spaces dedicated to such tests (social efficiency educators such as Bobbitt preferred they happen in the classrooms rather than create any spaces for them that could possibly end up just being underused). With this new approach to assessing knowledge acquisition in the era of scientific management, we slowly see new schools being built without those recitation spaces so central to pedagogy in the heyday of *The Yale Report*. Additionally, the emergence of professional educational administrators and specialist educators necessitated new ancillary spaces for their functions. Accordingly, more schools began to be built with more administrative type spaces for superintendents and principals (these spaces had never existed before, even during the common schools movement). Lastly, scientific management schoolhouses also demonstrate attempts on behalf of school designers to control growing and unprecedented numbers of students. Slowly, the small schoolhouse gave way to larger complexes with increasing numbers of pupils facilitated by the introduction of busing. These larger and more complex schools required advanced construction techniques and more fire-resistant materials, sparking a need for professional architects to assure the expansive needs. Inspired by calls of scientific management educators who sought to best manage increasing numbers of students, educational architects began to get caught up in designs that would help to control a school's population. See Table 2.2, for maps of these transformations in more detail.

1920–1950: Between World Wars

The roaring twenties was a time defined by new social and artistic freedoms as well as the Prohibition. This was an age of experimentation in popular culture for traditionalists and for emerging modernists (Gelernter, 1999). The cultural forces of experimentation that resulted in the popularity of jazz and of Art Deco impacted educational curriculum: experimentation in pedagogy was common during this period, particularly between the old and the new. Outside of education, the prosperity of the roaring twenties after the First World War came to an abrupt end as the Great Depression of the 1930s began to weigh on the nation. The lingering tensions of World War I were certainly not fully resolved and the post-war years sometimes only served to more deeply engender these tensions. But, turning back to education, these post-war years also saw the introduction of the school bus, enabling students who had traditionally walked to their local neighborhood schools to now ride the bus to bigger, more consolidated schools. With more students able to get to the increasingly larger schools built in earlier years in urban areas, one-room schoolhouses began to disappear in rural areas. To be sure, many educational reformers saw buses as a modernizing step and a way to give students access to a better education, but some parents objected to this change due to strong beliefs in neighborhood schooling (an objection that continues today).

Table 2.2 Translating the scientific management curriculum to spatial forms

Pedagogical directive	*Pedagogical activity*	*Program offering*	*Spatial form*
Academic	Listening, deciding, memorizing, and reasoning	Reading Writing Arithmetic	Classrooms
Vocation	Production, preparation, and distribution of commodities	Drawing Carpentry Forge shop Casting Pattern shop Machine shop	Specialty shops
Life science	Listening, deciding, memorizing, and reasoning	Physics Chemistry Biology Sociology	Laboratories
Family science	Listening, deciding, memorizing, and reasoning	Physiology Psychology Morals Intellect	Laboratories Classrooms
Citizenship	Democratic skills	History Civics	Classrooms
Leisure	Fancy, imagination, invention, taste	Literature Fine Arts Music, Painting, Sculpture Poetry Architecture Aesthetics Language Religion	Specialty classrooms: Art Music Studio
Accountability	Determining knowledge acquisition	Scientific testing	Recitation rooms Classrooms
School assemblies	Assembly	School population	Assembly Hall
Lunch	–	–	Cafeteria
Recreation	Physical exercise	Recess	Recreation rooms

Meanwhile, US architecture was spearheaded in this period by notable architects Frank Lloyd Wright and Richard Neutra, who laid the groundwork for modern design. But despite the introduction of new architectural styles and growing beliefs among educational thinkers at the turn of the century that schoolhouse design strongly affected the learning environment (Cutler, 1989), many schoolhouse designs in this period were simply reproductions of older, more traditional forms due to the need to meet building codes and to be functional. Accordingly, many schoolhouses in this period were masonry-clad steel and concrete-framed buildings (Gutman, 2008). Nathan Bishop School (see Fig. 2.10) and Central High School (see Fig. 2.11) are typical models of these massive masonry structures built in Providence and throughout US industrial cities. Nathan Bishop was designed by the architectural staff of the City of Providence, as part of the Works Progress Administration of the post-Depression Era. During this period, school health and safety was strengthened by the adoption of state regulations and codes (Kowalski, 2002). Despite these codes, many schools fell into disrepair (Cutler, 1989), as a result of the Depression (Button & Provenzo, 1989). But it was also in 1940, during the recovery period, that the first "modern" American schoolhouse emerged with the opening of the Crow Island School in Winnetka, Illinois (Tanner & Lackney, 2006). This school altered the direction of school design and was immediately recognized as a building that optimized the learning environment (Gutman, 2008). Carlton Washburn, the superintendent of schools, recognized the importance of pedagogically-driven design and he applied his research in the design of the Crow Island School (Brubaker, 1998). With these efforts, a new schoolhouse design was born (Tanner & Lackney, 2006). It was an informal small one-story brick masonry elementary school defined by a chimney clock tower, one main entry (not one for each gender), and was organized into administrative and teaching wings. It diverged from the multistoried brick tradition (Tanner & Lackney, 2006). This first modern school with its broad-minded and pioneering educational program focused on child-centered education and followed a post-war archetype design (Brubaker, 1998). It was the catalyst for inspirational scientific schoolhouse design (Blatner, 1948). Soon daylighting, furniture, and wall colors mattered, as well as impregnated woods, which became the preferred building material (Brubaker, 1998).

Turning back to curriculum, the 1930s notably saw the developmentalist movement focus more intently on teaching techniques, educational

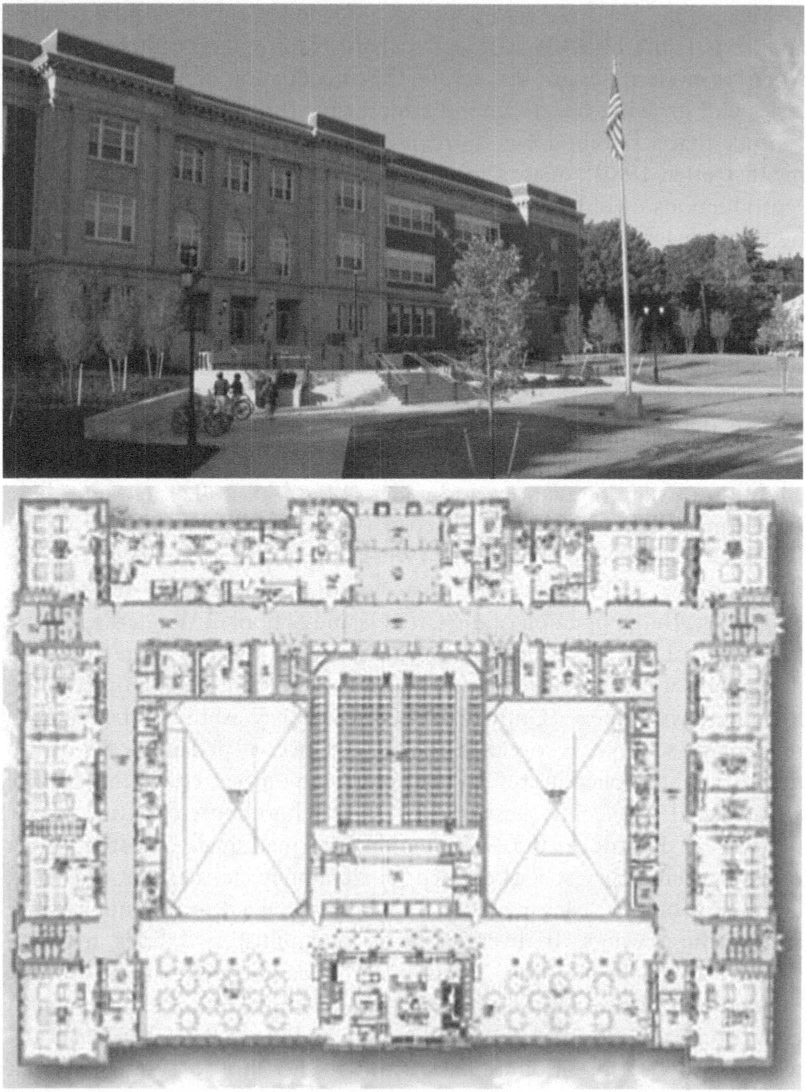

Fig. 2.10 Photograph and typical floor Plan of historically preserved Nathan Bishop Middle School in Providence, RI. (da Silva Photographer, 2013)

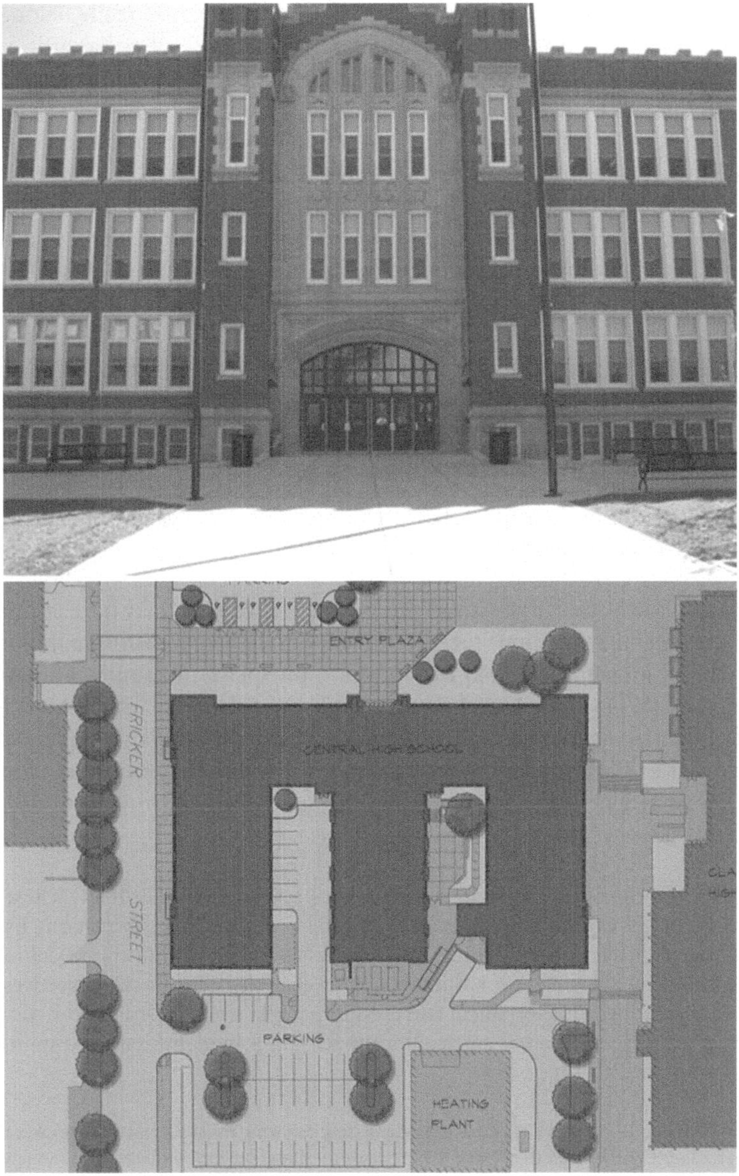

Fig. 2.11 Photograph and site plan of the restored Central High School (built circa 1931) in Providence, RI. (da Silva Photographer, 2006)

programs, and innovations (Cutler, 1989). But the period really belonged to reformers like Bobbitt: termed the "Golden Age" of social efficiency (Stillman, 2010), this era saw the realization of the movement's ambition to increase production in the nation at large. In this heyday of scientific management, a number of critical reactions to Taylorism emerged that unfortunately did not catch on. Of these, I would like to take up that of Mayo and Roethlisberger (Stillman, 2010). By following the scientific method of Taylorism, Mayo and Roethlisberger conducted a five-year study at a Hawthorne plant and arrived at a new conclusion. They found in a "primary work group" that the inter-relationships between workers and managers had more of an impact on productivity than the physical surroundings and economic benefits (Roethlisberger, 1941, p. 7). The statement based on their findings is worth quoting here:

> it is my simple thesis that a human problem requires a human solution. First we have to learn to recognize a human problem when we see one; and second, upon recognizing it, we have to learn to deal with it as such and not as if it were something else. (Roethlisberger, 1941, p. 7)

If Taylor had better understood this theoretical bias, he may have adjusted his scientific management theory to compensate for its shortcomings and may have, in fact, facilitated the common prosperity it sought. But while some like Mayo and Roethlisberger took up Taylorism with respect for scientific management's controlling consequences, others struggled with the order's stratifying results in education. In 1927, one of these reformers, Boyd Henry Bode, heavily criticized the theoretical underpinnings of social efficiency. He

> launched further criticism at the postulates formulated by Bobbitt, whose concept of curriculum impeded a progressive social transformation; by Charters,[23] who argued that it is impossible to apply the industry model to school; Snedden, whose reductive notion that the educational objectives were sociological determined; and even Kilpatrick, who, according to Bode, had presented a limited curriculum model and a fundamentalist position. (Paraskeva, 2011, p. 124)

[23] Following Bobbitt, W.W. Charters was a teacher who in 1923 wrote a book called *Curriculum Construction* that "set forth perhaps the most defensible theoretical framework in early social behaviorist writing" (Schubert, 1984, p. 44). But like Bode, Charters also argued that it was inappropriate to apply the assembly line production model to pupils in schools.

Bode's book, *Modern Educational Theories*, argued for an education that would re-center pedagogy around democratic priorities. In this vein, he advised curriculum that would nurture intelligence, student agency, and resistance.

In addition to Mayo and Roethlisberger and Bode, arguably one of the most important developments of this period was the emergence of "life adjustment" education, a movement that would come to dominate the curricular landscape before and during World War II just as the social efficiency doctrine began to lose its momentum. Emerging in the wake of social efficiency, life adjustment education was influenced in part by Bobbitt's and Charters' humanizing and efficient directives. Essentially, life adjustment education sought "to transform general education from subjects representing common elements of the cultural heritage, as Harris had advocated since before the turn of the century, to functional areas of living" (Kliebard, 1986, p. 220). It focused on designing curricula that would teach "life" skills such as personal hygiene, health awareness, and applications of technology. A key figure of the life adjustment education movement was Charles Prosser, a teacher and educational administrator. In 1940, Prosser was part of a Special Committee on Secondary Schools organized to prepare a report called *What High Schools Ought to Teach*. The report (along with those that that followed it, such as *Vocational Education in the Years Ahead* [1945]) argued that career education has not demonstrated to be the solution it was slated and that secondary curricula should be revised. As Pinar et al. details, "in *What the High Schools Ought to Teach*, the authors argued that a majority of students required an education not specifically directed toward college admission or a specific vocational role. The secondary curriculum ought to reflect the outlook of the majority of students" (1995, p. 145). The report's consensus, as Pinar discusses, is "consistent with the 'life adjustment'" (p. 145) movement. In step with the report, Prosser advocated for a curriculum that provided life skills that would prepare youth for adulthood, such as "home living, vocational life, civic life, and physical and mental health", (p. 114) to help youth best navigate an increasingly complex social environment. But before long, this new movement suffered many attacks that eventually came to a head in a full-scale assault on the intellectual respectability of public education. This assault incited "a whole rethinking of the progressive educational movement" and discredited life adjustment education to the general public.

At the close of this period, an educator named Ralph Tyler (who was also on the committee of *What High Schools Ought to Teach* with Prosser) incited a renewed interest in Bobbitt's concept of social efficiency theory, as it started to wane in populist thought (distracted as it was for a spell by the excitement about life adjustment pedagogies that marginalized many curricularists). Tyler's popular 1949 book, *Basic Principles of Curriculum and Instruction* solidified Bobbitt's theories in formal principles of pedagogy and evaluation. Crucially, *Basic Principles of Curriculum and Instruction* articulated four questions that Tyler argued educators should consider in designing their pedagogies. More specifically, his questions focused on establishing the goals of education, developing active behavioral experiences toward objectives, organizing these experiences to efficiently achieve the objectives, and evaluating whether or not objectives were realized. The assumptions of Tyler's programmed curriculum thus consisted of a change in behavior, the practice of behavior toward an automatic response that followed a linear model of cognition, an association and automatic response, acquiring scientific response based on stimuli, cumulative process through programmed curriculum, and it was applied universally. In general, Bobbitt's and Tyler's approach commoditized schooling by translating curriculum into a product that could be fabricated in an assembly line of schooling. Essentially, Tyler framed teaching and learning as caught up in a stimulus and the resultant linear response. His work positioned him as the "voice of both the scientific and rational curriculum" (Paraskeva, 2011). From Mayo to Tyler, the 1920s to the 1950s truly were a kind of "jazz age" of curriculum; a testament to how uncertain and complicated the school design landscape can be even in a period as assertedly "stable" as the Golden Age of scientific management.

The American Student

The varied and circuitous branches of American curricula and school architecture running up to, during, and in the wake of the nineteenth century surely impacted the students learning their lessons; dwelling in their schoolhouses. As I theorize in my introduction, the combined formative impact of curricula and school architecture—the school design nexus – is best theorized by the kind of "student" their norms anticipate. Taking this premise to task, this section begins to answer this book's driving question—what did it mean to dwell in America's nineteenth century schools?—by considering the (sometimes cumulative) formative work of the school designs this chapter has unraveled. Chapter 4, "School Design as Cultural (Re)production", will discuss the formative impact of American school design in depth. Here I only want to briefly wager the norms this history—defined on one side of the nineteenth century by *The Yale Report* and by scientific management on the other—has brought to bear on the "American student".

Working through this chapter's framework, it is clear that the pedagogies of *The Yale Report* were grounded in the Western ontological ideals of *reason*, budding in the age of British colonialization and used to justify the white hegemony these settlers ultimately established, and *liberalism*, inspired by the Enlightenment and formalized in American politics with Independence. Such cultural norms arose at the expense of suppressing Indigenous and African epistemologies and, with westward expansion and the slave trade. In 1828, the *Report*'s emphasis on classics, the arts, and science via rote and disciplinary pedagogies affirmed these early American norms: the classics, a site that would impart those Enlightenment commitments to reason while drawing only on the works of white, mostly male thinkers. In teaching students only by having them repeat what they were taught, the *Report*'s rote pedagogies, facilitated by the recitation rooms characteristic of the era's architecture, discouraged any critical thinking about these ideals and thus may have worked to limit student imaginaries—and with them, that of the nation's own—within the confines of historically white knowledges. Though the presence of debate rooms might suggest that the Report's pedagogies could indeed have fostered criticality, the kind of "reasoned" evaluations and interventions that the Enlightenment discourses of the eighteenth century advocated (from which Yale borrowed), all too often weaponized such reasonableness to construct racial stratifications in which the "white" subject was the most reasonable, and thus, the great "civilizer" of the others. Moreover, in refuting the specialization later championed by scientific management educators and instead emphasizing a broad, deep, and solid education, the *Report* exhibits a commitment to the American ideal of liberation. It's not that the *Report* truly offered any real liberatory potential, but rather that it imagined itself to do so (notably locating itself as one of the first formal "liberal arts" pedagogies in America) by introducing students to what its committee believed was a wide range of scholarly knowledge that—by not pinning students down to one subject or activity and instead letting them explore a number of different ways of thinking and being (that, as I make clear above, weren't really so different)—prepared youth to be reasoned agents in the nation's asserted liberatory public life. Taken together, these norms of *The Yale Report* and their historical legacies suggest that America's nineteenth century traditionalist/humanist school designs anticipated a student that was white, rational, and liberatory.

Meanwhile, the later doctrines of scientific management school design—namely: developmentalist theory, social meliorism, and social efficiency—complicated the formative work of *The Yale Report*. More specifically, in seeking to eliminate waste by employing strong supervision, empirical assessments, and control tactics, scientific management gave rise to a range of new pedagogical approaches that worked to filter students into jobs in which they would be highly productive (i.e. in which they would foster a stronger economy). This approach required students to specialize in different vocations or studies, with students who tested lower in IQ condemned to manual labor and students who tested higher prompted toward more managerial or intellectual positions—in both directions, such assertedly "objective" measures of aptitude discouraged students from deterring from their allotted occupational fate, effectively using the school to stratify society. To ensure such social control (which was, as noted above, also an attempt to manage growing populations), scientific management pedagogues and architects designed schools to discourage free movement and encourage compliance. Ultimately, school design in the era of scientific management normalized a student that was specialized, productive, socially stratified, and obedient. Together, the curricula and architecture of *The Yale Report* and scientific management worked to assimilate students into the primary needs of the nation in their respective eras. To be sure, with scientific management only really taking hold closer to the turn of the century, it didn't impact what it meant to dwell in nineteenth century schools as much as *The Yale Report* did. Nevertheless, getting a sense of the formative work of scientific management and the ways in which it developed or troubled the norms of *The Yale Report* remains central to understanding how nineteenth century school design influenced education into the twentieth and twenty-first centuries. To better unpack the intricacies of these formative moments in school design, I now turn to case studies in a "hotspot" of American educational history, Rhode Island.

References

Adams, C. F. (1879). *The New Departure in the Common Schools of Quincy and Other Papaers on Educational Topics.* Boston: Estes and Lauriat.

Barnard, H. (1839). First Annual Report, Connecticut Common School Journal, Case, Tiffany & Burnham.

Barnard, H. (1860). *School Architecture or, Contributions to the Improvement of School-Houses in the United States.* New York: Barnes & Burr.

Blatner, L. B. (1948). Trends in Materials and Design. *Review of Educational Research*, 18. Retrieved from http://www.jstor.org/. 5 Nov 2013.

Bobbitt, J. F. (1912). The Elimination of Waste in Education. *The Elementary School Teacher, 12*, 259–271.

Bobbitt, J. F. (1918). *The Curriculum.* Boston: Houghton Mifflin.

Bode, B. H. (1927). *Modern Educational Theories.* New York: Macmillan.

Brubaker, C. W. (1998). *Planning and Designing Schools.* New York: McGraw-Hill.

Burnham, W. H. (1883). *A Scheme of Classification for Child-Study. The Pedagogical Seminary 2*(2), 1892. Taylor & Francis.

Button, H. W., & Provenzo, E. F. (1989). *History of Educational Culture in America* (2nd ed.). Englewood Cliffs, NJ: Prentice Hall.

Charters, W. (1923). *Curriculum Construction.* New York: The Macmillan Company.

Cooledge, H. N. (1964). Samuel Sloan and the "Philadelphia Plan". *Journal of the Society of Architectural Historians, 23*, 151–154.

Cremin, L. A. (1970). *American Education: The Colonial Experience, 1607–1783.* New York: Harper & Row.

Cremin, L. A. (1988). *American Education: The Metropolitan Experience 1876–1980.* New York: Harper & Row.

Cutler, W. W. (1989). Cathedral of Culture: The Schoolhouse in American Thought and Practice Since 1820. *History of Education Quarterly.* Retrieved from http://www.jstor.org/. 8 Nov 2013.

Dewey, J. (1902). *The Child and the Curriculum.* Chicago: University of Chicago Press.

Dewey, J. (1916). *Democracy and Education.* New York: Macmillan.

Foner, E. (1995). *Free Soil, Free Labor, Free Men: The Ideology of the Republican Party Before the Civil War.* Oxford: Oxford University Press.

Gelernter, M. (1999). *A History of America Architecture: Buildings in Their Cultural and Technological Context.* New York: University Press of New York.

Gould, S. J. (1996). *The Mismeasure of Man.* New York: WW Norton & Company.

Graves, B. E. (1993). *School Ways: The Planning and Design of America's Schools* (C. A. Pearson, Ed.). New York: McGraw-Hill.

Greenough, H. (1843). American Architecture. *United States Magazine and Democratic Review, 13*, 206–210.

Gutman, M. (2008). United States School Buildings and Architecture. *Encyclopedia of Children and Childhood in History and Society*. Retrieved from www.faqs.org/childhood. 10 Nov 2013.

Hall, G. S. (1883). *The Contents of the Mind of Children*. Princeton, NJ: The Princeton Review.

Hansen, D. T. (2002). Dewey's Conception of An Environment for Teaching and Learning. *Curriculum Inquiry, 32*, 267–280.

Hearn, F. (2003). *Ideas that Shaped Buildings*. Cambridge, MA: The MIT Press.

Janowitz, M. (1975). Sociological Theory and Social Control. *American Journal of Sociology, 81*(1), 82–108.

Kliebard, H. (1986). *The Struggle for the American Curriculum: 1893–1958*. New York: Routledge.

Kowalski, T. J. (2002). *Planning and Managing Facilities* (2nd ed.). Westport, CT: Bergin & Garvey.

Kruft, H. W. (1994). *A History of Architectural Theory From Vitruvius to Present*. New York: Princeton Architectural Press.

Krugg, E. (1969). *The Shaping of the American High School, 1880–1920*. Madison: The University of Wisconsin Press.

Mann, H. (1842). *Sixth Annual Report as Secretary of Education of the Board of Education of Massachusetts*. Boston: State of Massachusetts.

Maslow, A. H. (1943). A Theory of Human Motivation. *Psychological Review, 50*(4), 370–396.

McClintock, J., & McClintock, R. (1970). *Henry Barnard's School Architecture*. New York: Teachers College Press.

Monk, D. M. (2006). *An Assessment of the Quality and Educational Adequacy of Educational Facilities and Their Perceived Impact on the Learning Environment as Reported by Middle School Administrators and Teachers in Humble Independent School District in the Humble Texas*. Texas A&M University.

Morrison, S. E. (1936). *The Founding of Harvard College*. Cambridge: Harvard University Press.

Nye MacMullen, E. (1991). *In the Case of True Education*. New Haven, CT: Yale University Press.

Orwell, G. (1949). *Nineteen Eighty Four*. London: Secker and Warburg.

Paraskeva, J. (2011). *Conflicts in Curriculum Theory*. New York: Palgrave.

Pinar, W., Slattery, P., & Taubman, P. (1995). *Understanding Curriculum*. New York: Peter Lang.

Prosser, C. (1940). What High Schools Ought to Teach: The Report of a Special Committee on Secondary School Curriculum. American Council on Education.

Rice, J. M. (1893). *The Public-School System of the United States*. New York: Arno Press.

Rice, J. M. (1912). *Scientific Management in Education*. New York: Publishers Printing Company.

Roethlisberger, F. L. (1941). *Management and Morale*. Cambridge, MA: Harvard University Press.

Ross, E. A. (1901). *Social Control*. New York: Macmillan.

Ruskin, J. (1849). *The Seven Lamps of Architecture*. London: Smith, Elder and.

Schubert, W. H. (1984). *Curriculum Books*. Lanham, MD: University Press of America.

Schubert, W. H. (1986). *Curriculum: Perspective, Paradigm and Possibility*. New York: Macmillan.

Sloan, S. (1861). *Villas and Cottages*. Philadelphia: J.B. Lippincott &.

Sloane, E. (1972). *The Little Red Schoolhouse*. Garden City, NY: Doubleday & Company.

Steiner, B. C., & Camp, D. (1919). *Life of Henry Barnard: The First United States Commissioner of Education, 1867–1870*. Washington, DC: Government Printing Office.

Stillman, R. J. (2010). *Public Administration Concept and Cases* (9th ed.). Boston: Wadsworth, Cengage Learning.

Tanner, C. K., & Lackney, J. A. (2006). *Educational Facility Planning*. Boston: Pearson Education.

Thomas, G. E. (2006). From Our House to the "Big House": Architectural Design as Visible Metaphor in the School Buildings of Philadelphia. *Journal of Planning History, 5*(3), 218–240.

Tyack, D. B. (1990). *The One Best System*. Cambridge, MA: Harvard University Press.

Tyack, D., & Cuban, L. (1995). *Tinkering Toward Utopia*. Cambridge, MA: Harvard University Press.

Tyler, R. W. (1949). *Basic Principles of Curriculum and Instruction*. Chicago: University of Chicago Press.

Upton, D. (1996). Lancasterian Schools, Republican Citizenship, and the Spatial Imagination in Early Nineteenth Century. *Journal of the Society of Architectural Historians, 55*(3), 238–253.

Urban, W., & Wagner, J. (2014). *American Education* (5th ed.). New York: Routledge.

Vincent, G. (1896). The Province of Sociology. *The American Journal of Sociology, 1*(4), 473–491.

Viollet-le-Duc, E. E. (1863). *Entretiens sur L'architecture* (Vols. 1–2). Paris. Translated by Henry Van Brunt as *Discourses on Architecture*, Boston. 1875.

Ward, L. F. (1883). *Dynamic Sociology* (Vols. 1–2). New York: D. Appleton and Company.

Ward, L. F. (1893). *The Psychic Factors of Civilization*. Boston: Ginn & Company Publishers.

Willis, G., Schubert, W. H., Bullough, R. V., Jr., Kridel, C., & Holton, J. T. (1993). *The American Curriculum*. Westport, CT: Greenwood Press.

Wriston, B. (1963). The Use of Architectural Handbooks in the Design of Schoolhouses from 1840 to 1860. *Journal of the Society of Architectural Historians, 22*, 155–160.

Yale College Faculty. (1828). *Original Papers in Relation to a Course of Liberal Education*. New Haven: Yale University.

Yarnall, J. (2005). *Newport Through Its Architecture*. London: University Press of New England.

Zinn, H. (1980). *A People's History of the United States*. New York: Harper Collins Publishers.

CHAPTER 3

Hotspot of Change: Case Studies in Nineteenth Century Rhode Island

Rhode Island and American Life

To really unfurl the formative work of the nineteenth century school design nexus, it is important to first complicate Chap. 2's conclusions with specific case studies to get a better sense of the nexus' granularities. As I've already suggested, Rhode Island schoolhouses stand as perfect subjects for such an examination. With Rhode Island a hotspot of American cultural change—its own transformations microcosms of those in the nation at large—the state's historic schoolhouses speak volumes to the complexities of nineteenth century American school design. More specifically, Rhode Island's rich heritage dates back to some of the most gruesome battles between settlers and Native Americans, making it perhaps unsurprising that the state was home to the first original colony to declare independence from British rule (which it did by setting the *Gaspee* schooner ablaze). But even before Independence, Rhode Island exhibited what would become primary American ideals: the lands now known as "Rhode Island" were initially founded in the colonial imaginary in the seventeenth century by Roger Williams as a refuge of religious freedom. Carrying this directive into Independence as one of the original states, Rhode Island solidified freedom of religion in the Constitution, giving rise to a key American ideology. Testament to its defense of religious freedom, Rhode Island is still home to one of the few examples of a multidenominational religious school space, the Newport High School (currently repurposed as

© The Author(s) 2018

J. da Silva, *School(house) Design and Curriculum in Nineteenth Century America*, https://doi.org/10.1007/978-3-319-78586-8_3

a youth center), once a public school that incorporated a dedicated Chapel as its architectural centerpiece. More broadly, the city of Newport is also home to some of the oldest surviving US architecture, not least of which are the famed designs of America's Gilded Age. But even well before the Gilded Age, Rhode Island (as previously noted) had already established itself as an American architectural hotspot: in the late eighteenth century, the state was proclaimed the "birthplace of the American Industrial Revolution" due to its being home to the first fully industrialized cotton spinning facility in the US, the Old Slater Mill in Pawtucket, built in 1783. Importantly, Slater Mill's innovative industrial architecture gave birth to a new paradigm in day-lighting design that would influence educational architecture at a national level, most obviously with the Lancaster School. More specifically, the architecture of the Old Slater Mill was inspired by early Puritan utilitarian building traditions, the need for an open floor plate, and the functional requirements of the structure's intended purpose (namely, the facilitation of a waterwheel shaft to propel machinery). Incited by similar requirements, the Lancaster School (as discussed in Chap. 2) emerged as a game-changing derivative of the Old Slater Mill. Later, in the late nineteenth century, Rhode Island's participation in the Chicago World's Columbia Exposition crucially put the state on the map as a leader in educational architecture—the exposition thus in a way representing the then-culmination of the state's early architectural achievements. At the event, Rhode Island exhibited an impressive display[1] on public education (RI Board of Education, 1894) that included many of the state's innovative schoolhouse designs. Some of these designs were characteristic of the social efficiency movement in educational reform that, as discussed in Chap. 2, was coming into popularity at the time. With the Exposition's exposure, Rhode Island's schoolhouse designs became national exemplars of American school architecture. Indeed, the year following the fair saw Rhode Island move even deeper into the epicenter of American school design with its establishment of two seminal industrial school designs, Newport's Townsend Industrial School and Providence's Manual Training School, both established in 1894. To be sure, with such a well-preserved and recognizably "American" past steeped in school design, Rhode Island cities and towns stand as exemplary sites to unpack the cultural and architectural developments that Chap. 2 surveys.

[1] In addition, on display was a bond copy of *A History of Public Education in Rhode Island, from 1636 to 1876* by Stockwell (2012), which was most useful in the preparation of this book.

Nineteenth Century Education in Rhode Island

During the nineteenth century, Rhode Island was a key site in the developments of the common schools, traditionalist, and scientific management movements of school design. Early on, Rhode Island was committed to creating free universal education. As far back as 1640, the area already had a number of public schools (according to the ceremonial documents from the 75th anniversary of the appointment of the Commissioner of Education in December 1920). Rhode Island's support of public education was solidified by the leaders of the City of Providence, who early on saw educating youth as the "first importance to every society" (Stone, 1876, p. 137–139). Along these lines, in the late eighteenth and early nineteenth centuries, Rhode Island took the lead in establishing free schools in the nation. In 1799, the Rhode Island General Assembly passed an act to establish free schools, which allocated state funds to each town (Stone, 1876). Following the passage of this act, new schools were built across the state (Cirillo, 1980). Important to note is that although these schools were publicly supported at the local (town) level, they were not free, and instead were funded by tuition or "rate bills". Take, for example, the way free schools operated in Bristol, Rhode Island: as early as the late seventeenth century, Bristolians required children's guardians to pay three pence each week for schooling and landowners were levied a tax for a local schoolmaster (Cirillo, 1980). In general, schooling at this time was held in private residences (with a sum paid to owners by the town). Around 1720, schooling was moved to be more centrally held in the courthouse on the Bristol common. Seven years later, the town bought a schoolhouse, and not long after, private residents built a new one-story school in 1702, but the first town-owned schoolhouse was purchased in 1727 and soon after a new one-story school was privately built in Bristol by residents in the Gothic style, designed to accommodate 60 students (Cirillo, 1980). During this period in Rhode Island at large, there continued to be—as there was during the colonial and revolutionary periods—one teacher assigned to all grade levels, with students of all ages working at their own pace and participating together in all lessons. Some loved this set-up: take, for example, one student who is quoted as saying that "[o]ne[-]room schoolhouses offered almost unlimited opportunity for gifted students to advance" (Graves, 1993, p. 22). In 1800, Providence established the "school law" of 1800, based on the State's 1799 act to establish free schools. Though the law was rather abolished three years later, that small amount of time was still enough to spark a dedication to free schools among Rhode Island's populace (Stone, 1876). In 1836, the state officially rekindled its commitment to public schooling by writing it into law (Rhode Island Board of Education, 1920). Even in the 1830s, Rhode Island was leading the nation at large in the common schools movement.[2]

During these early days of public education in the nineteenth century, schooling—from grammar to higher education—in Rhode Island, like that of the nation more broadly, was primarily characterized by *The Yale Report*'s Enlightenment-inspired traditionalist pedagogies. To briefly recap: *The Yale Report* was a curricular document penned by the faculty of Yale College in 1828 that argued for a traditionalist, liberal college education that was *broad* (exercising all faculties of the mind and balancing all branches of knowledge), *deep* (teaching through long-lasting, continuous, and close applications that required a steady, systematic personal effort), and *solid* (a pedagogy that would foster a cohesive mind that could hold a multitude of knowledge) (p. 6). To this end, *The Yale Report* advised teaching the classics, arts, sciences, and literature, arguing that such a general and liberal education would give students a strong intellectual foundation that would well prepare them for professional and civic life. Believing in the "mind as muscle" doctrine that suggested that vigorous, lengthy, and continuous exercises would expand the mind, the faculty advised teaching such content with disciplinary and rote pedagogies that fixed attention, directed thought, emphasized repetition and memorization, conducted analysis, facilitated a thorough and accurate discrimination of an argument's course, balanced evidence and judgment, and awakened the imagination (Yale, 1828). The most famous teaching methods from this period thus included lectures, recitations, and debates. Such methods posture teachers as trainers who fill students with knowledge—what educational philosopher Paulo Freire (1970) would famously later term "banking education".

For our purposes, it's important to note that each of these teaching methods required specialized fixed spaces in the school; the *Report*'s rote pedagogies could not be easily carried out outside such formal scholarly environments. The deeper point here is that there is thus a clear connection between the dominant philosophical traditions that frame

[2] Marking Rhode Island's commitment to common schooling was the exponential increase of schools in the state during the nineteenth century. The period saw the number of schools climb from 4 in 1800 to 51 in 1876 (Stone, 1876).

the Rhode Island traditionalist curriculum and the spaces in which that philosophy would be extended in the state. Accordingly, as I will argue throughout this chapter, Rhode Island schools of *The Yale Report* era markedly demonstrated the *Report*'s recommendations to disciplining the mind as muscle with rote pedagogies centered around the classics, arts, sciences, and literature. A typical nineteenth century Rhode Island's traditionalist classroom thus included: a large dictionary, global charts and maps, an encyclopedia, books in prose and science, blackboards, high ceilings, and a number of instructional apparatuses (to be sure classrooms also included those elements necessary for weathering the climate, such as stoves for heating). More specifically, primary grades (see Fig. 3.1) had age-appropriate blocks, color charts, and counting frames whereas classrooms for the higher grades had apparatuses that would facilitate more advanced studies of physical geography, physiology, natural philosophy, and other subjects in the sciences (Rhode Island Board of Education, 1880, pp. 118–120).

Fig. 3.1 A school room for young children. (Board of Education, 1898)

Figure 3.1 illustrates the high ceiling characteristic of classrooms of the period. To the middle left of the picture, just above the teacher's desk and chair (which is elevated on the framed platform), are a number of instructional apparatuses from a US flag to a clock, a counting frame, display charts, an alphabet chart, and a piano (some characteristic elements are indeed missing from this space, such as a dictionary, a globe, maps, and an encyclopedia). At the very front of the classroom there is a small group table with three student-size chairs. This student seating is fixed and characterized by wooden writing, storage, and seating surfaces with cast-iron supports frames typical of the era. The picture suggests that seating was provided for at least 35 students. The seating is placed close together to discourage student mobility. The seating scale from the picture would suggest that the seating was sized more for older primary students and not necessarily for students of just five or six years old. The student desks are empty and the room is very organized, centralized around the teacher's platform, with flags and picture frames helping to contribute to the normalization of the space. This positioning of the teacher speaks to the *Report*'s emphasis on discipline, which the teacher's visible governance would facilitate. The blackboards are filled with a prepared lesson plan in cursive writing. Notably, no artificial lighting was provided which would limit learning experiences on cloudy days. To remedy this issue, stations hang from the ceiling that provide space for candles (these stations could also be used for hanging visual displays). Moreover, the classroom entrance door—which was solid, adding some privacy to the space—helpfully incorporates an overhead operable transom light, which would allow for cross-ventilation and natural light to be exchanged between adjacent spaces, which may likely be a corridor. Managing the class's connection to the more public spaces of the school, the door stands as the ingress and egress into the domain of the classroom. In this particular case, the door is solid so that (unless the door is left purposefully open) it blocks out the rest of the school from the space, giving the classroom a semiprivate characteristic. This gateway from the public space to the privacy of the classroom is managed by the teacher—a management that reinforces her authority. Students were typically restricted from moving out to the corridors and the rest of the building unless they were given permission by the teacher, a practice that taught them to understand their movements as always predicated upon the will of a central authority figure. These power dynamics were critical to maintaining discipline and control as school populations grew so as to allow the instruction of large volumes of students to take place in a productive manner. On another (and final) note, the structural column that sits in the center of the space is testament to the limited construction technology available in the nineteenth century, such that the structural wood framing used at the time could not economically span the entire classroom. This kind of traditionalist school design, so inspired by *The Yale Report*, would prevail in Rhode Island for most of the nineteenth century, notably intensifying during Reconstruction. To be sure, the *Report*'s success in Rhode Island was due in part to its close ties with the common movement in which the state, as I detail above, was deeply involved. One of the most formative national leaders in Rhode Island common school education during the nineteenth century was Henry Barnard, who was a student at Yale College during the writing of the *Report*. As Chap. 2 details, during his time as Rhode Island's first Commissioner of Schools, Barnard championed the national common schools movement, the traditional pedagogies of *The Yale Report*, and school architecture that could support such a liberal education—projects he would later amplify in the nation at large as America's first commissioner of education and facility planner. Under Barnard, Providence accordingly reorganized public schools to offer a traditionalist liberal course of instruction. In order to carry out the city's ordinance, the appointed committee determined that new schoolhouses would be required. By 1842, these transformations would make Providence a national exemplar in school architecture (the plans of these schools showcased in Barnard's *School Architecture*). One of these new exemplars was the High School House in Providence. This model high school would later be converted into a normal school for the preparation of teachers, a site that will be discussed later in this chapter.

Though *The Yale Report*'s school design norms dominated nineteenth century education in Rhode Island they did not exhaust it. As Chap. 2 details, the last decade of the nineteenth century saw the rise of a new approach to education founded in the tenets of scientific management devised by Taylor and most famously developed by Dewey, Ward, and Bobbitt. More specifically, scientific management educational reformers sought to redesign schools to function as sites of social control—places in which to regulate or strategically shape the nation's growing population. To do so, they reconfigured the school around the industrial and scientific ideals of efficiency, empiricism, and production that were proving in commercial practice to be highly effective ways of managing large groups of people. Pedagogically, scientific management reformers thus called for schools (especially at the secondary level) to (1) test student aptitudes early on so as to quickly sort youth into programs that would train them for various roles in the nation's new industrial economy, (2) offer such professionalizing vocational programs, and (3) be overseen by educational administrators.

Emerging at the same time as these new ideas about school design, the *Committee of Ten Report* was much anticipated in Rhode Island. Up until this point, high school curriculum had remained substantially tied to the philosophies of *The Yale Report*, only slowly creeping in recent years toward offering more vocational opportunities. During this traditionalist period, Rhode Island high school course offerings were selectively itemized, scheduled, cataloged per subject and grade, and reconciled with recitation requirements (which usually ranged from three to four recitations per day, preferably conducted in dedicated recitation spaces) (RI Board of Education, 1894). The resultant course of study was that of the kind of college preparatory high school education traditionalists advocated, with primary course offerings such as English (composition, rhetoric, and literature), Latin, Greek, French, German (optional), mathematics, algebra, arithmetic, geometry (plain and solid), history (ancient, modern, British, civil government, and political economy), and science (botany, physics, chemistry, zoology or biology, geology, and astronomy) (Rhode Island Board of Education, 1894). Meanwhile, secondary course offerings also included music, elocution, free-hand drawing, and physical training. Taking on all these offerings, the high school day was divided into five periods of 50 minutes each (Rhode Island Board of Education, 1894). Rhode Island specifically emphasized this set of coursework in response to the entry requirements of Brown's College (now called Brown University), borrowed from *The Yale Report* (though coursework did from time-to-time vary based on the kind of education the instructor herself had received). But as scientific management took hold in education at the turn of the century, Rhode Island communities such as Newport and Providence became engulfed in this new curriculum. But the schools Rhode Island had designed for traditional pedagogies were no longer cutting it—scientific management demanded adjustments to schoolhouse design. Rhode Island thus began a new period in its educational architecture. Take for example, the fact that many of the state's schoolhouses of the scientific management era began to include spaces specifically for testing student intelligence and ability. Moreover, the new vocational focus of schooling required labs and shops in which students could practice the hands-on skills they would use as workers in the industrial economy.[3] Rhode Island high schools thus began to offer multiple tracks—different courses, departments, even schools—for students depending on their test results. Providence in particular, at the turn of the century, divided its high schools into four-year college preparatory programs; English departments (this one a three-year program); girls' departments (four-year); and training schools (three-year program) and Rhode Island at large also ran schools for the developmentally challenged, students who were deaf, and students in the care and control of state. Meanwhile, the heyday of scientific management also incited Rhode Island to mandate general science classes and physical education classes (Kowalski, 2002), a movement that also required new spaces for laboratories and recreation (sometimes the basements of existing schoolhouses [like those modeled after the Quincy Plan on the Bristol Town Common] were adapted for these purposes). During this period, growing enrollments also warranted additional classrooms and schools, while the creation of expert administrators necessitated new administrative spaces. To respond to these new demands, Rhode Island sometimes had to convert existing buildings (such as factories, stores, and warehouses) into schools (Graves, 1993). Trying to maintain some control on the rapidly changing school system, Rhode Island began to standardize school design in the form of a compact building mass organized by corridors that provided circulation and access to program spaces (these were shaped in the forms of capital letters "E" and "H"). Such plans fit on postage stamp sites while still accommodating specialized spaces such as gymnasiums, auditoriums, and libraries (Gutman, 2008). These standardized designs realize Ross' institutional methods of social control in the built environment of the school, essentially using architecture to manage the movements of the student population. For example, architects paid special attention to circulatory elements, such as halls and corridors: in step with the dream of social efficiency educators, these standardized schools exhibited narrow corridors that discouraged gathering and socializing by promoting quick and direct travel from one space to another, thus maximizing the time students would spend in class. Ultimately, Rhode Island's late nineteenth and early twentieth century schoolhouses—true to the era of scientific management—were largely concerned with controlling students while orienting them to fulfill those specific professional and civic roles reformers believed would most benefit society.

[3] During this period, new junior high schools opened that were also equipped with shops, kitchens, laboratories, and gymnasiums (Horn, 1915).

Having shaken out the two prevailing approaches to school design in Rhode Island in the nineteenth century, it is now time to turn to case studies of schoolhouses in some of the state's most well-preserved areas: Bristol, Newport, and Providence.

Case Studies

Newport

In 1828, the same year as the publication of *The Yale Report*, the town of Newport worked to raise revenue to create a city-wide schooling system founded on the Lancastrian or monitorial model of school design (Stockwell, 2012). The town's ambition emerged from a desire to offer "educat[ion to] the white children of the town who [were] not otherwise provided with the means of instruction" (Stone, 1876, p. 42). The town's efforts paid off: almost 30 years later, Newport was serving approximately 800 students in 17 schools (2 high schools, 4 grammar schools, 2 intermediate schools, and 7 primary schools) being taught by 22 instructors (Stone, 1876, p. 42).[4] The schools I unpack below emerge from this history.

Rogers High School, 1873
Built in 1873, the Rogers High School (see Fig. 3.2) was initially called the "Thayer School". By 1875, the building was rechristened with the name of a generous new benefactor, William Sanford Rogers (Stone, 1876).

In an extract from the school report published in the Rhode Island Board of Education's Annual Reports, Chairman Coggeshall praised Rogers and the accomplishments of the school's community in the construction of the new high school as follows:

> The crowning act of our school work of the year, has been the completion of the Rogers High School building. The joint Committee of the City Council and School board, in common with the citizens, may look to this monument of school architecture with pride, and with exceeding gratefulness to the noble benefactor, our son, William Sanford Rogers, of whom we may justly say, that if the scenes of his childhood and early manhood are no longer blessed by his presence, his benefaction remains, thereby consecrating his memory afresh, day by day, as it meets the eye of the citizen, as it holds within

[4] Notably, these statistics do not include the separate primary and grammar schools for persons of color.

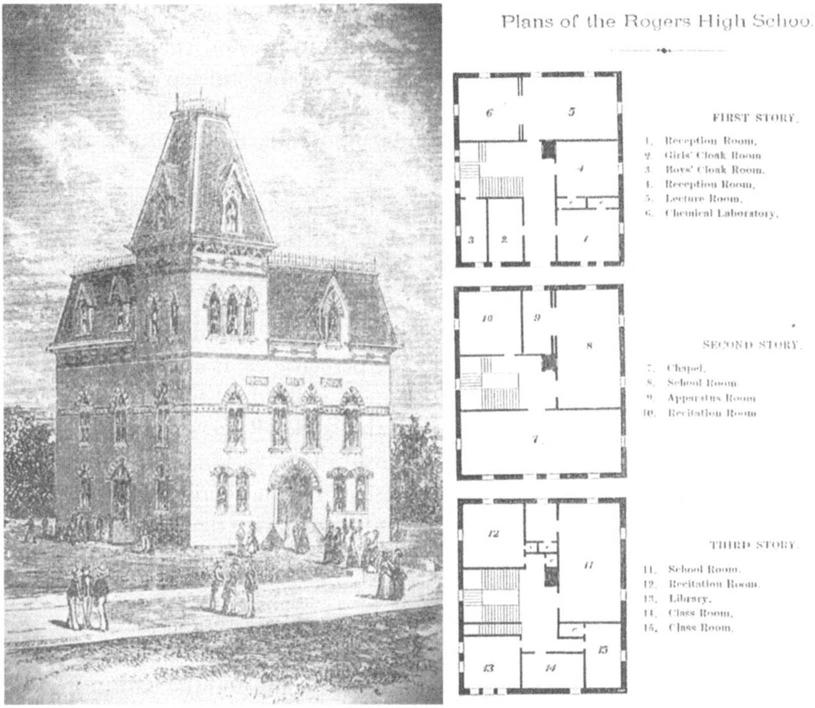

Fig. 3.2 A rendering and floor plans of the Rogers High School in Newport (1875). The building is of Venetian Gothic architectural styling and measures 53 by 60 feet. (Board of Education, 1875)

> its walls the teacher and student. Beyond this is the solid foundation on which it rests, a perpetual annual income of several thousand dollars, protecting its continuance and usefulness to generations. Within its walls are taught the needed fundamental elements of education for any avenue of life. Its corps of teachers, alive to the advance in scientific and classical knowledge, are placing the Rogers School in the front rank of schools of its class in our country. (Rhode Island Board of Education, 1875, p. 117)

In this quote, Coggeshall locates Rogers School within the norms of *The Yale Report*, using the report's "solid" buzzword to acknowledge the benefactor's standing gifts and describing the school's curriculum scientifically-based and concerned with classical knowledge. The school's architecture notably echoes Coggeshall's traditionalist sense of the school: Rogers School was fitted with an observatory, library, recitation room, chapel, chemistry laboratory, lecture room, school room, classrooms, and separate entrances and cloak rooms for boys and girls, along with a basement with eight feet of head space—altogether, the school was approximately 12,720 square feet (Rhode Island Board of Education, 1875).

Rogers School was notably built in the Venetian Gothic style, a very popular architectural style for Rhode Island schoolhouses that were similarly built between the 1870s and the 1880s to carry out traditionalist curricula (Rhode Island Board of Education, 1875). Reviving Gothic architecture with these schoolhouses was a way for Rhode Island to signal that its school design was inspired by the pedagogical norms of those great temples of learning in Britain (Oxford and Cambridge) and at home (Yale, Harvard, and Brown) built in the Gothic style. Rogers School demonstrates such Gothic styles most obviously in its façade, where balanced spiral column window frame jambs rest alongside Rosetta carved stone moldings framing the entry archway and a gargoyle (that could, perhaps, be said to represent the students) (see Fig. 3.3). In addition to such Gothic features, Rogers School also revealed the era's more modern construction techniques in its thin mortar joints and stone foundations.

Meanwhile, two elements of Rogers High School's programmed spaces stand out as being unique both within Rhode Island and the nation at large in this era: the observatory and the chapel. Though observatories were not very common in Rhode Island in the late nineteenth century, the course of study in Newport in 1865 at the high school senior class level did include "astronomy by lectures and frequent use of the telescope", arguably influencing the decision to put an observatory in Rogers School (Stockwell,

Fig. 3.3 Stone foundation, Gargoyle, and Windows at Rogers High School. (da Silva Photographer, 2014)

2012, p. 266). The observatory space was not shown on the floor plans, since it was on a fourth level, but it is projected to be located in the loft space in the turret portion above the library, which had windows on all four sides of the pitched mansard roof with access by way of a library-adjacent stair. Additionally, the school's chapel space was another fairly very uncommon feature at the time, given that the only course of instruction specifically related the use of a chapel in Newport at the high school level was that of "Moral Philosophy[5] lectures", which arguably could have been conducted in any other lecture room (Stockwell, 2012, p. 266). The chapel is visibly larger than a typical schoolroom, which suggests that it was built to accommodate a significant number of students (possibly the whole school population) at one time, indicating a significant commitment to religion. As I indicated previously, Rhode Island's commitment to religious freedom, deriving from the legacies of Roger Williams, was second to none nationally. Newport in particular was the home to the first synagogue in the US, which is still occupied today. A survey of public schoolhouse plans in recent historical educational architecture publications of McCormick in Ohio, and Gyure in Chicago reveals that chapel spaces are absent in public schools. Therefore, for the Rogers School in Newport to incorporate a (multidominational) chapel space is significant and reinforces Newport's pivotal role in shaping the national identity of religious freedom. It is worth noting that the chapel space is not elaborated by Coggeshall as unique, which could represent the hegemonic nature of the colonial curriculum residual in Newport at the time of the building's design. This could have been reinforced by higher education's Brown College or Harvard College connection with the transplanted European ideology, or it could have been influenced by the benefactor.

Rogers School continued to shape the lives of Newport students for decades. In 1907, the school moved to a new location in order to accommodate a growing population and the related directives of scientific management. Architect Creighton Withers expanded its classroom sizes and

[5] At the time, the Rhode Island Board of Education strongly believed that too little attention was placed on moral instruction in public schools, worried that it would undermine the foundation of good character (RI BOE, 1880). The Board felt that it was at odds with teachers on the issue of moral character, evident in its assertion that "our public school teachers seem to think that moral instruction is the last thing to be attended to" (RI BOE, 1880, p. 15). It is clear that the RI Board of Education at the time was aligned with *The Yale Report*'s doctrine of moral law. Perhaps the chapel space in Rogers School was designed to respond to these fears about the growing deficit of moral education in Rhode Island schools.

Fig. 3.4 Photos of the Thayer School built in 1873, now a Boys and Girls Club. In this recent photo, the mansard and turret roofs have been demolished and the building now supports a flat roof. (da Silva Photographer, 2014)

added administrative and recreation spaces (with Newport's other high school, the Townsend Industrial School, discussed below, offering plenty of space for vocational programs).

In sum, in its original form, Rogers School was a model traditionalist secondary school, its architecture surely influenced by Barnard's calls for schoolhouse form to respond more effectively to schooling's intended functions. Today, the school's original building has been repurposed to house the Newport Boys and Girls Club (see Fig. 3.4). It is fitting that a building designed to serve both girls and boys from 1873 to 1875 continues to perform such a service 140 years later.

Townsend Industrial School, 1894

The Townsend Industrial School (see Figs. 3.5 and 3.6) stands as a strong example of the shift in school design toward scientific management. More specifically, Townsend School's machine shop, forge room, carpentry

Fig. 3.5 Photograph of the Townsend Industrial School in Newport, RI (circa, 1894). (RI Board of Education, 1894)

room, wood turning room, moldering room, engine shop, cooking room, dress-making room, and sewing room exhibit the school's dedication to vocational programs. Moreover, the plan also introduces pronounced administrative spaces to Newport school design, made necessary by the emergence of the specialized educational administrators needed to evaluate and credit the student apprenticeships characteristic of the era's vocational programs. But Townsend's inclusion of classrooms suggests that it didn't completely negate traditional pedagogies but, rather, that it perhaps offered two educational streams—vocational and traditional—characteristic of the recommendations of developmentalist and social efficiency educators who yearned for schools to "sort" students.

The design for the new Townsend Industrial High School embodied the so-called Romanesque Neoclassical Revival style made popular by the great American Architect H.H. Richardson. Its robust proportioned forms demonstrate elements of Italian classical styling that contrast with its no-nonsense simplified floor plan. Its roof is essentially hidden from view

Fig. 3.6 Floor plans of the Basement, First, Second, and Third of the Townsend Industrial School in Newport, RI. (Board of Education, 1894)

behind the projecting horizontal roof edge cornice, reflecting Palladian and neoclassical formalities. The four-level building reads more like a two-story because it insets its basement level, which is situated within a strong one-and-a-half story water-table base aesthetically articulated by horizontal stone massed reveals and capped by a prominent horizontal stone band at the sill of the second-floor window units. Above this band are two stories of punched windows fitted into a masonry field terminated at its outside corners by stone quoin details that form two bookend massing pillars. Three formal entries are articulated in simplistic and subtle formations, which were uncharacteristic of the style (and so perhaps suggest a budgetary constraint).

The school building (see Fig. 3.7) is still in use today, but recently underwent some modern additions designed by the Massachusetts architectural firm, HMFH Inc., to transform the site into the community's state-of-the-art Thompson Middle School. As part of that historic restoration the Historic Townsend Industrial Schoolhouse portion now contains the Thompson Middle School administration suite on the ground floor, as well as a two-story library space. The addition houses the gymnasium and cafeteria. The historic building's Romanesque styling is gracefully echoed in the new addition's styling without literal replication. Both located on Broadway, the Townsend Industrial School and the 1907 location of Rogers High School converge as a telling landscape of the heritage of the once-thriving late nineteenth century fabric of Newport that stretches across Broadway's bustling streetscape.

Fig. 3.7 The Thompson Middle School addition to the existing historic Townsend Historic School in Newport, RI. (da Silva Photographer, 2015)

Bristol

Bristol is unlike many other Rhode Island communities, in that it has invested, in the last two decades, in the preservation of its historical school infrastructure and retained historical records from the nineteenth century.[6] This afforded my research a privileged perspective far beyond that which the visual data of renderings, photos, and plans might reveal—the past designs of schoolhouses so easily available in Bristol give a better sense of how these histories might continue to shape the work done in these schools today, a phenomenon I describe in Chap. 1 as "residual pastness". Bristol has a long tradition of naming its schools in honor of its key community figures. The schoolhouses located on Bristol's Town Common (see Fig. 3.8) were named after three of the four trustees of the original Bristol Grand Articles of 1680, namely: Byfield, Walley, and Oliver. These historically registered school buildings are located in Bristol's celebrated downtown alongside another historically significant and nationally registered building, a former statehouse, constructed in 1816 that today serves as the Bristol County Courthouse.

Byfield Memorial School, 1872

The Byfield School (see Fig. 3.9) is located on the Town Common on an acre of land in the southwest corner between High Street and Church Street. Constructed in 1872, Byfield was designed by Emerson, an architect from Lawrence, MA and modeled after the Coddington School in Newport (a prototype of the Quincy Plan discussed in Chap. 2). Byfield was Bristol's high school until the construction of the Colt Memorial High School (discussed below) in 1906.

Architecturally, Byfield School is almost a square, measuring 85 feet north/south and 70 feet east/west, and ringing in at 23,000 square feet. This square footage is divided over four stories (including a basement). The building is generally oriented toward the north and south, and is set

[6] The Rhode Island historical and heritage community, in reading this historical narrative, may be surprised to find from the middle of the nineteenth century onward that Bristol's public schools may have embodied the integrity necessary to be considered for National Registration status by the Secretary of the Interior and the Rhode Island Historical and Heritage Commission. Because many of the schools are still active in their intended purposes to this day, the schools built in the period this book interrogates embody a collective residual pastness in their additions, selective demolition and renovations over time, and connections with prevailing curriculum ideologies, such that I would recommend them for consideration of listing on the National Historical Register.

Fig. 3.8 An aerial site plan of the Bristol Town Common. (da Silva & Cordero, 2013)

approximately 30 feet from the street curb. The school rests on a granite water-table base and sills (each floor is approximately 5700 square feet), constructed of stones of varying widths. The exterior walls reflect a solid unreinforced masonry wall construction, which speaks to the era's desire to give public structures a sense of physical permanence. Typical punched fenestration openings are supported by arched granite lintels bearing on adjacent masonry brick walls at the first two stories, which maximize the day-lighting opportunities necessary to lighting the interior classrooms.

Fig. 3.9 The front façade of the Byfield School in Bristol. (da Silva Photographer, 2003)

The top story is wood framed and covered and handsomely adorned with a patterned-slate mansard roof—a traditional Gothic style—that gives the building a 2-½ story feel. The roof is set atop the brick masonry by a continuous ornamental banding with dentals, which, as a traditional style in the period, would have evoked a comforting familiarity for citizens, a particularly interesting stylistic feature given that this was in an era in which many yearned to have faith in government. The location of Byfield on the Town Common speaks to this trend of the community wanting to trust and support the public sphere; ideologies that played a large role not only in Byfield's construction but too in the success of the common schools movement more broadly. Moreover, like Rogers High School (the 1873 location), Byfield also employed such familiar Gothic styles which align to *The Yale Report* and its traditional underpinnings. On another note, Byfield's main entry faces High Street and consists of two single entrance doors hatted by granite arcades set side-by-side, designed as gender-specific entrances. Two other doors framed by wood with interior and exterior load-bearing masonry walls faced the Town Commons, offering separate entrances for teachers. This evident segregation of girls, boys, and teachers is consistent with the prescriptions of *The Yale Report* and the common schools movement. Meanwhile, at the opposite end of the common is another school, Walley Memorial, modeled after the Quincy Plan.

Walley Memorial School, 1896

Built in 1896, the Walley Memorial School (see Fig. 3.10) sits at the northwest corner of Bristol's town common, a site of the town's original "Common School" (also referred to as the "Old Brick School"), constructed in 1809. Bristol's common school was funded by the town itself, as well as St. Alban's Masonic Lodge, with each party paying half of the $1400 total building cost—a partnership that reflects a robust public-private relationship during the period. In this vein, the Old Brick School was located on the lower story, while the Masonic Lodge's headquarters used the top floor. This limited space pressed an addition in 1828 that doubled the size of the building to make room for classrooms on the upper story alongside the Masonic Lodge. In 1895, the Town sold the historic building at auction to a contractor named LeClair. LeClair demolished the building to make room for a new school, what would become Walley Memorial (Cirillo, 1980). Before the demolition, the school's famous bell was moved to the top of the Byfield School, replacing one that had been captured from an English merchant ship by the Privateer Yankee in the War of 1812 (Captain D'Wolf later presented this bell to the School of Bristol). The preservation of the Common School's bell echoes the scientific management ideologies emerging at the time that emphasized the importance of punctuality and time keeping.

Work began on the new Walley School in October 1895. LeClair hired William R. Walker & Son, an architectural firm in Rhode Island (designed numerous schools in the period as listed in Appendix), to design the new brick school (see Figs. 3.11 and 3.12). Completed almost a year later—after building costs of almost $25,000 (noticeably *much* more than the "Old Brick School" cost to build)—the new school was dedicated on September 16, 1896, and named after one of the original town charter founding fathers. Strategically located on the Bristol Common, Walley, like Byfield, spoke to the community's civic commitment.

Walley School was modeled after the Quincy Plan discussed in Chap. 2 and thus reflects the traditionalist architectural and pedagogical commitments of the Quincy Plan's period. Part of the reason Walley School was modeled after the Quincy Plan was that it was intended to be an elementary school

Fig. 3.10 Photos (front and rear) of the Walley School in Bristol, RI. (da Silva Photographer, 2014)

Fig. 3.11 A photo of the Walley School in Bristol. (RI Board of Education, 1895)

like the Quincy Grammar School. More specifically, the Rhode Island Historical Preservation Commission offers an exceptional description of the Walley School that is worth repeating here: "[t]he school's eclectic detailing includes Colonial Revival corner quoins in brown sandstone and a 25-foot, 2 level tower with an octagonal cupola and ornate weathervane; Italianate detailing includes Romanesque recessed entrances and round-headed windows in the pediment" (Rhode Island Historical Preservation Commission, 1990). Expanding this picture, the time-worn photograph and floor plan (see Figs. 3.11 and 3.12) depict that, viewed from High Street, the school's

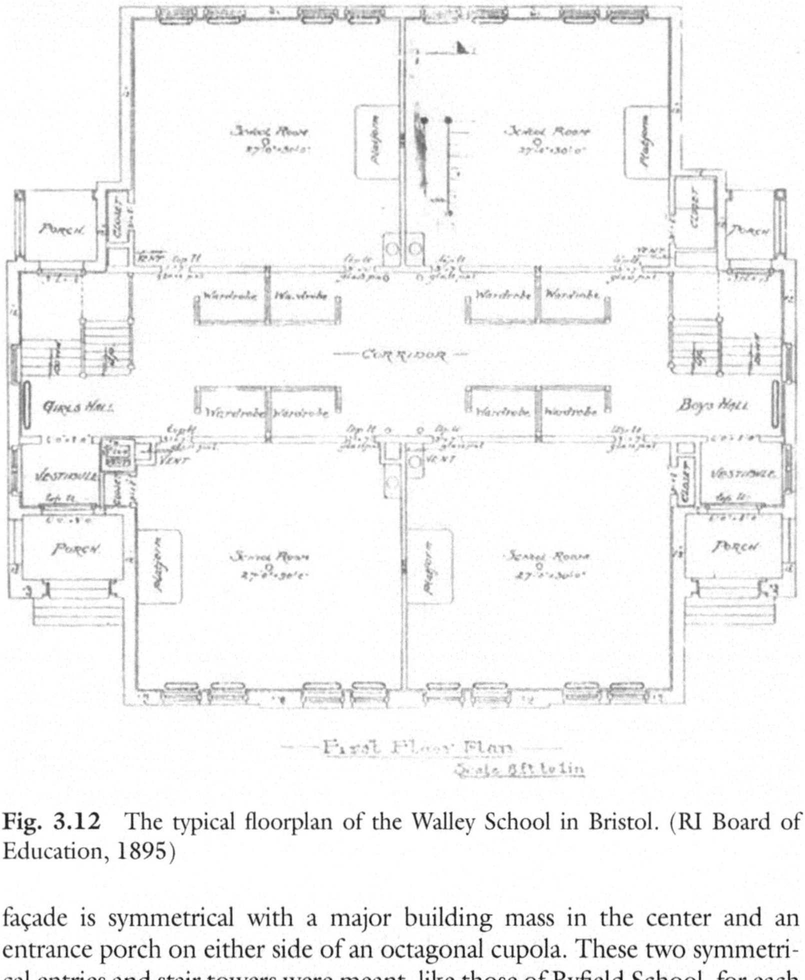

Fig. 3.12 The typical floorplan of the Walley School in Bristol. (RI Board of Education, 1895)

façade is symmetrical with a major building mass in the center and an entrance porch on either side of an octagonal cupola. These two symmetrical entries and stair towers were meant, like those of Byfield School, for each gender. These entries ultimately connect with a corridor containing wardrobe units that create pockets and that more resemble a gathering hall than a corridor. The major building mass is further divided into a dominant pavilion with a bay at either side by the pediment-like gable at the center of the façade. The center pavilion is sub-divided into bays by two pairs of windows. These massing configurations are intentional in that they reinforce scales proportional to the neighborhood and the traditional architectural styling popular during the period. The fenestration pattern is continued in the bays which each have a single window pair.

Notably, these schoolhouse architectural techniques—especially its platform classrooms, gendered entrances, and large corridors (cf. Figs. 3.1, 3.9 and 3.12) are more reflective of those ideologies of *The Yale Report* rather than those of the social efficiencists from the heyday of scientific management. So similar to Walley, Byfield also reveals this kind of consolidated school plan that follows those characteristics of schools in the era of *The Yale Report* and the common schools movement even though, as Kliebard (1986) makes clear, the heyday of scientific management was well in underway at the time of its construction. To be sure, it seems as if Byfield's community of builders were dedicated to replicating past designs—caught up in the early nineteenth century's traditionalist pedagogies—rather than build in step with the new prevailing curriculum ideologies that had already influenced designs like that of Townsend Industrial.

Oliver Memorial School, 1901

Five years after Walley School was built, another school modeling the Quincy Plan and also designed by William R. Walker & Son, Oliver Memorial School (see Figs. 3.13, 3.14 and 3.15), was constructed across the Bristol Commons at 151 State Street. Again, Oliver Memorial's location speaks to a sense that the purpose of the Town Commons was to offer the community shared public infrastructure dedicated to the common good. Oliver School's "postage-stamp" site is less than an acre. The site is occupied predominantly by the school's two-story building and is surrounded by single-family housing neighborhood to the north, east, and west, and by the Town Common just across the street to the south.

Similar to Byfield and Walley Schools, Oliver Memorial's Georgian Revival architectural detailing complemented that of the neighborhood's architectural aesthetics. Broadly, Oliver School is a two-story brick masonry building with a pitched wood frame roof with slate shingles. The overall dimensions of the building measure 76 feet north/south and 83 feet east/west for a total of 16,262 gross square feet, divided up by the basement (5455 square feet), first floor (5455 square feet) and the second floor (5352 square feet). The structure is a wood frame with interior and exterior masonry bearing walls on stone foundations of various widths. Meanwhile, the roof is comprised of wood rafters at various pitches, supported by heavy timber valley rafters. The façade is symmetrical, with a

Fig. 3.13 A photo of the Oliver Memorial School in Bristol, RI. (da Silva Photographer, 2003)

central five bay gable roof pavilion, and is flanked by two wings with hipped roofs containing double-arched entries with detailed rails that form balconies on either side (access to the building is off of State Street). According to the Rhode Island Historic Preservation Commission, a square steeple was removed in 1960.

In the school's floor plan exhibits six classrooms measuring 28 feet by 32 feet and gender- specific recreational spaces in the basement. Though these features—along with the fact that Quincy Grammar was its model—suggest that Oliver Memorial was built to facilitate traditionalist pedagogies, markedly, the school's floor plan does *not* have a number of the features that, as I discuss above, were common in schools inspired by *The Yale Report* such as recitation rooms, debate rooms, or a separate library. Instead, Oliver Memorial allocated this space for the teacher's use. The school's reduced program signals a minimal departure from the "mind as

Fig. 3.14 A photograph of the Oliver Memorial School in Bristol. (RI Board of Education, 1903)

a muscle" ideology and an incremental embrace of social efficiency, which, we might recall, encouraged school designs with spaces for educational administrators and specialist teachers. But the reality is that the extra room the school offers teachers may not actually represent the kind of administrative spaces for which scientific management reformers advocated—we don't know if the teacher's room was more than just that, if it represents the introduction of space for the master teacher or if it simply sought to provide teachers with separate restroom facilities. And so, these small moves alone are not enough to suggest that Oliver School's spatial form really departs significantly from *The Yale Report* or responds to the social efficiency ideologies of the heyday of scientific management.

Built nearing the end of the nineteenth century, Byfield, Walley, and Oliver schoolhouses all evoke a sense of residual pastness, their traditional designs constricting the scientific management education that would, in the

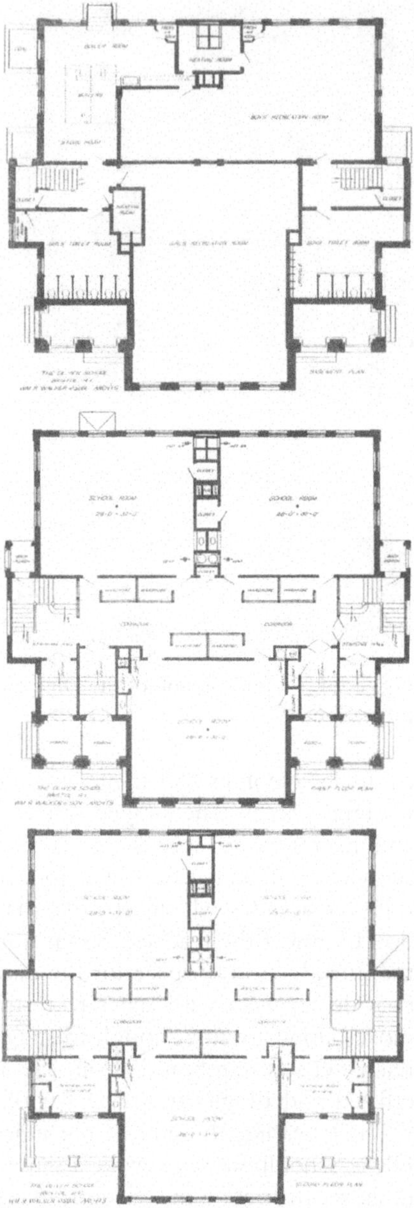

Fig. 3.15 The floor plans of the basement level, main level, and upper level of the Oliver Memorial School in Bristol. (RI Board of Education, 1903)

following years, fill their walls. Largely, the residual pastness of these Bristol schoolhouses speaks to the assembly-line like way in which they built (something that, rather ironically, reminds us that they were indeed erected during the heyday of scientific management), by which I mean that these schoolhouses were modeled on and barely deviated from an extant prototype (the Quincy Grammar School) and were built quickly and methodically. Perhaps this rapid and controlled approach to the design and construction of the schoolhouses accounts for the architects' failure to incorporate the emerging complexities of the curricular landscape in their plans.

But there was one intriguing way in which these Bristol schools spoke to the norms of scientific management. Borrowing from the Quincy Plan, the architects of Byfield, Walley, and Oliver all increased the amount of floor space available on the schools' very small Town Common lots by making the schools multistoried. This consolidated configuration evokes scientific management's commitments to efficiency. I explore just how efficient Bristol school plans were by dividing the gross area of the schoolhouse by the net area of educational space to determine the building's "efficiency factor" (see Table 3.1). The efficiency factor represents the relationship between program and overall building gross square footage. As a rule of thumb, I use a factor of 1.50 as a threshold of desired efficiency, which balances support spaces to program spaces. Plans with greater values than this threshold will thus be considered inefficient for the purposes of evaluating whether the plan is modeled after scientific management principles. More specifically, the program net square footage, the building gross square footage, and the social efficiency factor of seven schools built in the Town of Bristol in the later part of the nineteenth century and early part of the twentieth century in chronological order: Byfield Memorial School (circa 1872 at 23,004 gross square feet), Walley Memorial School (circa 1896, 17,531 gross square feet), Oliver Memorial School (circa 1901 at 16,262 gross square feet), Colt Memorial School (circa 1906 at 28,232 gross square feet), Reynolds Memorial School (circa 1918 at 28,518 gross square feet), Guiteras Memorial School (circa 1927 at 42,411 gross square feet), Andrews Memorial School (circa 1939 at 33,730 gross square feet).

Only the Walley (1.81), Reynolds (1.61), and Guiteras (1.82) schools approaches the desired ratio of 1.5. However, Oliver (2.33), Colt (2.42), and Andrews (2.37) do not reflect a trend toward the 1.5 efficiency of program area to building area. Despite a very subtle improvement in efficiency, this table does not illustrate a clear and obvious correlation of efficiency,

Table 3.1 Efficiency factor analysis of Bristol Memorial Schools

Memorial School	*Year built*	*Program NET square footage*	*Building GROSS square footage*	*Efficiency factor*
Byfield	1872	9512	23,004	2.42
Walley	1896	9682	17,531	1.81
Oliver	1901	6990	16,262	2.33
Colt	1906	11,663	28,232	2.42
Reynolds	1918	17,720	28,518	1.61
Guiteras	1927	23,249	42,411	1.82
Andrews	1939	14,252	33,730	2.37

synonymous with the progression from traditionalist to scientific management. But it is clear from the square footage totals that, in general, the size of the schools increased over time (from 1872 to 1939) ranging from 20 to 30, and then up to 40,000 square feet. These increases in schoolhouse areas reflect the increase in circulation space (such as the corridors that provided access to the increased program offerings). Notably, these increases in schoolhouse area do correlate with the shift in popular curriculum ideologies from *The Yale Report* to scientific management. But all in all, in surveying the development of schoolhouse forms in Bristol, it remains a struggle to identify any architectural elements that really speak to the ideals of scientific management. The building designs that followed Byfield, Walley, and Oliver—those of the Colt Memorial High School, the Reynolds Memorial School, the Guiteras Memorial School, and Andrews School—better embody something akin to a scientific management schoolhouse form.

Providence

Point Street Grammar School, 1874

Providence's Point Street Grammar school (see Figs. 3.16 and 3.17), is rather inspiring and worthy of a short architectural review. The Point Street Grammar boasts a very ostentatious and formal French Gothic design, its large scale (emphasized by its high sloping mansard roof forms and detailed central spire) dwarfing the modest two-story residences in its background. Inside, its Great Hall likely boasted a stunning cathedral ceiling. To be sure, the school exudes a sense of Bataille's monumentality[7]; it

[7] In *Oeuvres Completes* (1971), Bataille situates majestic architecture as conveying a sense of authority, importance, and power that encourages subjects to be submissive and obedient.

Fig. 3.16 A rendering of the Point Street Grammar School in Providence RI (1874). The building of French Gothic styling is located on Plane Street. (RI Board of Education, 1876)

seems it was designed to make a statement. This intense Gothic design notably recalls that of the Providence City Hall. The uncanny resemblance between and impressive style of the two buildings suggests that they were designed to convey a sense of a comprehensive and dedicated public sphere, similar to the schools on Bristol's Town Common, characterized by power. In its balanced monumentality, the Point Street Grammar School expresses values of permanence, rigidity, secureness, an immovability—values that echo the broad, deep, and solid norms of *The Yale*

He connects "ostentatious" architecture to the norms and ambitions of the Enlightenment and its admiration of imposing metanarratives of truth that inspire, and legitimize the rationality of calculated scientific processes. In short, Bataille's robust architecture dominates by drawing attention to its formative "monumentality", thereby impacting discourse, governmentality, and spatiality.

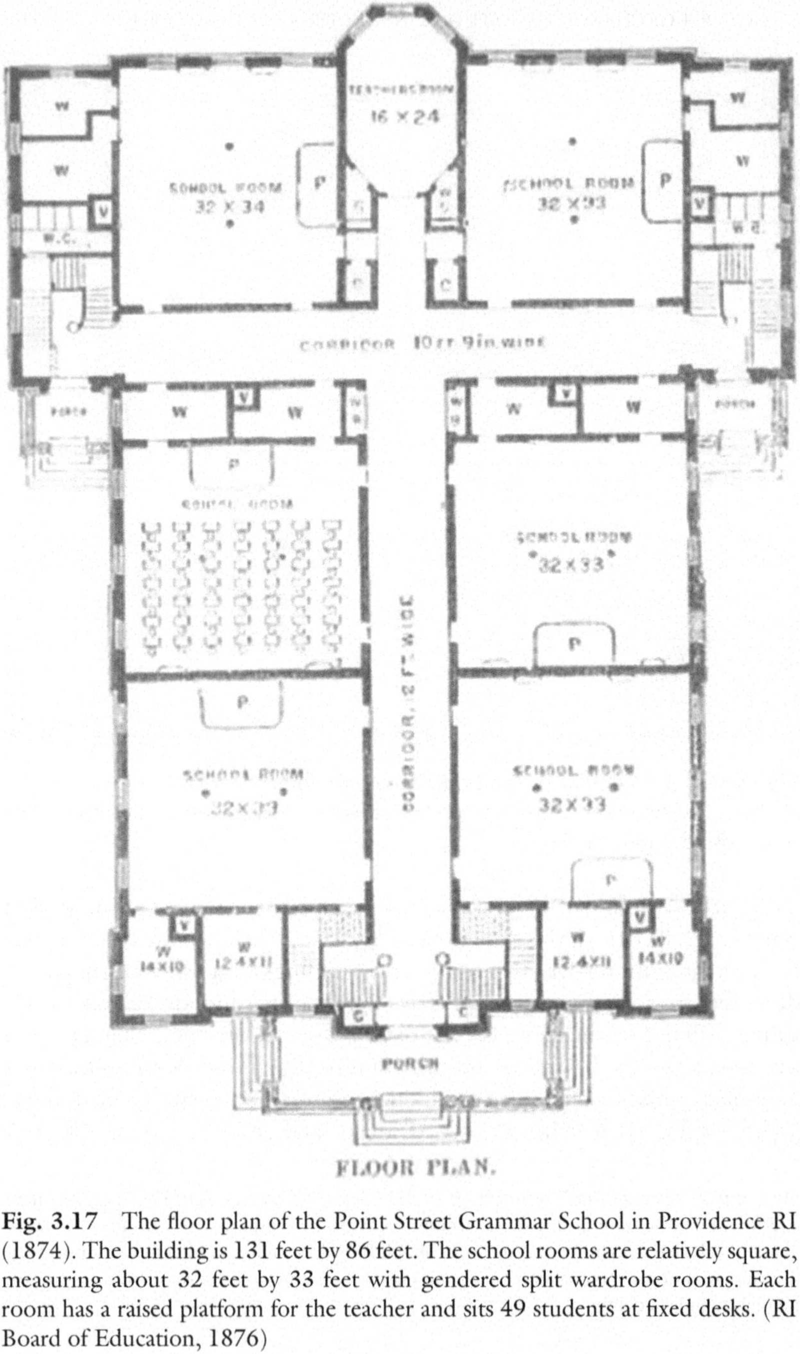

Fig. 3.17 The floor plan of the Point Street Grammar School in Providence RI (1874). The building is 131 feet by 86 feet. The school rooms are relatively square, measuring about 32 feet by 33 feet with gendered split wardrobe rooms. Each room has a raised platform for the teacher and sits 49 students at fixed desks. (RI Board of Education, 1876)

Report. In this vein, Point Street demonstrates many of *The Yale Report*'s basic spatial requirements. Most striking of these is that Point Street Grammar School is split in two by a cruciform corridor. This division creates gendered learning communities, each with separate entrances and program spaces.

State Normal School, 1879

To help shed light on the elements of *The Yale Report* that Rhode Island schoolhouses embodied, it is important to look at the architecture of the spaces that were used to train teachers. To be sure, the history of normal schools goes beyond the US; its origins lying in Europe with the American plan for the normal school "modeled in some features after the institution of Verhil, at Kruitzlingen, in Switzerland" (Barnard, 1851, p. 264). In the US, states introduced normal schools to prepare a force of teachers to improve the rapidly expanding common schools system. For Americans, the kind of quality education for which common school movement called required a quality *teacher*. In this spirit, the Rhode Island School Board of Education gathered to consider what norms should be formally applied to the teaching profession, concluding in an 1880 report that "past experience has proven that a good teacher must be a man of character and ability – that he should have a professional training like that of a clergyman or physician" (p. 8). Moreover, the Board argued that.

> The living teacher is the central utilizing force of the school, and therefore real and permanent improvement can be secured only by elevating the character of the teachers, and for this reason the instruction whose mission is to prepare them for their responsible duties, watched over with constant care, provide with the best instruction and management, and supplied with all the appliances needed to give it the greatest possible efficiency. (p. 51)

With this statement, the Board affirmed the importance of a properly equipped preparatory school for teachers. In making its case for professionalizing teachers, the Board crucially called for "commodious and well-planned buildings" (Rhode Island Board of Education, 1880, p. 8) that would facilitate their training.

But by the time the Board made their case the first normal school, the Rhode Island State Normal School, had already opened in Providence in 1864, established by the RI General Assembly. Predicting the aims of the Board's report, the school sought to establish norms and standards for teaching in Rhode Island by offering courses in instructional methods designed to train students to become primary school teachers. Over a decade later, in 1879, the Rhode Island Normal School moved from its initial quarters to a renovated high school building originally built in 1843 (Rhode Island Board of Education, 1880). This school was decommissioned and sold to the State by the City of Providence and the school district, and was located at the intersection of Benefit, Angell, and Waterman Streets (Rhode Island Board of Education, 1880). It opened with 134 students, mostly white females, and would later graduate two classes per year, with each graduate class in the first three years finding employment at the end of graduation (Rhode Island Board of Education, 1880).

The three-story building (see Fig. 3.18) was designed with a plain Roman and Greek revival aesthetic and brick masonry construction. The building's plain aesthetic was not without notice. In its 1880 report, the Rhode Island Board of Education's described it as "substantial, commodious, healthful and severely plain" (p. 57). The Board (1880) would go on to praise its plainness by insisting "a school building should be plain and simple in its structure", but criticize its lack of furnishings by commenting that "when suitably furnished, [it] will be worthy of imitation" (p. 57). In its original form, the building measured 56 by 76 feet, with later renovations adding an additional space that measured 42 by 32 feet (Rhode Island Board of Education, 1880). Notably, the State Normal School (see Fig. 3.19) supports three entries, one for teachers, one for male students, and one for female students. The main entry was located on Benefit Street facing south and was for the teachers. Meanwhile, the men's entry was located off of Waterman Street facing east, while the women's entry was off of Angell Street to the west, which required a sizable stair given Angell Street's acute slope. Perched on the hill of Benefit Street, the State Normal School's sense of place is noteworthy and deserves to be quoted at length here:

> Its distance from surrounding buildings allows the sunlight – that unfailing source of health and good cheer – to play through its halls and recitation rooms. The study hall commands a fine view of a large part of the city and the hills beyond. The proximity of the building to centers of travel, the railroad depot, the horse-car depot, and the steam boat landings; will be saving of money, and what is more, of time to the large number of pupils who reside at a distance from the school. But the great advantage of this building, when it is fully fitted for its purpose, is that it will enable the teachers and pupils to do more and better work in a given time. This building will

Fig. 3.18 A rendering of the third floor of the state Normal School in Providence. (RI Board of Education, 1879)

> allow the Board of Trustees to organize a more comprehensive course of study, so that more attention can be given to the common English brands, and those branches that directly aid in their teaching. (Rhode Island Board of Education, 1880, pp. 57–58).

Important to note is that the Normal school's trustees were all white men and that the school was headed by a white male principal. In contrast, many of the school's instructors and assistants were white women. On frequent occasion, lecturers from outside the school would come in to give lectures on specialized subject matter.

The facility on Benefit Street soon outgrew its useful life and became too small (Rhode Island Board of Education, 1891). The Trustees of the State Normal School in the quote below respectfully and urgently press the Rhode Island General Assembly for a new, more adequate facility for the Normal School. As the Board's report details, the trustees argued that:

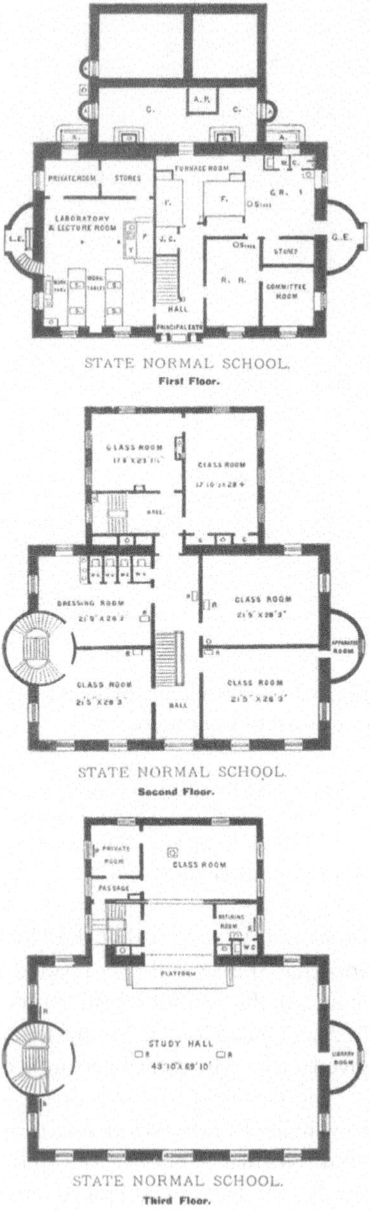

Fig. 3.19 Floor plans of the first floor, second floor, and third floor of the state Normal School in Providence. (RI Board of Education, 1879)

> The issues of the State will soon be in the hands of the children of to-day. What those children are to be depends upon the public schools, and those schools will be what we make them through the teachers whom we put into them. We have no time to lose, for at the best it will consume some two or three years to plan, erect and equip a suitable building; then come the three and a half or four years before the first class can graduate from those who begin with a new building; thus we have six or seven years at least before we can begin to reap the benefits of the new equipment, in the schools throughout the State. But in that time more than two-thirds of all the children in the public schools at the present time will have passed on and out and entered into daily life of the world. Surely then we ought not we must not wait. There can be no cause more urgent, no necessity more pressing. In the right settlement of this question are wrapped up the proper care and treatment of all other questions affecting the State; if we seize upon the golden opportunity to make the springs pure and wholesome, we may be sure that whatsoever streams flow forth therefrom will be pure and life giving. (Rhode Island Board of Education, 1891, pp. 56–57)

The Trustees' request would give birth to a new monumental building. This new form's materiality would go on to shape the pedagogical philosophies of teachers-training-teachers, a concept I take up in more detail in Chap. 4.

The Providence Manual Training School, 1894

Fulfilling the dreams of social efficiency educational reformers, a new school was built in Providence in 1894, the Providence Manual Training School (see Figs. 3.20 and 3.21), to house students (who would otherwise have attended Providence High School) completing studies in the English Department and in manual or vocational training. Since only one large student lavatory was provided in the basement, the school only admitted young men.

In design, the Providence Manual Training school embodied what was considered, at the time, an emerging "modernist" architectural aesthetic, a style that spoke to the empiricist and ordered norms of scientific management curriculum design (Rhode Island Board of Education, 1894, p. 2). For our purposes, this building takes on aesthetic elements that echo the Richardson's Marshall Field Wholesale Store in Chicago, demonstrating a powerful, simplistic, and functional style. Like Richardson's Marshall Store, the Manual Training school simply stacks its four floors (including its basement) in a box-like form, relying on the proportion, material delin-

Fig. 3.20 A rendering of the Providence Manual Training School in Providence, RI (circa 1892–1894). (Board of Education, 1894)

eation, and repetitive fenestration array of the façade for its monumentality. Strong visual corners were thickened to provide for a powerful embrace of the voided fenestration activities, while the building's empowering arch highlights its entrance. But unlike Richardson's Marshall Store, with its series of identical bays, the Manual Training School is broken up into manageable bays separated by a single fenestration or entry portal and caped with arches, culminating just under the flat roof cornice.

Fig. 3.21 Floor plans of the Providence Manual Training School in Providence, RI (circa 1892–1894). (Board of Education, 1894)

The school's internal spaces hardly informed this external shape, even though it housed many of the differentiated vocational spaces. Despite having to incorporate a room for the boiler plant and the electric engine room, the Manual Training school includes a "machine shop, forge room, pattern shop, a room for setting up machinery and performing experiments showing strengths of materials, etc., a lunch room and kitchen" (Rhode Island Board of Education, 1894, pp. 2–3). More specifically, the first floor provided four schoolrooms for the English department, which were isolated from the carpenter shop. The second level accommodated 100 students for the English Department, with two draughting rooms for 40 students, an optical room, physical laboratory, lecture room, apparatus and dark rooms for photography, and a museum room to house a collection of student work. The third level included a grand assembly hall with a stage, a laboratory for chemistry with prep and chemical storage spaces, an electrical room, and a lecture room with an inclined floor, oriented toward the lecturer. As I've already suggested, the vocational course of instruction at the Manual Training school differed from that at Providence High School, which focused on the more traditionalist pedagogies of a college preparatory curriculum. Courses at the Manual Training school thus included—as its architecture suggests—drawing, carpentry, forging, molding art/casting, and chipping, filing, and machining. Unlike other vocational programs that worked by giving students apprenticeships at commercial shops, the Manual High school sought to provide a "thorough insight into the character of the work done", while keeping students inside school walls (Rhode Island Board of Education, 1894, p. 12).

Though the Providence Manual Training School and, with it, the Townsend Industrial School both realize principles of scientific management in their architecture, this chapter's survey reveals that Rhode Island schoolhouses at large were designed in line with the norms of the traditionalist *Yale Report* even during the heyday of scientific management. Accordingly, this study suggests that school architecture in Rhode Island (a key indicator of school design in the nation at large) did not always develop with a consideration for the latest curricular trends; a finding that, as an educational architect, I have to admit is not an easy pill to swallow. In the chapter that follows, I consider the ways in which these schoolhouse forms limit or facilitate nineteenth century curricula to theorize the era's school design nexus as well as its formative impact on students and, through them, the world they would inherit.

References

Barnard, H. (1851). *Normal Schools.* Carlisle, MA: Applewood Books.
Bataille, G. (1971). *Oeuvres Completes* (Vol. 1–12). Paris: Gallimard.
Cirillo, S. (1980). *Bristol: Three Hundred Years.* Nashville: Franklin Graphics.

da Silva, J. P., & Cordero, M. A. (2011). FUNCTION Follows FORM: Building the Foundations for Student Achievement via "School as a Teaching Tool" and "Place-Based Learning". *Education Facility Planner, 45*(3), 24–28.

Freire, P. (1970). *Pedagogy of the Oppressed*. New York: The Continuum Publishing Corporation.

Graves, B. E. (1993). *School Ways: The Planning and Design of America's Schools* (C. A. Pearson, Ed.). New York: McGraw-Hill.

Gutman, M. (2008). United States School Buildings and Architecture. *Encyclopedia of Children and Childhood in History and Society*. Retrieved November 10, 2013, from www.faqs.org/childhood

Horn, P. W. (1915). The Junior High in Houston, Texas. *The Elementary School Journal, 16*, 91–95.

Kliebard, H. (1986). *The Struggle for the American Curriculum: 1893–1958*. New York: Routledge.

Kowalski, T. J. (2002). *Planning and Managing Facilities* (2nd ed.). Westport, CT: Bergin & Garvey.

Rhode Island Board of Education. (1871–1920). *Annual Reports of the Board of Education*. Providence: E.L. Freeman & Co

Rhode Island Historical Preservation Commission. (1990). *Historical and Architectural Resources of Bristol, Rhode Island*. Bristol, RI: Rhode Island Historical Preservation Commission.

Stockwell, T. B. (2012). *A History of Public Education in Rhode Island, from 1636 to 1876*. Lexington, KY: Forgotten Books.

Stone, M. (1876). *A Concise History of the Rise and Progress of Public Schools in the City of Providence*. Providence: Providence Press.

Yale College Faculty. (1828). *Original Papers in Relation to a Course of Liberal Education*. New Haven: Yale University.

CHAPTER 4

Structuring Sociality: School Design as Social (Re)Production

Asking after the political consequences of nineteenth century education in the US, this chapter takes up the ways in which the school designs outlined in Chaps. 2 and 3 structured the era's sociality. Embarking on such a journey, we must remember that all roads lead to and come from the student—the subject at the heart of such an analysis. To be sure, whatever the political consequences of nineteenth century school design might be, they are certainly caught up in how such designs produce a particular kind of subject. This idea is not new: in the twentieth century, French philosopher Louis Althusser famously argued that the mechanisms by which a society figures its schools deeply shapes its power dynamics; a theory known in short as Althusser's theory of "social (re)production".

Social (Re)Production: State, Economy, Culture, and Civil Society

Before discussing Althusser's theory in full, I want to step back for a moment to consider why school design has such a powerful impact on sociality. Though Althusser would argue that schooling is always, inevitably formative whether or not educational decision-makers ever deliberately intend(ed) to make it so, the history the previous chapters unpack makes clear that schooling has been deliberately torqued over the years to engineer particular social configurations. While the centuries reveal a number

© The Author(s) 2018
J. da Silva, *School(house) Design and Curriculum in Nineteenth Century America*, https://doi.org/10.1007/978-3-319-78586-8_4

of interesting ways that reformers have approached schooling as a method for social engineering, one of the most striking examples of this trend for our purposes emerges with school design's relationship to *assimilation*. Over the years, many reformers have geared school design, time and time again, to compel immigrants and new generations to take on subjectivities that sustain America's extant culture and stimulate the nation's economy. In other words, schooling has long been designed to enculturate students into the social order of civil society by equipping them with the necessary norms and aptitudes by which such a society measures its success—an educative process that requires schooling to intervene in and often delegitimize students' initial ways of thinking and being (Dewey, 1916). Though the school is only one of many formative institutions capable of such assimilative work, it stands as one of the most powerful sites for such socialization because the process of schooling is—by definition—a process of regulating the limits of thinking and being by which the inheriting generation will understand themselves, others, and the world. As I've argued throughout this book, inquiries into the specific norms into which school design interpellates students require a consideration not only of the curricula that impart such norms, but also of the *spaces* that house such pedagogies. In short: school design's socializing work is best determined by asking how it contours student "dwelling". Taking this to heart, this chapter unpacks the relationship between assimilation and what it meant to dwell in America's nineteenth century schoolhouses. Along these lines, it was Dewey who first pointed out, in 1916, the determinedly assimilative function of schooling in the US. In the years since, many acclaimed philosophers, cultural historians, and educational theorists have further unpacked the nuances of school design as an assimilative process. Of these scholars, Habermas (1962), Foucault (1972), Bowles and Ginitis (1976), Willis (1977), Bourdieu and Passeron (1977b), Giroux (1984), Bauman (1992), Apple (2004), and, of course, Althusser (1970) have most provocatively theorized the ways in which schools act as formative sites for civil society. But their works share another register that make this theoretical base all the more meaningful: these scholars crucially take up Dewey's recognition with a social justice framework that considers how schooling, as formative, creates and/or stabilizes social disparities and inequalities. Taking the work of these scholars to task, my next section applies their theories to unpack how nineteenth century school design assimilated students and mobilized them as producers of particular modes of sociality with an eye for how such processes connect to the era's inequities.

As I argue above, such an analysis focuses on how school design anticipates a particular kind of "student". For these scholars, theorizing this "student" requires travel down a number of roads of inquiry, each characterized by one of the three pillars of civil society (which notably correspond to salient strands of schooling [Giroux, 2001]) namely: state, economy, and culture—those apparatuses that make up the public realm, wherein the schoolhouse is situated and acts as one of civic life's most formative institutions. Accordingly, whatever the mutually formative impact of nineteenth century school architecture and curriculum might be, it is necessarily answerable to the state, economic, and cultural conditions that characterize this conjuncture. To be sure, these roads are all caught up in the broader context of civil society. In step with this sense, Bauman (1992) argues that because the birth of education and civil society occurred simultaneously, it is important for any work on education as social production to understand the school as located within the public realm (p. 3). Just as in architecture, where walls are the boundaries that contain the core elements of the space, we can better understand the role education plays in sociality if we understand the state, the economy, and culture not as wholly separate influences, but rather as beholden to the broader civic realm they contour together. In the same view, it is the *interplay* of these three pillars that informs the ideological and spatial school design nexus that shapes student dwelling.

In the nineteenth century, American society was defined by a system of state government predicated on the liberal promise that the administration would guarantee the space for businesses and private citizens to thrive. The state assertedly performed this role by regulating commerce and values. In this scenario, the business sector primarily supported the state by producing commodities, generating revenues, and distributing incomes—in short, by creating the kind of thriving private economy that legitimizes the birth of a liberal state in the first place. Meanwhile, the cultural sector's role was to supply private labor for production, inform values, and intervene in policy. In the antebellum era, the church and the school had the headiest cultural impact at the local community level on civil society. Meanwhile, during the industrial revolution, the mill added another prominent American cultural influence. For our purposes, it's important to note here that both of these eras saw the rise of those prevailing curricula I detail in Chap. 2 related to *The Yale Report* and scientific management. It is with this more holistic understanding of these state, economic, and cultural roads in mind that I want to break down their nineteenth century nuances.

But before investigating the different but related roles of state, economy, and culture in social (re)production in more detail, it's important to establish a sense of the *discursive* quality of America's public realm to better understand the formative nature of these roads: for Dewey (1916), the public realm is made up of groups of individuals affected by an idea and/or action, in which the idea and action are *collective* rather than *private*. In other words, in this scenario, individuals come together when they are affected not just by their own personal needs, but by those of their community at large. Further, Habermas (1962) describes this realm as *purposeful*: public opinion and public interest help form policy and legislation, a configuration in which individuals come together into what he calls *social will formations*. Such formations are effected by a collective idea and action. For our study, we might more precisely understand Habermas' social will formations as giving rise to particular modes of school design; certain kinds of pedagogy and architecture thus emerge as consequences of public interest and consensus. But notably, Habermas makes clear that there is never just one kind of "consensus"—rather, there are always a number of publics emphasizing different norms with many often in play at any one time; certainly, such pluralities are evident in the myriad oscillations of schoolhouse design and curriculum ideology Chaps. 2 and 3 survey. Accordingly, in theorizing social will formations, Habermas emphasizes that such formations are always *dynamic* and *issue dependent*. Answerable to the shifting nature of the spatial and temporal elements of their issues, formative publics are ever-changing. In 1828, *The Yale Report* stood as one of these social formations, while by the mid-century the common schools movement—led by Mann, Barnard, and the friends of education (Reese, 2001)—stood as another. In the late nineteenth century, scientific management reform—informed by Dewey, Tyler, and the National Education Association—emerged as a new formation in stark contrast to Yale's traditional pedagogies. Notably, at times these publics had to resist attempts made by officials to bring schooling completely under state control. It was in response to issues like this that Hauser (1999) reinforced Dewey's argument that civil society is defined by the effect of the idea or action (values) by confirming that a "context of shared meaning" (Hauser, 1999, p. 234) is necessary to legitimate any will formation. While nineteenth century schooling did exhibit a number of moments of relatively stable configurations, I'm not so sure—as I detail more fully in below sections—that American citizens, fractured in this period by inequities and tensions across racial, economic, and gendered lines, ever enjoyed such shared contexts. Rather, such moments of stability more accurately reflect the fact that those who held the power in schooling—primarily, as I've detailed throughout this book, white, well-educated, middle-and-upper-class men—shared such a semantic foundation and excluded (purposefully or not) those who held other systems of meaning from having any influence in school design.

Extending Habermas, Foucault (1972) affirms that this socializing public realm is indeed always discursive by asserting that it is configured, at least in part, by purposeful conversation through a variety of communicative mediums that formalize consensus about collective issues (i.e. curricula and school architecture) and create public opinion (common sense). This so-called discursive space in civil society is informed, informs, and legitimizes discussions within the state, economic, and cultural apparatuses through shared participation. Theoretically, this participatory space discursively realizes and fosters the social will formation, which is fundamental to the democratic process and the creation of public opinion. But important to note is that participation in such a process is always predicated upon having a number of basic competencies: individuals must be skilled in discourse, which requires them to have a command of things such as ordinary language (speech), mathematics (symbol), gestures, and rituals. Without these skills, subjects are often excluded from discourse, their voices silenced in the public realm. These biases of assertedly democratic participation illuminate why, as I argue below, nineteenth century schooling was so slanted to support America's white, Western hegemony despite the nation's racially and culturally diverse population.

I now want to delve more specifically into the first of the "roads" that so characterize the public realm: the state sector. Giroux (2001) argues that Gramsci (1891–1937) completed the most informative work on the state's role in social reproduction. More specifically, Gramsci (1971) expanded Marxist and Weberian thought by bringing state domination into conversation with their theories of manufactured belief systems (i.e. hegemonies) of consent. Considering Marx's and Weber's work, Gramsci argued that social will formations (publics) are not free to form outside this controlling hegemony and so that such discursive norms reflect the standards of their contemporary hegemony, always influenced by the state. Moreover, Gramsci made another crucial contribution to social reproduction theory by making clear that such reproductions rely on *class* as a key means to preserve civil society's extant norms: he argues that the hegemonic ideology and infrastructure in capitalist societies encourage the middle class to accept, or, worse yet, support, a ruling-class public that is really counter (if not completely detrimental) to the middle class's best interest. For Gramsci, the *state* is the structural tool that makes such oppression possible: he locates the state's policies and institutions as preserving extant socio-economic inequalities and its ruling-class politics as reinforcing the interests of this already economically-dominant culture. In short, Gramsci argues that the state nurtures ideological constructs of class relations in civil society by building such socialities into political economics as a kind of hidden curriculum. Within this framework, schooling that reiterates such normative class biases will reproduce such an economic hegemony, thwarting individuality and facilitating student socialization into a culture that violently pacifies their agency. In 1977, Willis underscored the reality of Gramsci's theory with a study of non-ruling-class male students that showed that when such students resisted the ruling-class interests of their schooling, it repressed their economic opportunities and further reproduced their already-marginal class status.

Meanwhile, theories of economic reproduction developed by thinkers like Althusser (1970) and Bowles and Ginitis (1977) expand Gramsci's work on the state as a vehicle of social reproduction. First, Althusser articulates the role of economy in his famous "Ideology and Ideological Apparatuses" (1970). In this essay, Althusser argues that economic configurations like capitalism are maintained despite their exploitative consequences by norms that *reproduce of the relations of production*, a phrase he uses to indicate the stabilization (through repetition) of the basic dynamics of the capitalist industrial economy. According to Althusser (1970), the reproduction of the relations of production is secured by the legal-political and ideological superstructure and by the exercise of state power by what he terms *repressive state apparatuses* (RSA) and the *ideological state apparatuses* (ISAs). First, "repressive state apparatus" signifies any governmental entity that can take on a repressive or liberating role, that orients the political conditions of the reproduction of relations of production to become relations of either exploitation or emancipation (Althusser, 1970). For Althusser, these RSAs are often violent and oppressive, using physical force to constrict the agency of subjects. Some examples of RSAs include, as Althusser details, "the Government, the Administration, the Army, the Police, the Courts",[1] et cetera. These apparatuses can then secure by

[1] Louis Althusser. "Ideology and Ideological State Apparatuses," in *Lenin and Philosophy and Other Essays*, trans. Ben Brewster (New York: Monthly Review Press, 1971), 137.

repression or liberation the political conditions for the action of "ideological state apparatuses". ISAs are, as their name suggests, state apparatuses that work to orient the population in particular ways, not through physical force but through *ideology*, which is to say, by common sense. While he makes clear that the church has historically been a primary ISA, Althusser pivotally argues that the school is *the* modern ISA and, moreover, that as such the school works in service to the economy. Accordingly, Althusser situates education as a vehicle for preparing the workforce by training workers to develop the skills necessary to complete the kinds of work the contemporary economy demands and by making sure workers exemplify the approaches, values, and customs (e.g. the necessary self-control and reverence essential to sustaining the existing economic engine) necessary for maintaining the ruling-class' hegemony.

In the nineteenth century, as today, individuals occupying similar economic ranks—mostly defined by family income—were recognized as belonging to certain stratified classes. Different kinds of lifestyles were associated with different classes—you lived as you could afford to live. Accordingly, the ways one dressed, spoke, et cetera were recognized as indicators of one's economic/social class (I extrapolate on the significance of these divisions in my discussion of Bourdieu's concepts of "cultural capital" and "habitus" below). In other words, social behaviors were (and still are) recognized as the result of being part of a particular class. To this end, in the nineteenth century, there were four basic "classes": *enslaved, lower, "middling", and ruling class*, each characterized by different amounts of economic, social, and political capital (Blumin, 1989). The degree of such capitals a subject possesses determines his or her advantages, connections, and opportunities to types of distributed networks. This in turn organizes his or her access to earnings, wealth networks, and the degree of control he or she has over others. Up until reconstruction, African Americans were enslaved, deprived of basic human rights. Even after reconstruction, many scholars have well made clear, an era in which blacks were professedly "free", African Americans were continually subject to structural racisms that limited their agency in a close degree to that accomplished by enslavement. Meanwhile, poor whites made up the lower class, which included the working class who labored for something below a living wage. Lower class families notably suffered from a chronic absence of social and political opportunities. These stifled opportunities and access to wealth strained the sustainability of impoverished families. These strains undercut accessibility to other networks and supports, and placed a greater reliance on family networks, which further limited access to capital—poverty, a vicious circle. Caught up in these politics is a deficit model that unjustly normalizes the impoverished as an "underclass" who just hasn't worked hard enough to be financially secure.

In the antebellum era, the middle class was not firmly yet established. Instead, there were the "middling" folks, individuals who engaged in manual work such as small farmers, skilled workers or artisans, and shopkeepers (Blumin, 1989). It was not until the industrial revolution in the later part of the nineteenth century that the middle class really emerged, though the concept of the "middle class" emerged as early as the American Revolution. The eventual formation of the middle class was a product of the creation those white-collar non-manual labor wage earners—e.g. managers—during the industrial age. More specifically, the industrialization and theories of scientific management that so characterized the latter half of the nineteenth century swept up the majority of the American population into workplace dynamics that required a large number (66%) of "blue-collar" and a smaller number (33%) of "white-collar" workers. For the white-collar worker—that archetype of the middle class—independence and success correlated with individual expertise. The emergence of the middle class and their accumulation of wealth would go on to redefine their residential dwellings. The middle class caused homes to become bigger, with more spaces dedicated to specialized activities. More precisely, the emergence of the middle class along these industrial lines meant that social, professional, and financial mobility no longer depended on earning a patronage but, rather, upon earning qualifications, upon developing an expertise. This inspired a sea-change in the ways in which society approached children's socialization and education: in addition to taking on such norms themselves, middle class parents also encouraged their children to develop new character traits and values that better aligned with such employment landscapes of accomplishment and decorum. These new discursive traits emerged in contrast with the more bullish and aggressive characteristics of an entrepreneurial disposition and instead trended toward conservative, small business-minded sensibilities and pleasing a higher authority like a company director (Blumin, 1989). With modernity demanding this kind of non-manual workforce, competition for such middle-class opportunities compelled subjects to become more qualified than ever before, which meant they needed to attain more education. Primary school was no longer an adequate level of preparation; high school graduation became the essential gateway to prosperity (Blumin, 1989). The ruling class fueled by urbanization and growth in slavery, farming (cotton), manufacturing (factories), transportation (railroads), and banking, were the captains of these industries. Their wealth was a product of family status (the older the wealthier). Schooling thus became deeply tied to the politics of class in America. Such a consideration of class structures is so important for our study because it makes clear that the economic structures of the state deeply shape the power dynamics between communities and, accordingly, agency. Taking to task such dynamics, Althusser's work compels us to consider the ways in which all elements of school design—from curricula to the training of the teacher, from room assignments to the design of the classroom—intervene in such economic structures of capitalist production.

A few years later, Bowles and Ginitis (1977) expanded Althusser's economic reproductive theory, particularly with regard to education as an ideological apparatus. Bowles and Ginitis (1977) articulated that schooling functioned as Althusser argued (as a reproduction of labor power) because it was designed to sort cognitive and technical aptitudes. In more precise terms, they suggested that schooling facilitates the social division of labor by splitting youth up early on in their lives into different and economically stratifying paths defined by such seemingly innocent markers as "college prep", "vocational studies", and "home economics". Further, these reproductions transcend and squash students' extant identities by normalizing certain values, temperaments, and ways of being that maintain institutional social relations that are aligned with archaic social divisions of labor. Bowles and Ginitis call this phenomenon the *correspondence principle*. This principle views schooling as a corresponding mirror of society, the classroom a site to indoctrinate students with the dynamics of the workforce and class system by teaching particular skills, values, and norms. These relations program students to serve a myriad of economic roles. Such roles are determined by tests that measure their ability to meet the norms of each position, professional aptitudes defined by students' attitudes, temperaments, and socio-economic positions. Bowles and Ginitis call this sorting the "hidden curriculum". For our purposes, what's crucial to grasp about the hidden curriculum is that it inculcates students to succeed in the established social economy according to their aptitudes and as such shapes a student's identity and future role in society according to the economic demands of the student's day. Together, Althusser and Bowles and Ginitis contribute to our understanding of reproductive theory by emphasizing its role in civil society's economic realm through their concerns with ideology, the correspondence principle, and the hidden curriculum.

While these theorists greatly unpack the economic register of social reproduction, they fail to more fully articulate the cultural one. More legibly taking up the role of culture in social reproduction, Pierre Bourdieu (Bourdieu & Passeron, 1977a) builds on the state and economic theories of Gramsci, Althusser, and Bowles and Ginitis by linking domination and class with culture. More precisely, Bourdieu focuses on the cultural power dynamics at work in civil society, how these dynamics deny subjects particular opportunities, and how they manifest within epistemological and ontological constructs (Bourdieu & Passeron, 1977b). Against theorists of economic reproduction, Bourdieu argues that cultural capital—i.e. one's ability to know and demonstrate particular things associated with a particular class (e.g. to dress or talk in a ruling-class way)—plays a larger role in one's social position than how much money is in one's coffers. Accordingly, Bourdieu suggests that what he calls "symbolic" power dynamics—those relations of power predicated not necessarily on money, but on the ways in which we recognize each other as having differential kinds of *cultural* worth—maintain the ruling class' control over the social order. Within this framework, schooling *appears* as an equalizer—its assertedly fair and objective persona and relative isolation from the state or economic ruling interests suggesting that it works meritocratically, that it rewards hard work. But to be sure, any inequities in schooling only intensify cultural capital in certain areas while inhibiting it in others. For Bourdieu, schooling empowers the work of *cultural capital* by normalizing its competencies—those sensibilities of style, thinking, and temperament most frequently exhibited by the ruling class. While different kinds of schooling in different areas certainly contribute to unequal distributions of cultural capital, these uneven competencies are also typically shaped by, as Bourdieu makes clear, those dispositions common to one's family. Those norms of our lives, like our family's style, influence what Bourdieu calls our *habitus*—that is, our most frequent way of being, evident in our character, taste, and sensibility, among other traits. Our habitus always exists in relation to those ways of thinking and being that are hegemonic in our society. In this way, if our habitus fails to align with our society's norms of cultural capital—with those social practices and knowledges popular ideology deems most worthwhile—it stands as a vehicle for a subject to endure a symbolic violence—"symbolic" because normalized in everyday culture and "violent" because such a misalignment marginalizes subjects without cultural capital simply because they did not inherit or have not been able to embody the upper-class decorum rooted in those white (British) colonial norms brought to the US by early settlers. For our purposes, Bourdieu's theory underscores how school design might disempower students who don't express the norms of the dominant culture. For example, students going to a school that prioritizes certain cultural competencies (e.g. those associated with white, upper-class hegemonies) that don't align with one's habitus will be marginalized by virtue of not having any "capital" in their school's "culture"—schooling in this case emerging as a microcosmic indicator of the way in which Bourdieu's theory operates in society at large. The cultural competencies prioritized by nineteenth century school design (which I discuss in more detail below) were rooted in the era's broader cultural commitments. More specifically, as I've articulated throughout this book, nineteenth century American culture was variously defined by its white, Western Puritanical origins, commitments to moral, economic, and technological progress, and an emphasis on personal liberty that heralded the infamous "bootstraps" mentality (irrespective of whatever structural forces might be unfairly working against a subject). Thus far, I have contextualized reproduction theory by the boundaries of civil society—state domination, economic mirroring, and cultural capital, which forms the place of schooling within the public realm. These boundaries create and shape the public space that remains, which positions schooling at the intersectional plane of the schoolhouse and the public realm. What remains is the spatial membrane of the schoolhouse that houses student dwelling. As I've described, Althusser argues that this formative sphere is not just physical, but ideological. Ideologically, the space is governed by the curricula (intentional and hidden), which form the relations of reproduction through social control and socialization on behalf of preserving civil society. It is critical to take up such ideological norms of curriculum before we move on to consider their relationship to the physical schoolhouse form.

Ideology and Curriculum

It should come as no surprise that the primary strains of nineteenth century curriculum I'm concerned with unpacking here are those best exemplified by the traditional commitments of *The Yale Report* and the industrially predicated pedagogies inspired by scientific management. As I've discussed throughout this book, these two paths of American curriculum each emerge from long debates—what Habermas would locate as social will formations—about what constitutes "knowledge", what kinds of and whose knowledge are most worthwhile, and what the central functions of public education should be. Such concerns have consumed the curriculum theory and studies landscape in the US for over a century (see, e.g. Giroux, 2012; Kliebard, 1986; Paraskeva, 2011; Pinar, Slattery, & Taubman, 1995; Schubert, 1986; Watkins, 2001). The discursive consensus in education on what knowledge is most worthwhile becomes a "course of study", more formally termed the "curriculum" (Willis, Schubert, Bullough Jr., Kridel, & Holton, 1993). Michael Apple (1979) in his seminal work *Ideology and Curriculum* expands this discussion to social justice by exposing the importance of whose knowledge is most worthwhile. Such decisions about curriculum are value-based and often revolve around three basic points: subject matter, societal values, and the reformer's ambitions for the individual learner (Willis et al., 1993). Accordingly, a primary focus when designing a curriculum is how it might work in the interest of fostering *productive* learning (Pinar et al., 1995). As Chap. 2 details, American education derives from the industrious and determined European—but primarily British—influences of early settlers, which for our purposes first emerge most legibly in education with the constitution of Harvard College—founded over a century before the nation itself (Morrison, 1936). These transplanted roots were grounded in Enlightenment ideologies that were themselves tied to notions of Caucasian privilege. In *American Education: The Colonial Experience,* Lawrence Cremin (1970) described the foundation of the Harvard curriculum as rational, humanistic, religious, and classical in language (focusing on Latin and Greek). It included the study of philosophy, science, history, mathematics, and politics, subjects that were primarily taught by oration, narrative, and debate. The omission of "ethics" in this curriculum may not have been innocent. Harvard's early curriculum—so influential on later pedagogical developments in the US such as *The Yale Report*—was silent with regard to diverse ethnicities, preferring a white elitist perspective. Below the tertiary level, schoolhouses in this period were ungraded and made up of only one room. They were primarily for white students, this slant due, at least in part, to the racial homogeneity of colonial villages. By the time *The Yale Report* was written in 1828, challenges to this traditional curriculum were developing, because such curricula failed to take the popular working-class reality into consideration. Almost a century earlier in 1749, Benjamin Franklin portended this challenge in his "*Proposal Relating to the Education of Youth in Pennsylvania*" (Willis et al., 1993), in which he advocated for higher education to become more career-oriented. As I detailed in Chap. 2, in response to Franklin's proposed reforms and their later advocates, in 1828 the Faculty of Yale College issued "*Original Papers in Relation to a Course of Liberal Education*", otherwise known as *The Yale Report*. Widely publicized, *The Yale Report* reinforced humanistic-traditionalist curriculum in an attempt to quench growing calls for more vocational-based reforms (Willis et al., 1993).

The Yale Report (and the centuries of curricula later inspired by it) prioritized a classical, Western, notably white canon that emphasized ideals of "reason" (mobilized in many ways to secure a white hegemony); the hope being that such a pedagogy would "produce" a student with a "mind richly stored with general knowledge, [and] an elevation and dignity of character, which gives him commanding influence in society, and a widely extended sphere of usefulness" (p. 15). In short, the *Report*'s pedagogues hoped to produce an industrious and powerful citizen who possessed a broad knowledge base. But this assertedly "humanistic" curriculum was deeply concentrated on the contributions of *white* scholars (embedded in the Kantian ethos of human as subject), suggesting that it reared citizens to reiterate historically white values, practices, and aspirations. To be sure, "white" curriculum was not new, even in the nineteenth century. The Western humanists whose traditions inspired Harvard's, Brown's, and Yale's, seminal curricula enjoyed a long history of prominence in Europe and, with British and Dutch imperialism, in those nations colonized by the West long before the nineteenth century. Tracing the humanistic tradition back to its roots, Aloni (1999) locates it in the classical traditions of ancient Greco-Roman notions of *paideia* (learning) and *humanitas* (kindness, culture, refinement). In other words, intellectual traditionalists developed their curricula from the western intellectual history beginning with the ancient Greco-Romans. The book, *Great Treasures of Western Thought*, written by Adler and Van Doren and published in 1977 (Schubert, 1984) aptly captures this adoption. The book makes clear that Western thought mainly focused on promoting the great ideologies of the classics and practicing the disciplines of knowledge that, according to Adler (1981), centered on ancient obsessions with approaches to ideals of "truth, beauty, goodness, liberty, equality, and justice" (Schubert, 1986, p. 15). Traditionalists believed that this content would encourage inheriting generations to uphold (if not develop) the kind of liberal humanistic thought upon which American democracy was assertedly predicated (Schubert, 1986). Of course, as Chap. 2 discusses, traditionalists felt that such classical concepts were best taught in their original language—an affinity underscored in *The Yale Report*. Accordingly, students were taught to prioritize Latin. One could say that the curriculum's emphasis on these historically elitist languages and consequent omission of any of its students' other languages is a clear indicator of Western ideological reproduction. I wish to recall here my own experiences in K-12 education during which we were only allowed to communicate in English and sometimes in French, despite the number of students in the school of Portuguese decent. This deliberate negation of native language works to eradicate the non-Anglo and non-Western histories and backgrounds caught up in these tongues, a process I experienced firsthand. Further, this normalized humanistic act of linguistic and, not unrelatedly, cultural marginalization decouples youth from a supportive diaspora and attempts to fill the void with a new culture that the student is often ill-prepared to receive. Despite these consequences (or perhaps to ensure them), humanist pedagogies hold that by studying subjects such as gymnastics, grammar, rhetoric, music, mathematics, geography, natural history, and philosophy *only* as they emerge in the Western canon, a student can become more virtuous, nurture his/her mind, and become a more complete person (Schubert, 1984). More specifically, the Humanistic cosmology implies the following three fundamental premises:

> The first is philosophical, consisting of a conception of man—men and women—as an autonomous and rational being and a fundamental respect for all humans by virtue of being endowed with freedom of will, rational thinking, moral conscience, imaginative and creative powers. The second tenet is socio-political, consisting of a universal ethics of human equality, reciprocity, and solidarity and a political order of pluralistic, just and humane democracy. The third tenet is pedagogical, consisting in the commitment to assist all individuals to realize and perfect their potentialities and "to enjoy", in the words of Mortimer Adler, "as fully as possible all the goods that make a human life as good as it can be" (Aloni, 1999, p. 1).

The conception of what it means to be human, possessing rights of freedom based on equity and societal commitment to foster human possibility, is fundamental and, as such, these concepts must inform those spaces we create in our society. However, these ideals were always slanted with white norms, pressing youth with different ideas of "morality", "reason", or the "good" to pathologize their historic non-white standards and instead assimilate into those prioritized by their humanistic education. In step with these ideals, *The Yale Report* expresses humanistic philosophical, socio-political, and pedagogical notions of education as facilitating the "complete" person. And so, humanistic education emerged in nineteenth century America promising a "completeness" paradoxically predicated on the student's destruction of one way of being for another and on the student's broader pathologization of non-white and non-Western subjects (e.g. most notably in the nineteenth century, Native Americans and blacks) in his/her community—a process that shored up the settler's white hegemony. Moreover, the *Report*'s rote pedagogies encouraged students to swallow such content without criticism, schooling youth into merely reiterating—and thus empowering—the Western status quo.

Rejecting this classical curriculum not for its racism but because it did not directly support capital accumulation, those pedagogies predicated on scientific management so popular in the late nineteenth century championed a shift in education so that it would instead teach youth the skills the nation's burgeoning industrial economy required of its workers. Interestingly, it was in this era of scientific management that many scholars first identified the formal beginnings of "curricula" as a field in itself (see, e.g. Beyer & Liston, 1996; Franklin, 1794; Giroux, Penna, & Pinar, 1981; Jackson, 1992; Kliebard, 1986; Schubert & Lopez Schubert, 1980; Tanner & Tanner, 1980; Willis et al., 1993). This history is best underscored by the emergence of such publications as: *Laggards in Schools (1879–1946)*, the *Cardinal Principles Report (1918)*, and the publication of Bobbitt's *The Curriculum* (1918). Perhaps most important to unfurl for our inquiry is Bobbitt's book, a text primarily devoted to applying scientific management "to the general principles of making curriculum decisions" (Willis et al., 1993, p. 1). In this vein, *The Curriculum* (1918) argued for pedagogical models that were always empirically organized and measurable. Bobbitt's argument emerged more precisely in response to the cult of mental discipline (the faculty psychology of the mind as a muscle) so dominant at the time, inspired by *The Yale Report* and affirmed by Eliot (1834–1926) and the National Education Association *Reports* of the committees of ten (1893) and fifteen (1895), which argued that the mind was to be exercised by memorizing and reciting (Kliebard, 1986). In step with Bobbitt against the humanists were, as I detail in Chap. 2: the developmentalists (child-centered pioneers led by Hall, Parker, and Dewey), the social efficiency educators (a group that yearned for education to make society easier to "run", led by Rice, Snedden, and Finney), and the social meriolists (educators committed to social change and social justice, led by Ward). The product of these scuffles in education reform was the birth of the heyday of scientific management pedagogy, an order inspired by Taylor's *Principles of Scientific Management* (1911) that approached education as a vehicle to support social efficiency and the Gross National Product (GNP). More specifically, as I detail more fully in earlier chapters, Taylor's theory was based on economic practice and workplace structures, which were specialized and made routine with strong supervision and control that focused on effectiveness, efficiency, and mass production (Pinar et al., 1995). Curricula accordingly became predicated on sorting youth early on by "aptitude" tests that would determine the kind of vocational education they would receive so as to optimize their strengths in the economy. Such a pedagogical style is a poignant reflection of Althusserian economic reproduction theory because it operates by directing, with cognitive assessments, students from blue-collar households into trades, and students from white- collar households into white collar—especially, in this era, management-style—work. What scientific management education frames as a difference in "aptitude" is thus more accurately a manifestation of what Bourdieu located as the cultural capital students inherit from their families.

Accordingly missing in the curricula based on scientific management were any commitments to criticality or capaciousness: students were taught to be specialized and efficient by strict teachers and administrators, a set-up that taught the inheriting generation to obey and respect authority early on. Such an educational configuration was deeply strategic for America's capitalist economy: by training youth to become fast, compliant, and effective workers, the nation's factories could produce more commodities than ever to turn the profits they craved. Where traditionalist education still existed at this time, it was similarly considered to be answerable to industry, thought of as a means of training youth with white- collar cultural capital to become managers. To be sure, such a classical education would have, after Bourdieu, given emerging adults the cultural capital necessary to move in the higher (but not really ruling) class circles managers enjoyed and into which workers were denied entry, such a habitus working to affirm the social stratifications upon which the factory relied. As a result of these pedagogical directives, by the end of the nineteenth century, schools had essentially become sites in which to train youth to devote their lives to rapidly accumulating capital—not for themselves, but for the ruling class. Between *The Yale Report* and scientific management and their respective pedagogical legacies, by the later part of the nineteenth century, a number of different social will formations about what curriculum "should be" were at play in the field of education, complicating what Habermas might approach as the nation's pedagogical discourse and its consequences. What can be taken away from this quick journey through America's nineteenth century curricular ideologies? To be sure, such a survey makes evident that in this period American schooling normalized white, Western epistemologies as well as efficient and stratifying skills and dispositions that supported capital accumulation.

The Schoolhouse Form and Dwelling

Such struggles over the American curriculum gave birth to a number of notable schoolhouses over the course of the nineteenth century, such as the "vocational" normal schoolhouse, that are well worth taking up. But before unpacking this architecture, I want to briefly review the significance of the built environment for our study. Despite the fact that we all live or dwell in buildings daily, human subjects rarely think about the creation, shape, style, and construction of their shelters as they cross their thresholds. Buildings are so common to one's everyday existence that they often go unnoticed. However, the physical environments (both built and natural) in which we dwell undeniably shape what it means to exist in fundamental ways. These physical environments influence how we engage, transverse, communicate, and identify in our everyday lives. In brushing off the hegemonic covering of temporal dust and exposing the bare architecture of the schoolhouse form, we can get a sense of the ways in which schoolhouses may have interacted with the curricular norms of their period, knowing that such designs can sustain, erode, and complicate the intentions of curricular ideologies. To be sure, it is important in these theorizations to look out for the work of residual pastness, which is to say to be attentive to the ways in which an older schoolhouse form might snag the hopes of the curricula that were introduced after it was built, that were never considered in its design.

Together, the discursive interactions of the curriculum and the schoolhouse inform what it means to dwell in nineteenth century schools and Gert Biesta in *Beyond Learning* (2006) contributes to this interplay by drawing attention to the fundamental limitation of Humanism. According to Biesta (2006), modernity's curriculum is reflective of a Kantian rationality of human as "subject" and ignores the essential ontology of "being" human. He credits Ernesto Laclau (Laclau & Mouffe, 1985, p. 94) with proclaiming Martin Heidegger's (1949) "being of man", Michel Foucault's (1973) "end of man", and Emmanuel Levinas' (Levinas & Nemo, 1985) essence named "Man", as a death, rebirth, and death of Humanism (1996, pp. 33–34). He proclaims a new language of learning after the "death of the subject" as the birth of "coming into presence" similarly to Heidegger's "dwelling" (1996, pp. 33–54). In this way, he exposes Humanism's silencing of the student's essence of being, within a deficit model of what the student lacks (as previously noted as the Freirean "banking model" of teaching) rather than what she or he brings into the classroom. Thereby, advocating for a curriculum and a schoolhouse form that supports the student not as a subject, but as one coming into presence- dwelling. He draws attention to the singularity of the student coming into presence in a world of pluralities (countering Humanistic norms of a dutiful homogeneous student soaked in critical reasoning, individual freedom, and benevolent progress) sponsoring ontology of dwelling through diverse relationships with others that are unlike her or his unique individuality, which in short considers the student as a "who" rather than a "what". In step with humanism, the Yale Report curriculum was a fitting gateway to scientific management, since they share in common the cultivation of the dutiful student as a "what"—a being of social construction. In this social construction, the student is potential "capital" rather than someone coming into "presence" into a school in a world different from her or him. In this scenario, the context of schooling plays a reduced role and explains the omission of the schoolhouse from the prevailing curriculum discourse.

While many educational thinkers unsurprisingly negate the pedagogical role of the schoolhouse itself, some have made clear that it is absolutely critical to education. Notably, taking this gap to task in 1938, Dewey was the first pedagogue to tackle the environment as a central theme in education. For him, the way the environment in which schooling takes place interrelates with the student *is* the educational experience. Dewey's understanding powerfully anticipates Biesta's schema of "coming in to presence" and the German philosopher Heidegger's schema of "dwelling". More specifically, Heidegger offered insightful theoretical reflections on the environment and being, arguing that "dwelling" is a fundamental form of being that occurs at the intersection of ground and sky (physical environment). For Heidegger, it is at this horizontal spatial juxtaposition between the heaven and earth that architecture realizes "dwelling", and he thus credits the building as constituting the place wherein dwelling appears. Dwelling (1949) establishes a meaningful relationship between one's self and the environment, similar in many respects to Dewey's notions of experience and education. Drawing from these works, I want to posit that, as I have argued throughout this book, the formative impact of education is not only answerable to the norms of its curriculum, but rather also those of its architecture. Indeed, schooling's formative impact ultimately emerges as the shared influence of both, curricula and architecture, a normative pressure that I argue is best characterized as an "ideo-spatial school design nexus". The norms of any school design nexus determine what it means, as Heidegger says, to "dwell" in that school. Considering what dwelling means in any particular school is so important because, as Dewey reminds us, a student's education is not a preparation for the future, so much as it is life itself, making schooling, and within this, especially the often-overlooked role of the schoolhouse, absolutely *primary* to experience. It is *in* dwelling that a subject concretizes a presence and identity, and thus it follows that the ways in which we dwell deeply shape our subjectivities. In other words, educational dwelling matters because it teaches a child *what* it means to be, *how* he or she *should* be, and how he or she fits into their immediate community and world at large.

In this vein, Norberg-Schultz argues in *Intentions in Architecture* (1965) that architecture might best be approached as a cultural phenomenon inspired by psychological and sociological senses of how subjects should live, learn, and work. Norberg-Schultz's architectural theory was based on the human reproduction of the work of architecture and on the conceptual inspiration of noted architectural theoreticians, such as Giedion, Rohe, and Mumford. Norberg-Schultz's approach helps give form, purpose, and means to the built environment because it draws attention to the impact a building might have on those who dwell within it. Considering architecture as thus reflective of a culture's normative aspirations, architectural historian Gifford (1966) insisted that studying architecture can shed light on the dominant ideologies and the culture of a place in time. More specifically, Gifford (1966) details that

> [a]rchitecture involves delimited concepts with comparatively well-focused history, theory, criticism, and practice – as against the concepts that cluster around 'nature', 'the soul', 'man', 'society', and so on; consequently, a study of architectural concepts offers the student of culture or the student of ideas a glimpse of direction in the flux of ideas and attitudes, not unlike the glimpse of direction that dye poured into a current of a stream affords. (p. 16)

These literatures convey a logic that architecture matters, not only because it impacts modes of dwelling, but, because as such it has a normative impact on sociality. While these theorists underscore the ways in which architecture emerges as a form that *follows* function and thus highlight the ways in which buildings are designed to foster specific socialities, the reverse is also true: function can—and often does—follow form. As my concept of residual pastness underscores, buildings are often used for many things other than those functions that initially inspired their forms. The architecture of a building can thus complicate or inhibit its dwellers' intended activities within the building—for example, the recitation rooms of *The Yale Report* do not facilitate the kind of technical work scientific management pedagogies so prize. And so, when we consider the formative impact of architecture in theorizing the ideo-spatial nexus of any school design, it's important to always ask how its form facilitates or limits popular contemporary functions. With these architectural nuances in mind, let's return to this book's opening question: what did it mean for students to dwell in America's nineteenth century schools?

Power Relations in Nineteenth Century American Schools

Let's begin to take up this question by recalling the norms of nineteenth century school architecture to establish the groundwork necessary for theorizing the ways in which the era's ideo-spatial school design nexus intervened in its white, ruling-class, and capitalistic hegemony. McCormick (2001) provides an exceptional account of the evolution of educational institutions from the eighteenth century to the present, offering an important roadmap for considering how changing educational ideologies inspired the form of schoolhouses and how schoolhouses, in turn, can limit or encourage various curricula. Over the course of the nineteenth century, McCormick details, subscription schools gave way to public schools; a shift that prompted the disappearance of one-room schoolhouses and the wide-spread rise of *graded* schools. As schooling became state-controlled and "common", previously isolated schools were amalgamated into large centralized school districts which, by the end of the nineteenth century, relied on male educational administrators to run smoothly, administration here a striking new development, where previously women teachers had been the sole educational authorities in the school. Notably, these transformations make more evident the ways in which, as Althusser argued, schooling became the dominant ideological state apparatus over the church: as state control and funding made education more pervasive, schools became institutions more common than churches in every jurisdiction, with homogenous governance structures such as administrators and standard curricula enabling the teaching of the same ideas across vast and different geographies, in a similar style to the way standard religious texts disseminated norms. To be sure, such shifts in educational reach and style inspired new forms of educational architecture that would best facilitate these emerging hopes of schooling.

In this vein, nineteenth century schoolhouses embody that myriad of architectural styles and techniques I survey in Chap. 2 from Gothic, Federal, Greek Revival, Italianate, Victorian, Romanesque, Georgian, Second Renaissance, and Art Deco (McCormick, 2001). Crucial to note when considering the formative power of such structures is that these styles are answerable for not only the period's educational expectations but also its technological abilities and, more important, its aesthetic ideals. Unpacking the aesthetic ideals reflected in many of the century's school designs reveals that such designs demonstrate a hidden curriculum that advances patriarchal, ruling-class, and Western norms. For example, in the *Evolutionary Chart of Design* (1979), Loewy makes clear that those changes in architectural style evident in nineteenth century schoolhouse architecture reflect shifts in patriarchal expectations of feminine appearance—essentially mobilizing architecture to affirm the norms of "beauty" that torque the common sense of what kinds of women, as gender theorist Judith Butler (1993) would put it, "matter" in any stylistic era. Architectural design thus stands as part of a larger humanistic aesthetic complex that restricts women's agency by encouraging them to preoccupy themselves with their appearance and that presses them to appear only in those *specific* ways the male gaze of "the moment" might find pleasing—a reductive common sense of the feminine, to be sure.

Loewy's chart of aesthetic evolution also screams of class biases. Praised styles are often those popular among the white ruling class—the group who had the luxury of purchasing highly priced, custom-built homes and high-fashion clothing. Accordingly, school architecture in this way can notably work to normalize ruling-class values over other aspirations. But this bias also adds another layer of inequity to schoolhouse design: if a school building could demonstrate the architecture du jour (a costly endeavor), it became more revered, received more attention than those in communities that could afford to construct new buildings, that were forced to use those structures that may have been built for other purposes and, moreover, whose pedagogies will thus be restricted by the work of residual pastness. Students educated in the more stylish buildings thus not only received the benefit of a more easily facilitated education but, moreover, developed the cultural capital that comes from attending school in a prestigious building that inevitably introduces its subjects by very virtue of their being there to the respected artistic traditions its architecture embodies. In short, these design sensibilities speak to a culture of a white elite hegemony that at times objectified women and failed to give voice to the needs and styles of poor, non-white, and working-class people in the US.

Moreover, many thinkers such as Kruft, Hearn, Burchard, Bush-Brown, Gelernter, Sykes, Nesbit, Ching, and Gifford have also underscored how those architectural styles popular for nineteenth century US schoolhouses support a Western hegemony by chronologically categorizing America's architectural ideologies within the history of Western design. For example, in *Form, Space, and Order* (2007), Ching defines epistemic art in the development of architecture. This Western epistemological concept, fixated on architectural style, is typically found in popular texts on architectural history. It organizes prevailing architectural styles, which typically relate to the subjective anthropocentric thinking that informed the culture of the day, into periods. These styles and periods can be outlined as the Greek Revivals (1760–1830), Gothic Revivals (1830–1865), Functional (1865–1900), Organic (1900–1920), and Functional Beauty (1920–1950) made popular by architects T. Jefferson, H.H. Richardson, L. Sullivan, F.L. Wright, and W. Gropius, respectively, just to name a few (Gifford, 1966). It should not be surprising that US schoolhouses are Western epistemological institutions that contribute to the production, reproduction, and resistance of the knowledge and beliefs of the communities in which they reside. Therefore, it seems fitting to harken back to the ancient roots of Western civilization and architectural theory. According to Vitruvius (30 B.C.E.) schoolhouses, like other architectural structures, embody three critical characteristics: *firmness* (which speaks to shelter, safety, and egress), *commodity* (which speaks to the building's ability to satisfy the functional purpose of the institution), and *delight* (experiential, emotional, and responsive). Echoing classical Vitruvian tripartite theory *The Yale Report* calls for an education that is *broad, deep, and solid*. However, both of these classical humanistic tenets are silent with regard to experiential social interactions with others, instead they focus on the subject matter—category of knowledges and forms.

Further, the Western architectural norms exemplified by historians of architectural theories, such as Hearn, Kruft, and Ching, just to name a few (as well as those previously illuminated by Loewy, Gelernter, and Gifford), are embedded in humanism's classical rationality of aesthetic subjects and less so on the experiential elements of dwelling. These scholars reductively categorize the architecture as object and assess the degree of aesthetic cohesion and completeness of designs related to a particular grouping or style. For example, Fil Hearn's *Ideas That Shape Buildings*, distinguishes "the fundamental topics of architectural theory as universal underpinnings, conventions, principles, and convolutions", uprooted from antiquity reveals a fixation on "classical orders" of beauty and proportion (2003, p. 335). Further, the timeline of treatises starts with the classical works of Vitruvius in Rome in 30 B.C.E, silencing the plethora of non-Western theories and heritage before and occurring alongside (Hearn, 2003, pp. 337–341). Similarly, Hanno-Walter Kruft in *A History of Architectural Theory: From Vitruvius to the Present* discloses categorically a character of architectural theories as a "written system of architecture" centered on a traditional consistency of humanistic meaning based on man's proportionality (1994, p. 15). Ching deviates slightly from these norms by establishing a design vocabulary that engages the classical aesthetics by way of point, line, volume, proportion, scale, circulation, form and space, which represents a slight shift to the experiential nature of architecture, but nevertheless is still silent with regard to criticality of social justice. Exploring these past humanistic architectural constructions of form reveals a Western architectural tradition of objectification. It lacks an experiential theory of coming into presence of the dweller within its spaces or whose voices are missing from these constructions. In deconstructing these elitist architectural theories and reversing the attention from the walls to the spatiality left behind, the opportunity for the social justice experience provided by these forms can be better understood and becomes more answerable to the question what it means to dwell in their spaces. This relative silence of social justice in these Western elitist architectural theories facilitates the omission of whose ideologies these theories represent, surely not those of the Other; socially producing and reproducing the norms and stifling potential emancipatory opportunities.

Expanding on the experiential elements silenced by Humanism, Foucault (1977) makes clear that educational spaces can further limit student agency with the famous interpretative lens he provided to illuminate how power dynamics operate within spatial forms. The links between the actual physical space, the operational framework of that space (what he terms "governmentality"), and the discourses surrounding dwelling in that space, form what Foucault calls an *archeological tripartite of power dynamics* (1977). For Foucault, this tripartite plays a powerful and often-overlooked role in modernity's rationalization and management of subjects and those it abjectifies as "Others" (I more fully discuss the concept of the "Other" below). To better understand the conceptual connections and applications of Foucault's spatiality—which, for our purposes, involve how the theory speaks to the formative power of the schoolhouse (Hennon, 1999). To expand Foucault's theory, I'd like to bring it into conversation with the seminal work of Georges Bataille. His theories on architectural representational duality meaningfully develop the workings of the relationship Foucault argues exists between the discursive, governmental, and physical realms and the Other. While Foucault, as Hollier (1992) succinctly summarizes, focuses primarily on the ways in which buildings can subtly exercise a *panoptic* kind of *governance* by embodying an "architecture that sees, observes, and spies, a vigilant architecture", that demonstrates "insinuating concavity that surrounds, frames, contains and confines" (Hollier, 1992, p. x), Bataille (1971) makes clear that "ostentatious spectacular architecture", meaning those styles which are "convex, frontal, [and] extrovert[ed]" as well as "externally imposing"—those styles designed with the intention of wanting "to be seen" (Hollier, 1992, p. x)—similarly suggest that architecture can also work less subtlety to convey a sense of authority, importance, and power that encourages subjects to be submissive and obedient. More specifically, in *Oeuvres Completes* (1971), Bataille situates majestic architecture as tied to the humanistic norms and ambitions of the Enlightenment. For Bataille, such imposing and ostentatious architecture expresses the Enlightenment concept that modernity should revere similarly imposing metanarratives of truth, narratives that derive from, inspire, and legitimize the Enlightenment's rational love of order and evaluative processes. While Foucault's panoptic architecture oppresses being (dwelling) by emphasizing surveillance, Bataille's ostentatious architecture oppresses being (dwelling) by "draw[ing] attention to itself" and by masking surveillance (Hollier, 1992, p. x). Such architecture draws attention to its power to change "documents" into "monuments" (Foucault, 1971, pp. 138–139). In other words, for Bataille, "great monuments rise up like levees, opposing the logic of majesty and authority to any confusion: church and state in the form of cathedrals and palaces speak to the multitudes, or silence them" (Bataille, 1991, pp. 171–172). Bataille terms such formation of ostentatious architecture "monumentality", a concept that provides a new register in Foucauldian theory about how discourse, governmentality, and physical space shape the subject's being (dwelling). Speaking likewise of the relationship between the Enlightenment and architecture's interpellative power in *Discipline and Punish* (1977), Foucault wagers that the movement's emphasis on *control* inspired architectural styles that managed populations by schooling them into disciplinary norms. Such forms of governmentality would come to replace, Foucault details, older methods such as torture. More precisely, Foucault locates the most striking example of architecture as a kind of disciplinary control mechanism in the rapid growth of the *prison*. For Foucault, the prison worked as a disciplinary spatiality because it incorporated the mechanisms of *examination*, *normalized judgment*, and *hierarchical surveillance*. Taken together, Bataille's and Foucault's work on architecture as monumental, panoptic, and disciplinary speak to the repressive dwelling role of architecture in society (Hollier, 1992).

Applying these mechanisms of control (examination, normalized judgment, and hierarchical surveillance) to questions of school architecture illuminates the ways in which schools sometimes demonstrate prison-like qualities that speak to their relationship with discipline and control. By asking the question of how nineteenth century schooling might work in step with a system of power based on discipline and control, it becomes clear that the pedagogies in question do so by focusing on the disciplinary controls of lectures, recitations, and memorizations. Here, control is just caught up not only in the judgment of what a student has mastered, but also in what the student has not understood.

In this deficit model, the lack of achievement of the standard is represented as deviant and abnormal, which Foucault (1977) represents as the normalized judgment mechanism that stratifies populations. *The Yale Report* establishes the classics as a requisite standard of education and purposefully excludes other pedagogies and, in doing so, establishes the normalized standard. In the execution of recitation, the standard is reinforced through the metanarrative of truth embedded in modernity and the pedagogical process of rote learning the *Report* believes will achieve the norm of memorization of classical curricula. The evaluation of the recitation/examination reveals what the student knows or does not know in line with what the pedagogy expects and then works to control her or his next steps in her or his journey to acquire the normalized "truth". These next steps of control are hierarchically observed, for example, by fixing student seating and establishing raised trainer platforms that facilitate the enhanced surveillance of all students. Like Foucault, Jeremy Bentham provides a concept of the ***panopticon*** that speaks to this concept of control. Bentham's model locates the educational administration as a network of observers collaborating together in a hierarchical order. In this modern panoptic context, prisons and schools exhibit similar characteristics of disciplinary control. Students, for example, are disciplined and controlled by being constantly under surveillance, an arrangement that has, as my introduction underscores, has now become much normalized. Negotiating constant surveillance and so threatened by the sense that someone is "always watching", students self-regulate—they discipline and control themselves in the face of the surveillance apparatuses to which they are subject (Foucault, 1977). Though different, Bataille's attractive and Foucault's repulsive conceptual polarities are both critical of the controlling, repressive work of the panoptic built environments Bentham details (King, 1996). Together they form a boundary that is critical of the space of schooling that is discursive, administrative, and physical (Hennon, 1999). This geographical dwelling within the resultant fixed school form subjugates non-normative ontologies and epistemologies through the power dynamics of discourse, curriculum, and physical space (in contrast, e.g. to those more possibilistic spaces like that of an open field, a mountaintop, a dense forest, or a majestic canyon).

To more fully unpack how these architectural norms emerge in nineteenth century school design in relation to such theories, let's turn to the more specific examples the previous chapter lays out with case studies in Rhode Island. To quicken our analysis, I'd like to begin with one of the most powerful educative sites of social reproduction—those school designs used to facilitate *teacher training*. Pedagogical training is the site where what knowledge was most worthwhile was concretized before it was distributed to countless classrooms, as such teacher training sites are nerve-centers of queries into education as social reproduction. Accordingly, teacher training stands as what Althusser, in "Ideology and Ideological State Apparatuses" (1970), would have qualified as a primary means of reproducing the conditions of production. In preparing the teacher, we are preparing the facilitator who cultivates the student's humanity and/or enculturates them into a repressive or liberating social order and what is in between. Teacher education thus shapes the ways in which teachers enable students to dwell, an arrangement that makes clear that because students are cultural actors, it intervenes in the norms of society. And so, to unpack this cultural reproduction let's look at the forms provided for training the teachers who teach the students the so-called truth. Rhode Island was certainly a hotspot in the training school movement as exemplified by the large presence of teacher education centers in the communities of Newport and Providence. Accordingly, I'd like to begin theorizing how school design worked as social (re)production with an analysis of Providence's famous State Normal School.

Providence's State Normal School and Social (Re)Production

The State Normal School in Providence, RI, as I detail in Chap. 3, was inspired by the Swiss focus on teacher training. Inspired by this European drive to standardize teacher education, the Rhode Island General Assembly opened the state's first normal school in the capitol by mid-century, aptly named the "State Normal School", to establish standards for teaching and to train youth primary school teachers that upheld such standards. As Chap. 3 makes clear, the Board argued that teacher training was so important because the teacher was really understood as the force at the heart of the school in this period and thus, that educational reform should focus first and foremost on teacher training. While it's certainly true that teachers play deeply important roles in schooling, such a parochial sense of education detrimentally distracts from the student. More specifically, in omitting the student, the Board reiterated the disciplinary and controlling slant of *The Yale Report* that fixated on subject matter while negating the student's experience and interest, those facets of education that Dewey would later earmark as intensely important in the *Child and Curriculum*.

While the Europeans provided the encouragement for the broader concept, it was other US normal schools that inspired the more precise designs of the Providence normal school. The normal school of Bridgewater, MA, built less than a decade before Providence's, is one famous example of the generalized idea of the "US normal school" because it was one of the first and was showcased in Barnard's seminal *School Architecture*. This school was decorated in the architectural style of the Greek revival, with Doric column pilasters that gave it a masculine monumental presence and an architectural majesty that suggested that whatever was happening inside its walls was deeply significant. These classical architectural styling also located the education that would take place within the building firmly in the *Western* tradition. Moreover, the floor plans reflect a pedagogy that instructs by example. Of particular note is the monitorial nature of the

Normal School Room layout, which could facilitate an apprenticeship mode of instruction and adds some credence to the claim that the monitorial method of school administration based in discipline and control was exported from Europe and adopted in the US. This layout of the Normal School Room has three platforms for three teachers and leads directly to two recitation rooms. These aesthetics were typical of early normal schools of the period and read very much like the one-room schoolhouses they were built to replace. Important to note is that these floor plans demonstrate an affinity for those banking model (or "rote") pedagogies favored by *The Yale Report.* More specifically, the floor plans encouraged instructors to stand at the head of the class on a platform (as would be customary in an actual common school at the time), symbolizing their authority and encouraging the class to learn from their lectures rather than from any kind of collaborative or inquiry-based work. The Bridgewater Normal School, like many schools of the period, had separate entrances and stairs for males and females, affirming the era's divisive gendered politics. Meanwhile, the upper level exited through stairs at either end down to the Model School Room and Laboratory at the lower level. This adjacency makes the transition from lecture to model practice seamless. The Model School Room was situated adjacent to the laboratory and chemical room and opened to spacious hall entries. This floor plan thus embodied the reproduction elements necessary to prepare the future teachers to work in many schools during the common schools era.

While like many normal schools of the period, Providence's State Normal School—detailed in Chap. 3—echoes Bridgewater's design in many ways, it also stands as a more striking example of the tensions between the schooling movements associated with *The Yale Report* and scientific management as social will formations of the era. In fact, the State Normal School might be best described as a transitional design caught in between traditionalist education's emphasis on cultural capital and the capitalistic imperatives of pedagogies inspired by scientific management. Built in 1879, the State Normal School echoed the three-story square style of the seminal grammar schools built all along the East Coast in the earlier part of the century. It housed a laboratory and lecture hall, with a number of classrooms, along with a study hall. Interestingly, then, the State Normal School was an institution designed for *vocational* education—namely, teacher training—but designed in the style of grammar schools inspired by *traditionalist* pedagogies.

With Providence (and Rhode Island more broadly) a leader in the nineteenth century's seminal professionalization and standardization of education, it should come as no surprise that the state's first normal school would quickly outgrow its usefulness. As Chap. 3 details, the nation's intentions to expand schooling to meet the needs of the common school movement, the burgeoning population, and the industrializing economy certainly warranted more teachers, and this demand compelled the construction of a much larger facility. The second State Normal School (see Fig. 4.1) was built to be a state-of-the-art institution, equipped to serve 250 students at a time (though the school soon introduced a "second shift" of students to double the number of attendees). The building itself was made up of three floors and a basement and designed in a monumental Renaissance style with robust detailing, an aesthetic favored by many schools of the period and considered to be a rather "simpli[stic]" design in its day (RI Board of Education, 1899, p. 4). The second floor housed the normal school (RI Board of Education, 1899, p. 4). Notably, this space included the normal school's "commodious and handsome" study hall, "furnished with opera chairs" and laid out in a shot-gun style with a "spacious and attractive" library and a connecting platform. This platform was the central focus of the building's architecture, made clear by its Renaissance ornamentation (RI Board of Education, 1899, p. 6). The normal school's floor also included recitation rooms, English literature rooms, and science rooms in the style of that traditionalist school architecture common to sites that favored the curricula of *The Yale Report*. The third floor housed the museum room (36 by 72 feet in size), chemistry, mathematics, and drawing rooms, as well as space for "the literature societies of the institution" (RI Board of Education, 1899, p. 6). Meanwhile, the first floor accommodated a "model" school of 750 school students disbursed into kindergarten, primary, and grammar groups (RI Board of Education, 1899, p. 4). The entire first floor served the model Kindergarten school and younger students, it's a large and airy 36 feet by 72 feet Kindergarten room well-lighted and equipped to serve up to 48 students (RI Board of Education, 1899, p. 4). Notably, the central portion of the school made room for administration. This administrative section is more detailed than the symmetrical classroom wings on either side, indicating the state's dedication to scientific management's emphasis on managerial structures. More specifically, the central portion accommodates the trustee's rooms and offices on the second floor and the gendered reception rooms on the first floor.

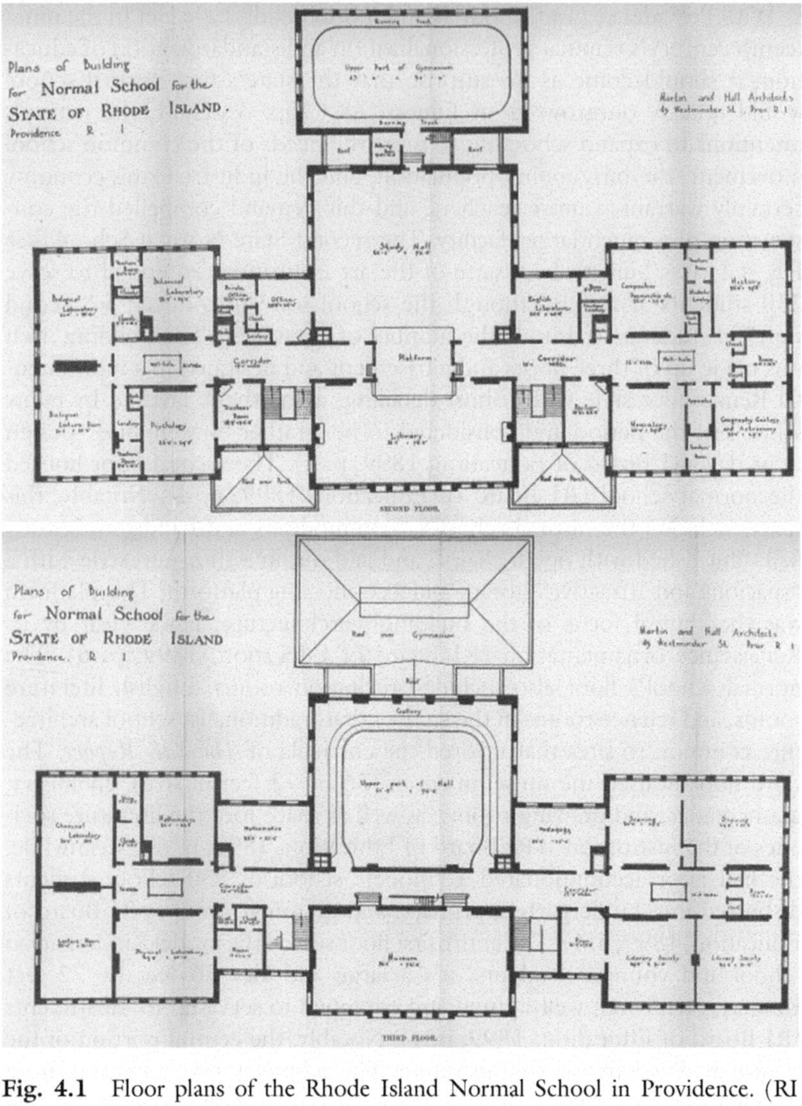

Fig. 4.1 Floor plans of the Rhode Island Normal School in Providence. (RI Board of Education 1899)

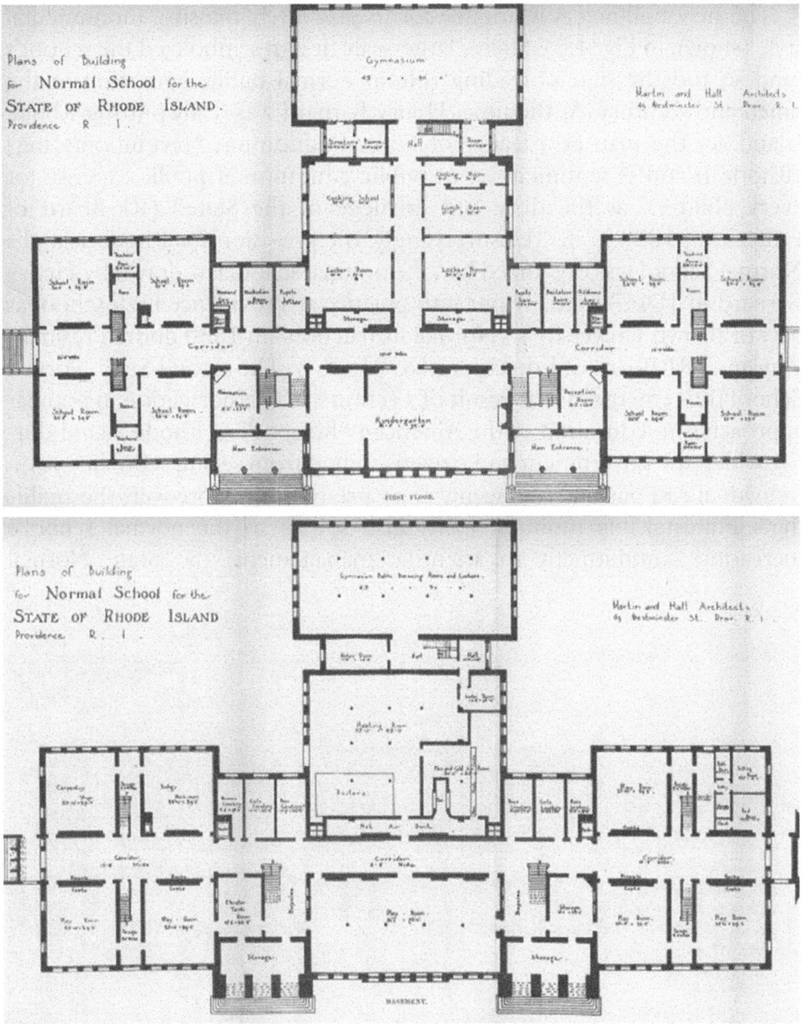

Fig. 4.1 (continued)

The new building was notable for its absolutely massive, monumental style (shown in Fig. 4.2). Such a large-scale design symbolized the school's (and so too the state's) leading role in normal public education in the nineteenth century. At the time, Henry Barnard was really putting Rhode Island on the map as a leader of normal education, "revolutioniz[ing] [Rhode Island's] sentiment … of public education at public expense for every child … as the duty and privilege of the State" (RI Board of Education, 1899, p. 5). Unsurprisingly, the provision for Rhode Island's Normal School was organized by "the original school law drawn by Henry Barnard in 1844" (initially put into practice at Providence high school as part of Brown University's "Normal instruction" in 1850 under President Wayland [RI Board of Education, 1899, p. 6]). The second State Normal School thus emerges as the result of a century of transformation in popular approaches to education in the American "hotspot" of Rhode Island during which the government and citizens shifted from seeing schooling as an individual responsibility to seeing it as a state duty. Moreover, the building's unmistakable monumentality also speaks to the normal school's increasing commitment to scientific management: the State Normal

Fig. 4.2 A rendering of the Rhode Island Normal School in Providence. (RI Board of Education, 1899)

School's increased emphasis on "industrial education" and "manual training" made it the model gateway for the nation's embrace in the next century of scientific management curricula (RI Board of Education, 1899, p. 5). Reflecting this commitment, the normal school's huge, imposing architecture echoed scientific management's celebration of authority—the school was clearly, as Bataille put it, made to be *seen*. Its large scale dwarfing students, the second State Normal School impressed a sense that the school was a supreme power, an institution to revere and obey.

This shift in design from the first more traditionalist, grammar-school style to one that used a big scale to emphasize its commitments to discipline and control was not, as I suggest above, abnormal for the period: by the end of the nineteenth century, monumentality had become a common trend in design. Echoing the formative work of the school at a wider level, monumental buildings were popular in the industrial era for their ability to house large numbers of workers and machines that could produce great amounts of commodities at once. Intentionally or not, such architecture was, like that of the second State Normal School, *imposing*, a style that sent the message that workers were powerless next to and thus subject to the entities that owned such leviathan buildings. At the level of education, this blanketing industrializing trend catalyzed a wide-spread transformation in school architecture (related, to be sure, to contemporary economically-inspired changes in curricula): the capitalistic imperatives of the new industrial economy demanded that education be remodeled to more directly support America's GNP. As I've stated several times, borrowing from the then-popular theories of scientific management that were optimizing factory production, reformers began to design curricula that would similarly prepare students to become efficient and obedient workers—disciples of capital accumulation. Such an ambition called for schooling to teach students to revere capital as a driving objective of their labor, or at the very least, to teach them to respect and obey capital's immediate "lobbyists"—factory managers. Efficient workers, to the proponents of scientific management, were those who would get the job done quickly and properly with little fuss. In Foucauldian (Foucault, 1972) terms, industrialization was thus "phenomena of rupture, of discontinuity" (p. 4), an "incidence of interruption" (p. 4) in the US' classically inspired educational culture—a superstructure to, as I discuss in Chap. 2, the nation's classical base—that had up to this point been hegemonic.

Two other things are important to note about the second normal school's design. First: in step with monumentality's interruptive discourse was the more *vocational and efficient* tone of the new design: corridors had become thinner and more streamlined, encouraging students to move from space to space, from task to task with little distraction. In short, the vocational elements of the school's design supported the industrial function hinted at by its monumentality by normalizing for students a complete concentration of their attention to the task-at-hand, to efficient productivity, that defining norm of scientific management. And second: recalling Loewy's chart, it's also helpful to consider that school architecture came together with the gendered politics within schools to reproduce the patriarchal social norms already characterizing American society: within the normal school and those scientific management school designs that followed, male administrators worked at the heart of the school to direct the movements of female teachers who were placed at its extremities, driving home with this spatial organization the patriarchal sense that men controlled and were at the center of sociality, directing women's movements at its margins. This organization speaks to school design's broader patriarchal history: in the nineteenth century there was no diversity in educational decision-makers: they were traditionally white, middle-class males. Despite the user's central role in schooling, students, teachers, and other staff had no input in policy or architecture (as this chapter makes clear, the schoolhouse instead was formed and operated on norms that silenced user voices). Rather, decisions regarding design were made by an appointed building committee and selected architects, roles that were traditionally available only—again—to white, middle-class males. In turn, school policies were also developed by white middle-class male administrators, boards, and legislators. Manuscripts of the Rhode Island Board of Education's Reports from the 1870s through to the 1920s make clear that the board was not concerned with educating the people of color. Meanwhile, in this period, teaching was approached as a woman's profession, a bias connected to limiting norms of femininity as "naturally" nurturing, which was believed to be good for students. The exclusion of teachers' voices and favoring of administrator's voices in school design was thus a carefully coded formula to exclude *women's* voices from having any formative impact.

In short, the second State Normal School's school design nexus encouraged mostly women teachers in training to obey a patriarchal authority. Upon entering the workforce, "authority" would become the male administrators that were rapidly populating schools (emerging as similar presences to factory managers, with similar objectives to keep a tight ship), as well the standards set by the nation and the states to manage the growth of common schools. By teaching teachers to reiterate—and only reiterate, never criticize or trouble—the directions of these authorities, such a nineteenth century school design worked to ensure the easy management of the school system: intimidating teachers into conformity early on in their education would make it easier to control what was taught across America's vast geographies. Such a standardization of schooling would have a large impact on sociality. The State Normal School's focus on standardizing education and churning out as many accordingly professionalized (read: "normalized", "obedient") teachers as quickly as possible made clear that teaching was now considered a "training", rather than a "scholarly" role—a shift that, as I discuss in more detail in my conclusion, many thinkers have charged as contributing to the anti-intellectual tone of twenty-first century American education.

Meanwhile, the school's pedagogies—developed versions of those delivered at the first normal school—supported the repressive educational tone conveyed by its architecture. As I argue in my discussion of the first State Normal School, at this time, pedagogies for teacher training stood at a strange intersection of traditionalist education and scientific management. On the one hand, the style of teaching teachers was based primarily in the skill-and-drill leanings of *The Yale Report* and the content was primarily centered around those traditionalist subjects the *Report* famously defended. But part of the curriculum was also devoted to establishing and teaching professional norms—to knowledge about the nuances of the act of teaching itself. Such methodological foci were taught by rote and then practiced by teachers-in-training in classrooms. This standardization of teacher training speaks to the assembly-line style of scientific management education: the goal with normal schools was to educate as many teachers as effectively as possible to support the growth of the common school system, a key part of facilitating the rapid expansion of the nation at large. As such, the normal school sought to provide not only a high-level liberal arts education that would ensure teachers had a strong command of the traditionalist knowledge normal schools asked them to impart to their future students, they also supported the production of more teaching professionals, delivering at the same time the kind of vocational education many proponents of scientific management adored. In short: sitting at such a strange intersection of nineteenth century pedagogy, the State Normal School imparted the classical topics of *The Yale Report* using scientific management techniques to facilitate the efficient diffusion of such traditionalist curricula across the growing nation.

With teachers taught as such, it becomes more evident why, as I detail in Chaps. 2 and 3, the typical Rhode Island traditionalist classroom in the nineteenth century so embodies the principles of Freire's banking model of education favored by *The Yale Report*. These models of education support social production because, as Freire argued, they indoctrinate the pupil with whatever knowledge the teacher (as authority) presents as "truth". In other words, banking education manufactures a hegemony in which the teacher takes the position of being the only wise and learned in the room, positioning students as unknowledgeable, as ignorant. The teacher then shares his/her knowledge with the students, who must "bank" this "deposit". The norms of this "truth" become the norms by which the pupil negotiates the world—these norms, in short, constitute the pupil's subjectivity. By reiterating these norms in his/her daily practice within and beyond the schoolhouse, the pupil makes them part of, indeed solidifies them as a common sense, in his/her culture's broader sociality. For example, as I detail above, the knowledge of classical languages and literature that teachers graduating from the normal school would have taught their students covered only the Western epistemological canon. With the banking model of education, the student would have been taught to absorb these epistemologies uncritically and revere them as "truth". Therefore, the limits of the pupil's knowledge are characterized by white, Western norms: as a consequence of *The Yale Report,* these pupils engage their surroundings with the belief that what "is" begins and ends with the West, their imaginaries recognizing any other kinds of knowledge as abject—as not only unqualified, but, worse yet, bad or as not mattering at all. This kind of Western-centric pedagogy stands as a form of social reproduction that thus reinforces Western hegemony by teaching students to not take seriously and to reject any other ways of thinking and, as such, to similarly pathologize those subjects constituted by such abject epistemologies. In other words, the normal school's emphasis on the classical curricula of *The Yale Report*—reinforced and encouraged by architecture that supported the rote learning historically wedded to such traditionalist subject matter—taught students to affirm a hierarchical dichotomy between the "West" and "everyone else" (e.g. including but not limited to the "East") and to then indoctrinate their *own* students with this bias as well. To be sure, such stratification has long characterized American society. Many scholars (most famously Edward Said) have argued the US has historically secured itself as a world power by encouraging its own citizens and those communities it colonizes to understand themselves within such a racist hierarchical dichotomy; to understand the "West" as the wise bringer of civilization and Othered communities as backward, uneducated, and savage. This constructed imbalance would legitimate American imperialism for centuries. By teaching only Western epistemologies with the rote pedagogies that discourage the kind critical thought that inspires subjects to think beyond the given, the traditionalist norms of this normal schooling thus reproduced the ideological conditions upon which the US' white hegemony—already burgeoning by the 1800s—relied. The strong presence of such stratifications today—evident, for example, in the lack of public resistance to manifestations of the West/Other "civilizing" norm (e.g. the 2017 Presidential Muslim ban; the never-ending war on terror)—underscore the cultural power of such biased foundations of American school design.

While many Rhode Island schools thus not unsurprisingly demonstrate traditionalist classrooms, some also show an affinity for the norms of scientific management with new forms of architecture that made room for the administrators that would take on part of the authoritative role previously played by the master teacher (something the second normal school naturalized for new teachers with its central administrative hub). This shift was largely supported by the creation of normal schools. With the creation of the teacher training schools that power dynamic began to change. The move from teacher to master teacher, headmaster, and then administrator significantly impacted the teacher workplace first and the student experience second. With the introduction of the administrator, the workplace dynamics of the teacher shifted to staff and supervisor, a reflection of the scientific management and social efficiency ideologies. This teacher workplace transition gave birth to the growth in teacher organizations and unions. These power struggles were at the heart of the various curriculum ideological committees and reports previously discussed. In breaking down this workplace relationship to a simple power dynamic between the administration and the teacher, it becomes very similar to any other workplace relationship between the management and staff. These transformations effectively streamlined—and so quickened—the process of "banking" education. As such, this shift would only further empower the work teachers, reared with the traditionalist pedagogies normal schools so emphasized, as missionaries of a ruling-class Western hegemony.

In tracing such dialectics between the pedagogies deriving from *The Yale Report* and scientific management, it's also important to consider the ways in which such oscillations more broadly relate to those historic power variations that, as I discuss above, Foucault (1976) outlines in *Discipline and Punish*. Here I'm thinking more specifically about Foucault's sketches of the shift from absolute strategies of punishment, such as public displays of torture produced by the governing body, to more non-absolute and more scientific-based solutions, such as those approaches of imprisonment popular at the turn of the nineteenth century. For Foucault, the latter shift to disciplining and controlling the soul by writing particular ways of thinking and being as "deviant" was more oppressive that simply punishing the body. This claim crucially deepens our existing insights about the reproductive work of nineteenth century school design: Foucault's historical framework illuminates the ways in which *The Yale Report*'s pedagogies similarly work to discipline and control pupils: the traditionalist norms discussed above make "deviant" non-Western epistemologies, with the teacher's authority giving her a role of "control" that encourages students to discipline and monitor themselves and others for such allegedly pathological ways of thinking. The monumentality of the school design reinforces this sense for the students that they are subject to the power of the teacher, the school, and the knowledge that these authorities distribute.

Together with the pioneering social efficiency training schools case studies discussed in Chap. 3, in Newport (Townsend Industrial School, circa 1894, see Figs. 3.5, 3.6, and 3.7) and Providence (Providence Training School circa 1894, see Figs. 3.20 and 3.21), the second State Normal School in Providence produced and reproduced the scientific management curriculum. It's inclusion of spaces for vocational education (e.g. carpentry, cooking school) asserted Rhode Island position as an epicenter of scientific management in the US in the nineteenth century.

This analysis of nineteenth century school design as a form of social (re)production suggests that this generation of American schools normalized patriarchal power relations while fostering an obedient, uncritical student steeped in the ideologies of ruling-class Western hegemony. Schooling thus functioned as an institution that supported the nation's dominant ideology, with all its knowledge forms and skills, and, in doing so, deepened extant racial and economic stratifications and state social controls. From this vantage point, school design provides a window into reproduction theory at work and the impact for non-white students of civil society who were excluded from opportunities for social mobility. In doing so, it reveals the soul of nineteenth century popular culture, making evident its exclusive homogeneous aspirations and values despite its democratic professions.

Looking back on what it meant to dwell in nineteenth century schools by taking "[a]rchitecture, combining as it does technology, economics, and aesthetics, [as] a peculiarly sensitive reflector of the ideas-complex" (Gifford, 1966, p. 15), helps us to better understand the nature of today's troubled schools and the marginalizing civil society they support. Before moving on, we might pause to recall how this analysis speaks to a broader theoretical framework that might be applied to the late modern classroom to better understand contemporary school design's general role in social reproduction. More specifically, this example makes clear that it's important to approach the classroom as a domain ruled by a teacher who normalizes a particular discursive practice that is encouraged (and sometimes, though not in this example, complicated) by the architectural design. Just as the mill town communities, which sprawled out along the Blackstone River Valley in northern Rhode Island during the late nineteenth century (now a national park), provided housing for workers based on their lot, and so schoolhouses were so shaped and select curriculum so delivered according to the student's lot. This transformation was taking place in the later part of the nineteenth century, as society embraced a culture of discipline and control. In this context, the architecture and the prevailing curriculum pressed the teacher to normalize a patriarchal Western hegemony. These ideologies shape the mental spatiality of the student and in turn formulate his or her identity, which informs the students' place in society. As this chapter makes clear, class, race, and gender stand as meaningful lenses with which to criticize the formative work of curricula and architecture. Accordingly, in critically taking up curricula and school architecture, it is important to think about how these sites intersect with matters of race, class, and gender especially because (even today) schools and pedagogies are most often, as I've already articulated, designed by teams of white males. Accordingly, the normative "student" is constructed from the get-go out of a politics of structural inequity that empower discriminations based race, class, and gender. And yet these divisions were, especially after scientific management became popular, falsely framed as the consequence of individual strengths and weaknesses, the resultant hierarchy thus approached not as a reiteration of the nation's already-extant white hegemony, but a "meritocracy". In this multiplicity of subjection, students are variously empowered, indentured, assimilated, and transformed by prevailing classroom rituals that regulate contradictory duties. As normalizing, this social reproduction—produced by the social will formation that is the school stakeholders, reproduced by the teacher—necessarily produces "Others". To be sure, a nation that prides itself on ideas of freedom and equality cannot continue to produce and (re)produce the repressive stratification of the "Other".

Othering

Briefly: the "Other" can be defined as an abject, an individual framed as non-normative by particular arrangement of power, by particular biased, naturalized conceptions of what it means to embody the "right" kind of class, race, gender, et cetera. The Other is thus contextualized within a framework largely defined by "models of assimilation and association, civilization and culture or state and subject" (Anderson, Jenson, & Keller, 2011, p. 2). Deepening this sense of the Other, Bell Hooks (2000) offers an explanation of how one of these biases works by detailing the way in which class plays a meaningful role in such exclusionary politics. She writes: "[c]lass involves your behavior, your basic assumptions, how you are taught to behave, what you expect from yourself and from others, your concept of a future, how you understand problems and solve them, how you feel, think, act" (p. 103). All these telling ideologies are nurtured within the walls of the schoolhouse by the mutually formative impact of architecture and the prevailing curriculum.

In reflecting on Heidegger's notion of dwelling, we might recall that Others are so marginalized in part because they are those who have been historically excluded (already "Othered") from decision-making processes about curricula and the built environment. Dominated by white men, architecture and curriculum theory situate the Other within schooling environments that limit, rather than fuel, the Other's autonomy by writing off the Other's ways of thinking and being, by delegitimizing the Other's voice, norms that limit the Other's agency. Recalling the discussions of earlier chapters, nineteenth century curricula and design nexuses primarily silence *non*-white, "*un*"reasonable, and "*un*"American epistemologies and ontologies—"reason" and "Americanity" historically written onto only white patriarchal subjects. More specifically, nineteenth American culture and curricula wrote women, immigrants, and people of color as *un*reasonable (popularly writing women as "hysterical" and immigrants and people of color as "savage") and accordingly capable of nurturing the nation *only* by supporting the aspirations of assertedly reasonable local white men; abandoning their other senses of self for traditionalist Eurocentric and patriarchal norms. In other words, the schoolhouse, as an icon of cultural artifacts formed by human intention, becomes a political site that in the nineteenth century restricted student identities to support a white, ruling and upper-middle class, Western capitalistic at the expense of the agency and dignity of any one who didn't fit into this mold.

Resistance

While the school can act to reproduce and so bolster a culture's extant configuration by interpellating students into its norms, in *Theory and Resistance in Education,* Giroux (2001) argues that schools are never simply sites of repression, but also always sites of contestation. Public education has the capacity, if not always the will, he reminds us, to become more pluralistic and possibilistic. While the nineteenth century ideo-spatial nexus of school design popularly assimilated students into the nation's white elite hegemony, schooling in this period nevertheless had the capacity to counter such a trend, to emancipate students and foster in them something other than the terrible inequities of class, race, and gender to which it most popularly gave rise. In this vein, many counter-cultural education reformers have worked over the centuries to expose and trouble such formative processes, to give voice to what nineteenth century American education determinedly made "Other". This next section unpacks the most significant of these contributions.

For our purposes, the first of these radical curricula emerged as a direct response to those pedagogues Schubert (1986) calls the *conciliators*, namely: those reformers who embraced Tyler's *Basic Principles of Curriculum and Instruction* and Bobbitt's *Curriculum.* Critically connecting curricula with social, economic, and political ideological paradigms, is Watkins (1993), who shines a light on the segregative racial dynamics of American curricula. More specifically, Watkins (1993) highlights the marginalization of blacks in American schooling and proposes a way to make the US curriculum more responsive to the African American educational experience, a movement he calls "the black curriculum orientation". Importantly, Watkins (1993) recognizes that curriculum has

> evolved under socially oppressive and politically repressive circumstances involving physical and intellectual duress and tyranny. Black America's socio-educational development is thus distorted, unnatural, and stunned. The black response to servitude and exclusion has run the gamut from capitulation to accommodation to outright defiance. (p. 322)

These social and political historical realities emerging from "the dynamics of colonialism, American apartheid, and discriminatory exclusion" have marginalized black epistemologies and ontologies in education (Watkins, 1993, p. 322). For example, recent findings about the involvement of established institutions in the nineteenth century in slavery (such as documented in the Report of the Brown University Steering Committee on Slavery and Justice [2007]) speak volumes to an institutional legacy of racism. Further, the triangulation of Atlantic commercial trade routes, which included the trade of African slaves, makes clear that Rhode Island and America more broadly played a heavy role in the violent oppression of black people to shore up white wealth and power. Family accounts of the wealthy and influential Colt dynasty (Colt Memorial School endowment) of Bristol, RI, offer more tangible examples of these kinds of oppressions, even after the Civil War (Tracey Center, 2018). In theorizing an anti-racist intervention in such educational politics, Watkins highlights Emoungu's (1979) dialectic lens, which crucially illuminates the two suppositions upon which racist approaches to education are founded: those norms embodied by the "educational adaptation model and … [the] cultural-educational deprivation model" (Watkins, 1993, p. 322). More specifically, the education adaptation model signals those pedagogies based on the violent and normalized notion that racial differences are natural and that therefore each race needs a differentiated curriculum, which in the nineteenth century emerged as "literary education for Whites and utilitarian education for Blacks". Meanwhile, the latter model relies on the "culture of poverty" assumption which locates black people as culturally deficient (Watkins, 1993, p. 322). In response to such racist educational norms, Watkins (1993) articulates six curriculum orientations (that somewhat overlap with those proposed by Kliebard, Pinar, and Schubert) that intervened in these racial politics cemented by nineteenth century schooling: "functionalist, accommodationist, liberal, reconstructionist, Afrocentrist, and Black Nationalist" (p. 322).

First, the *functionalist* curriculum was generally practical, concerned primarily with preparing students for those duties it considered central to "real" life, which was aligned with the scientific management curriculum. Pedagogically, this curriculum advocated for "learning … through imitation, recitation, memorization, and demonstration" (Watkins, 1993, p. 324). Meanwhile, the *accommodationist* curriculum,

> often called the 'Hampton-Tuskegee' model of education[,] ... emphasized vocational training, physical/manual labor, character building and a social science packaging, suggesting the acceptance of racial subservice for Negros[. This approach] was promoted by northern corporatists (King, 1996) and popularized by Washington [, thinkers who] ... were linked ideologically to colonialism, segregation and subservience. (Watkins, 1993, pp. 324–327)

Liberal education orientations were optimistic. Borrowing from humanist traditions, liberal pedagogues figured education as a prerequisite to a harmonious democratic society and supported the creation of black colleges (Watkins, 1993). Accordingly, the liberal curricular orientations did not accept race as an impediment to black educational achievement. Rather, it charged slavery as creating structural inequalities that seemed like natural facts and asserted in contest that blacks and whites possessed the same capacities for teaching and learning (Watkins, 1993). In this way, black liberal education emerged in step with the liberal progressive pedagogies for which Dewey advocates in *Democracy and Education* and *Experience and Education*.

On another note, *Black nationalists* called for more resistant pedagogies that denaturalized America's white hegemony by exposing "international slavery, colonization, the debasement of Africa, and the mistreatment of African People scattered throughout the world" (Watkins, 1993, p. 329). Black nationalists asserted that culture was a binding force, shunned assimilationism (calling instead for a parallel black society), and "argue[d] for an educational system around which Black people [could] unite in the present day" (Watkins, 1993, p. 330). The coursework revolved around black Studies, a discipline that took up black politics, economics, aesthetics, experience, art, poetry, literature, and history (Watkins, 1993). This black nationalist and separatist orientation was the seed for the contemporary Afrocentrist viewpoint that advocated for the recalling and the rebirth of the African people and continent (Watkins, 1993). This viewpoint rejects those Western ideologies and linear modes of inquiry rooted in positivist and empiricist scientific notions and instead embraces more circular African epistemologies (Watkins, 1993). It also repudiates representations of blacks in public schooling in the US more broadly as submissive and as making up an "underclass" and instead advocates for an Afrocentric curriculum that covers a temporal period beginning with ancient Egypt and only ending with the present

(Watkins, 1993). Provocative as the Afrocentric orientation may be, it left unchallenged the socio-economic infrastructure of oppression. Taking up this absence is the last black curriculum orientation, social reconstructionism (Watkins, 1993). This radical group—its popular theorists including Counts, Hook, and Rugg—filled in this gap by questioning the capitalist order (Watkins, 1993). The *reconstructionists* approached social progress as predicated on redressing unjust social, political, and economic modes of production. Such calls for democratic socialist reforms connected the reconstructions with the progressive education movement. Moreover, their views greatly spoke to those of DuBois, a key figure in anti-racist education in the era. DuBois famously advocated "a curriculum that would criticize capitalism, promote democracy, propagate common schooling, foster emancipatory thinking, support societal transformation, and seek a higher civilization"—all of these things were "part of the Reconstructionist education program" (Watkins, 1993, p. 334). DuBois' (1932) educational philosophy takes up issues around the relevance of curricula and the political consequences of its treatment of general knowledge, experience, and technical training. Douglas, Truth, and Washington are thinkers who also made important pioneering contributions to this discourse, but whose work often goes unrecognized. In particular, Washington's contributions to curricula have been inexcusably neglected given that he established an entire school (the Tuskegee National Industrial Institute) driven by the "project method" well before Kilpatrick's article, and the "laboratory" idea six years before Dewey's 1910 work, *How We Think*. In fact, student projects at Tuskegee included constructing the school's buildings. Further, the innovative and pioneering ideas of Douglas, Du Bois, Truth, and Washington would come to reinforce the influence of the autobiographical approach later expanded by Pinar. The black curricula orientations Watkins articulates have appeared and continue to progress both apart from and as part of greater curricula movements. He also, crucially, makes clear that any anti-racist education must consider not just the obvious workings of the curriculum, but also the workings of the "hidden" curriculum (a by-product of the intended curriculum and reflective of norms, values, and beliefs transmitted in the classroom and other socially constructed discourses according to Philip Jackson [1968a, 1968b]) and its relation to race and ethnicity (Watkins, 1993). While Watkins' discussion offers a primer in anti-racist education, Pinar offers a deeper sense of how schooling might be accordingly redressed.

More specifically, Pinar (2006) provides a theoretical framework that highlights those formative aspects of curricula we must be attentive to in order to intervene in its politics. Namely, Pinar delineates curriculum studies as engrained within dominant and subordinate epistemologies that frame ideological modes of inquiry (Pinar, 2006). For Pinar, "the curriculum theory field has forgotten what existence is" and "will remain morbid until it remembers"—meaning, until it plants the seed for alternatives ways to conceptualize curricula (Pinar, 1975, p. 396). However, much the scholarship that "derives from the work of Tyler, Kliebard, Huebner, and Macdonald, as well as others, has explained why Tyler's [scientific management] rationale and, hence, that tradition are not viable" (Pinar, 1975, p. 397). Influenced by the oppressive landscape and the banking model painted by Freire (1970), in *Curriculum Theorizing: The Reconceptualists* (1975), Pinar highlights that "a third group's work can be characterized as revisionist or reconceptualist in function" (p. 397). This group, which is mostly uncoordinated and emphasizes Marxists social theory elements such as ideology, class, and hegemony, is described by Pinar et al. (1995) as follows and is worthy of quote at length:

> Macdonald, Huebner, Kliebard, Eisner, Greene, Berman, and Klohr opposed behaviorism, scientism (a reduction of forms of knowing to quantifiable ones), dehumanizing technology, and an oppressive, alienating bureaucratization of the schools. These curricularists first attached behavioral objectives, then bureaucratization, the disciplines-centered orientation, and quantified, standardized evaluation and measurement of learning (Huebner, 1964). This challenge – largely uncoordinated – represented the first stage of the Reconceptualization, as the traditional field, for a few, became static and limiting. (p. 184)

Pioneered by Pinar, Macdonald, Apple, Giroux, Mann, Huebner, Greene, Phenix, and Willis, reconceptualist education focused on autobiographical, psychoanalytical, and de-constructional approaches responsive to the lived experiences of everyday educators and students and attuned to how these experiences were shaped by historical, political, cultural, social, racial, and gendered power dynamics (Pinar et al., 1995). These perspectives departed from the dominant and largely bureaucratic traditionalist and scientific management curricular orientations field that fixated on repetition, standards, efficiency, stratification, and procedures. Instead, reconceptualists were devoted to deconstructing the norms of curriculum and reimagining pedagogy in ways that made it more truly democratic (Pinar et al., 1995). In this new schema, curricula needed to emerge from and be responsive to a multiplicity of viewpoints within the educational experience. Following Pinar's notion of "currere" (Pinar, 1975, p. 400), reconceptualists approached and evaluated curricula for their historical, political, racial, gendered, phenomenological, autobiographical, aesthetic, theological, and international facets (Pinar et al., 1995). Following this radical roadmap Pinar provides, DuBois, Hooks, Truth, and Watkins advocate for new kinds of education that enable every youth to realize his or her full potential and that encourage more peaceful and just modes of co-existence. They emphasize, in taking on this project, educators must also embrace the responsibility of being attentive to and intervening in the damaging politics of oppression that characterize the American landscape, that stratify our society. In addition, Jane Addams (Hull House founder), Ida Wells (anti-lynching activist), and Sojourner Truth (anti-slavery) exemplify Feminists responses to patriarchal and ruling-class norms of nineteenth century through class-based resistant pedagogies employing sympathetic understanding and dignity (Addams, 1907, 1909). Though radical scholars and pedagogues have valiantly taken on this responsibility over the years, the biases of nineteenth century school design continue to shape the educational landscape in the twenty-first century (Ross, 1997). The white, Western, patriarchal, and ruling-class norms of the era's education were so central to the emergence of America's common school system and normal schools that these marginalizing ideologies deeply defined the very foundations of modern schooling in the US. With education, as this chapter makes clear, a key site of social reproduction, these school designs bolstered the hegemony of white elites in America. Recalling the violence inherent to such a power imbalance, it is imperative to take seriously the calls made by the above radical theorists to orient schooling so that it nurtures the well-being of *all* publics. Inspired by this responsibility, the next chapter surveys the late modern legacies of nineteenth century school design and considers what changes might be made to current curricula and school architecture to transform education so that it fosters the kind of equity upon which democracy relies.

References

Addams, J. (1907). *Democracy and Social Ethics*. New York: Macmillan.
Addams, J. (1909). *Youth in the City*. New York: Macmillan Co.
Adler, M. J. (1981). *Six Great Ideas*. New York: Macmillan.

Aloni, N. (1999). Humanistic Education. In M. Peters, P. Ghiraldelli, B. Žarnić, & A. Gibbons (Eds.), *The Encyclopaedia of Educational Philosophy and Theory*. Retrieved from http://eepat.net/doku.php?id=humanistic_education. 19 Nov 2013.

Althusser, L. (1970). Ideology and Ideological State Apparatuses. In B. Brewster (Trans.), *Lenin and Philosophy and Other Essays* (pp. 121–176). New York: Monthly Review Press.

Althusser, L. (1971). *Lenin and Philosophy and Other Essays*. New York: Monthly Review Press.

Anderson, W., Jenson, D., & Keller, R. (2011). *Unconscious Dominions: Psychoanalysis, Colonial Trauma, and Global Sovereignties*. Durham, NC: Duke University Press.

Apple, M. (1979). *Ideology and Curriculum*. London: Routledge & Kegan Paul.

Apple, M. (2004). *Ideology and Curriculum*. London: Routledge Palmer.

Bataille, G. (1971). Architecture. In *Oeuvres Competes*, 12 Vols. Paris: Gallimard

Bataille, G. (1991). *The Accursed Share, Volume 1: Consumption* (R. Hurley, Trans.). New York: Zone Books.

Bauman, Z. (1992). Survival as a Social Construct. *Theory, Culture & Society, 9*, 1–36.

Beyer, L. E., & Liston, D. P. (1996). *Curriculum in Conflict*. New York: Teachers College Press.

Biesta, G. J. J. (2006). *Beyond Learning: Democratic Education for the Human Future*. Boulder, CO: Paradigm Publishers.

Blumin, S. M. (1989). *The Emergence of the Middle Class: Social Experience in American City, 1760–1900*. Cambridge, UK: Cambridge University Press.

Bobbitt, J. F. (1918). *The Curriculum*. Boston: Houghton Mifflin.

Bourdieu, P., & Passeron, J. (1977a). *Reproduction in Education, Society and Culture*. London: Sage Publications.

Bourdieu, J., & Passeron, J. C. (1977b). In J. Karabel & A. H. Halsey (Eds.), *Reproduction in Education: Power and Ideology in Education*. New York: Oxford University Press.

Bowles, S., & Ginitis, H. (1976). *Schooling in Capitalist America: Educational Reform and the Contradictions of Economic Life*. New York: Basic Books.

Bowles, S., & Ginitis, H. (1977). The Marxian Theory of Value and Heterogeneous Labour: A Critique and Reformation. *Cambridge Journal of Economics: JSTOR, 1*(2), 173–192.

Brown University Steering Committee on Slavery and Justice. (2007). *Slavery and Justice: The Report of the Brown University Steering Committee on Slavery and Justice*. Downloaded at https://www.brown.edu/Research/Slavery_Justice/documents/SlaveryAndJustice.pdf. 1/7/2018.

Burchard, J., & Bush-Brown, A. (1966). *The Architecture of America, a Social and Cultural History*. Boston: Little, Brown and Co.

Butler, J. (1993). Critically Queer. *GLQ: A Journal of Lesbian and Gay Studies*, 1, 1738, Academia.edu.
Ching, F. D. K. (2007). *Architecture: Form, Space, and Order*. New York: John Wiley & Sons.
Cremin, L. A. (1970). *American Education: The Colonial Experience, 1607–1783*. New York: Harper & Row.
Dewey, J. (1900). *The School and Society*. Chicago: University of Chicago Press.
Dewey, J. (1916). *Democracy and Education*. New York: Macmillan.
Dewey, J. (1938). *Experience and Education*. New York: Macmillan.
DuBois, W. E. B. (1932). Education and Work. *The Journal of Negro Education, 1*(1), 60–74.
Emoungu, P. A. (1979). Socioeducational Ideologies of Black Education. *The Journal of Negro Education, 48*(1), 43–56.
Foucault, M. (1971). *Orders of Discourse* (Vol. 10). New York: Sage.
Foucault, M. (1972). *The Archaeology of Knowledge and the Discourse on Language*. New York: Pantheon Books.
Foucault, M. (1973). *Birth of Clinic: An Archaeology of Medical Perception*. New York: Pantheon Books.
Foucault, M. (1976). *The History of Sexuality Volume 1: An Introduction*. London: Allen Lane.
Foucault, M. (1977). *Discipline and Punishment: Birth of the Prison* (A. Sheridan, Trans.). London: Allen Lane.
Franklin, B. (1794). *Proposals Relating to the Education of Youth in Pennsylvania*. Philadelphia, PA: Franklin.
Freire, P. (1970). *Pedagogy of the Oppressed*. New York: The Continuum Publishing Corporation.
Gifford, D. (1966). *The Literature of Architecture: The Evolution of Architectural Theory and Practice in Nineteenth-Century America*. New York: E.P. Dutton & Co., Inc..
Giroux, H. A. (1984). *Ideology, Culture, and the Process of Schooling*. Philadelphia: Temple University Press.
Giroux, H. A. (2001). *Theory and Resistance in Education: Towards Pedagogy for the Opposition*. Westport,CT: Bergin & Garvey.
Giroux, H. A. (2012). *Education and the Struggle for Public Values*. Boulder, CO: Paradigm.
Giroux, H. A., Penna, A. N., & Pinar, W. (1981). *Curriculum & Instruction*. Berkeley, CA: McCutchan Publishing Corp.
Gramsci, A. (1971). *Selections from Prison Notebooks* (Quinten Hoare and Geoffrey Smith, Ed. and Trans.). New York: International Publishers.
Habermas, J. (1962). *The Structural Formation of the Public Sphere: An Inquiry into a Category of Bourgeois Society* (Thomas Burger, Trans. 1991). Cambridge, MA: MIT Press.

Hauser, G. A. (1999). *Vernacular Voices: The Rhetoric of Publics and the Public Sphere*. Columbia, SC: University of South Carolina Press.
Hearn, F. (2003). *Ideas that Shaped Buildings*. Cambridge, MA: The MIT Press.
Heidegger, M. (1949). *Existence and Being*. Chicago: Henry Regnery.
Heidegger, M. (1996). *Being and Time*. New York: State of New York Press.
Hennon, L. (1999). *School Architecture, Curriculum and Pedagogy*. Washington, DC: ERIC.
Hollier, D. (1992). *Against Architecture: The Writings of Georges Bataille*. Cambridge, MA: The MIT Press.
Hooks, B. (2000). *Where We Stand: Class Matters*. New York: Routledge.
Huebner, D. (1964). *A Reassessment of the Curricular*. New York: Bureau of Publication, Teachers College, Columbia University.
Jackson, P. W. (1968a). *Life in Classrooms*. New York: Holt, Rinehart and Winston.
Jackson, P. W. (1968b). *Life in Classrooms*. New York: Teacher's College Press.
Jackson, P. W. (1992). Conceptions of Curriculum and Curriculum Specialists. In P. W. Jackson (Ed.), *Handbook of Research on Curriculum* (pp. 3–40). New York: Macmillan.
King, R. (1996). *Emancipating Space: Geography, Architecture and Urban Design*. New York: The Guilford Press.
Kliebard, H. (1986). *The Struggle for the American Curriculum: 1893–1958*. New York: Routledge.
Kruft, H. W. (1994). *A History of Architectural Theory From Vitruvius to Present*. New York: Princeton Architectural Press.
Laclau, E., & Mouffe, C. (1985). *Hegemony and Socialist Strategy: Towards a Radical Democratic Politics*. London: Verso.
Levinas, E., & Nemo, P. (1985). *Ethics and Infinity*. Pittsburgh, PA: Duquesne University Press.
Loewy, R. (1979). *Evolutionary Chart of Design 1930*. Woodstock, NY: Overlook Press.
McCormick, V. (2001). *Educational Architecture in Ohio*. Kent, OH: Kent State University Press.
Morrison, S. E. (1936). *The Founding of Harvard College*. Cambridge, MA: Harvard University Press.
National Education Association. (1893). *Report of the Committee of Ten Secondary Schools*. Washington, DC: Government Printing Office.
National Education Association. (1895). *Report of the Committee of Fifteen on Elementary Education*. New York: American Book Company.
Norberg-Schultz, C. (1965). *Intentions in Architecture*. Cambridge, MA: MIT Press.
Paraskeva, J. (2011). *Conflicts in Curriculum Theory*. New York: Palgrave.
Pinar, W. (1975). *Curriculum Theorizing*. Berkley, CA: McCutchan Publishing Corporations.

Pinar, W. (2006). *Race, Religion, and a Curriculum of Preparation*. New York: Palgrave Macmillan.

Pinar, W., Slattery, P., & Taubman, P. (1995). *Understanding Curriculum*. New York: Peter Lang.

Reese, W. J. (2001). *America's Public Schools: From the Common School to "No Child Left Behind"*. Baltimore: The John Hopkins University Press.

Ross, A. S. (1997). Jane Addams, "Utilization of Women in City Government". In Alice S. Rossi (Ed.), *The Feminist Papers: From Adams to de Beauvoir* (pp. 604–612). Boston: Northeastern University Press.

Schubert, W. H. (1984). *Curriculum Books*. Lanham, MD: University Press of America.

Schubert, W. H. (1986). *Curriculum: Perspective, Paradigm and Possibility*. New York: Macmillan.

Schubert, W. H., & Lopez Schubert, A. L. (1980). *Curriculum Books*. Lanham, MD: University Press of America.

Tanner, D., & Tanner, L. N. (1980). *Curriculum Development*. New York: Macmillan.

Taylor, F. (1903). Shop Management. *Transactions of the American Society of Mechanical Engineers, 24*, 1337–1480.

Taylor, F. (1911). *The Principles of Scientific Management*. New York: Harper.

Tracing Center: James DeWolf and the DeWolf Family. Downloaded at http://www.tracingcenter.org/resources/background/james-dewolf/. 1/7/2018.

Tyler, R. W. (1949). *Basic Principles of Curriculum and Instruction*. Chicago: University of Chicago Press.

Vitruvius, P. M. (30 B.C.E.). *De architectura*. Roma. (M.H. Morgan, Trans.). Cambridge, MA, 1914; Reprinted, New York, 1960.

Ward, L. F. (1883). *Dynamic Sociology* (Vol. 1–2). New York: D. Appleton and Company.

Watkins, W. (1993). *Black Curriculum Orientations*. Cambridge, MA: Harvard Educational Review.

Watkins, W. (2001). *The White Architects of Black Education*. New York: Teachers College Press.

Willis, P. (1977). *Learning to Labor*. Lexington, MA: D.C. Heath.

Willis, G., Schubert, W. H., Bullough, R. V., Jr., Kridel, C., & Holton, J. T. (Eds.). (1993). *The American Curriculum*. Westport, CT: Greenwood Press.

Yale College Faculty. (1828). *Original Papers in Relation to a Course of Liberal Education*. New Haven, CT: Yale University.

CHAPTER 5

Conclusion

Contrary to what its marginalizing work suggests, America has historically approached schooling as a means for building a better society. From the centuries-old common schools movement to our modern push for science, technology, engineering, and mathematics (STEM), US education has most often developed as a constructive response to the day's demands—the politics of the period, of course, always determining what constitutes such a "constructive response". In other words, the hopes America has pinned on its education system over the centuries have always been answerable to the nation's contemporary values. To be sure, such values are always complicated, shaped as they are by a myriad of formative forces—from economic drivers (e.g. the demands of emerging industries to, more recently, calls to close gaps in wealth), to more philosophical norms (e.g. morals, customs, lifestyles, identities, and forms of expression, often answerable to Independence and the American Dream), to the whims of the governmental institutions that administrate and legislate the limits of schooling. In short, as Tyack and Cuban (1995) put it in *Tinkering Towards Utopia*, the field of US education has long been concerned with "devising educational prescriptions for specific social or economic ills".[1] And yet, despite such seemingly good intentions, the nineteenth and early

[1] David Tyack and Larry Cuban, *Tinkering Toward Utopia* (Cambridge: Harvard University Press, 1997), 2.

© The Author(s) 2018

J. da Silva, *School(house) Design and Curriculum in Nineteenth Century America*, https://doi.org/10.1007/978-3-319-78586-8_5

twentieth century reforms inspired by *The Yale Report* and the imperatives of scientific management oriented education gave rise to a deeply exclusive politics: as I hope my earlier chapters have made clear, the norms of American school design developed and stabilized in the 1800s in ways that anticipated and interpellated students as Eurocentric, rational, liberatory, specialized, productive, socially stratified, and obedient subjects. To offer a quick review of the development of this school design nexus, Table 5.1 charts this history.

More specifically, the table's rows divide this history into four key periods between 1760 and 1920, each defined by significant changes in culture, architecture, curricula, and administrative structure. The first three periods (1760–1900) are deeply marked by *The Yale Report*'s paradigmatic influence: the first cultural period, "the age of Revolution", was largely defined by the optimism surrounding the birth of America as an independent nation. The years surrounding American independence were saturated with—an at least asserted—dedication to building the new nation upon the Greek's gilded democratic principles. During this period, America's affinity for such classical norms thus reached across architecture and curriculum. To demonstrate its commitment to classical principles, the government began to design many new civic structures in the Greek revivalist style—in the period to follow, educational buildings would come to similarly take on Greek revivalist style to echo these same commitments. The defining curricular document of the nineteenth century, *The Yale Report* (produced by the Faculty of Yale College in 1828) affirmed and detailed the nation's early love of classical education—what would come to be known in the history of American school design after the *Report* as "traditionalist" curriculum. This traditionalist curriculum called for a general liberal education, or, as the *Report* put it, one that was "broad, deep, and solid". More specifically, the *Report* suggested that such an education should teach the sciences, classical languages, and the arts. Holding steadfast to the contemporary claim that the mind was a muscle, the *Report* argued that rote pedagogy was the best way to deliver such an education. In the years that followed, these traditionalist pedagogical goals became the primary approach to schooling in the US. School architecture quickly developed to facilitate the *Report*'s pedagogy. The nineteenth century saw many schools built with lecture halls, recitation rooms, debate rooms, and small laboratories that would facilitate such pedagogies. Prioritizing such a classical education—one that championed the often racially predicated (or, at least, racially mobilized) Western norms of Enlightenment reasoning

Table 5.1 An overview of the history of US culture, architecture, and curricula from 1760 to 1950

US cultural, architectural & curriculum history								
Culture		*Architecture*		*Curriculum*				
Period	*Cultural period*	*Architecture (Gifford)*	*Architect (Gifford)*	*Curriculum documents (Willis)*	*Curriculum author (Willis)*	*Date (Willis)*	*Curriculum ideology (Kliebard)*	*Administrative structure (Tyack)*
1760–1830	The Age of Revolution	Greek Revivals	T. Jefferson	Yale Report	Faculty of Yale College	1828	Humanists	School-based
1830–1865	Expansion and Realignment	Gothic Revivals	H.H. Richardson	Common Schools	Henry Barnard	1839		Decentralization
				Selection Among Studies	Horace Mann	1842		
1865–1900	Industry & Turmoil	Functional	L Sullivan	Committee 10 & 15	National Education Association	1893		
1900–1920	Modernity, Diversity	Organic	F.L. Wright	Child & the Curriculum	John Dewey	1902	Child Study	Centralization
				Cardinal Principles	National Education Association	1918	Social Efficiency	Admin. Progressives
				Scientific Method	Franklin Bobbitt	1918	Social Meliorists	Science/Experts
1920–1950	Between World Wars	Functional Beauty	W. Gropius	Experience & Education	John Dewey	1938		
				8-Year Study	Wilford M. Aikin	1942		

(norms thought to be central to liberal governance)—American schooling began to anticipate a student that was white, rational, and liberatory.

But it was really in the second significant period, "expansion and realignment" (1830 to 1865) that Enlightenment sensibilities—by then well developed in Europe—took root in the American psyche. At the same time, education became a more formal discourse and the common schools movement emerged in earnest, making the period a foundational one for American schooling. This period was also defined by a Gothic Revival architectural style (notably of the architect Richardson) that incorporated the transcendentalists' organic sensibilities. The Gothic revival in this period was often employed to signal the nation's growing power and prosperity and dedication to using such growth to improve the social, especially in the field of education. More specifically, this trend emerged in school design with the "common schools" movement, influenced by *The Yale Report* and driven by Barnard. This second period thus developed the first period's traditionalist approach to school design by attempting to make it universal—of course, "universal education" in the nineteenth century still signified "white". Next, the third period, which stretches from 1865 to 1900, was a time of "industry and turmoil". This era crucially saw the National Education Association (NEA) assemble the Committee of Ten and the Committee of Fifteen to review the extant curriculum. Both committees would ultimately call for education to continue to reinforce the traditional curriculum of *The Yale Report*. Meanwhile, the functional and modernist sensibilities in architecture began to take root, amplified by the work of Louis Sullivan and continued by his apprentice Frank Lloyd Wright—architectural developments that would really come to fruition in school design in the following era of "scientific management". The reports of the committees of ten and fifteen came at a time when many reformers were already considering how education might best adapt to, learn from, and facilitate America's increasingly robust industrial economy. The committees' traditionalist recommendations were greatly criticized by these industrially-inspired groups who believed that the classical curriculum failed to prepare youth to take on roles in the new economy. These calls for vocational education would define the next period in this history, the age of "modernity and diversity", that ran from 1900 to 1920. Inspired by the advances in method, management, and science of the Enlightenment and the Industrial Revolutions, reformers in this period called for education to be newly predicated on the dictates of "scientific management", hoping such an education would prepare inheriting generations to take on the demands of America's growing industrial economy, to develop the young nation as a global capitalist epicenter. Accordingly, curricular works of this period included, but were not limited to Dewey's *Child and the Curriculum* (1902), which was furthered by child study progressives; the NEA's *Cardinal Principles* (1918), which inspired social efficiency progressives; and Bobbitt's *Scientific Method* (1918), which was embodied by social meliorist progressives. Similarly, this era was architecturally, as I suggest above, marked by an organic architectural sensibility epitomized by the work of Wright and the pragmatic. Accordingly, schooling was designed increasingly around sorting students for specific roles in the economy, imparting the necessary skills for those jobs, and delivering this education as efficiently as possible. The administration of schooling thus became more centralized and was spearheaded by scientifically driven administrative experts (an arrangement that would continue well into the twentieth century). Districts began to build schools that moved the student body as efficiently as possible, preventing congregations or distractions. Such schools were also newly designed with rooms in which students could practice and so learn particular vocations—from metal work to sewing. With scientific management, school design developed an eagle-eyed focus on sorting and training youth to be obedient and efficient workers.

Throughout all these periods the vast majority of decision-makers were white middle-class men, while the majority of educators were female and the pupils were ethnically and economically more diverse, though schooling was racially segregated (if youth of color were educated at all). To be sure, this decision-making arrangement is not reflective of so-called "American" democratic values. Because the ruling minority shaped a public schooling system that served the majority, schooling popularized the white, male, middle and upper-class sensibilities and interests of curricular scholars and school builders as general "American" norms. Such a homogeneous concentration of power not only limited the input of marginalized groups, but also assimilated them into the working norms. The dogmatic approach to pedagogy evident throughout the eras of both *The Yale Report* and scientific management suggests that education became a key site of cultural reproduction rather than a site of resistance or possibility. In this way, American education historically worked to reiterate and stabilize the nation's founding economic and racial disparities—legacies of settler colonialism and slavery—by inhibiting any behaviors or thoughts that were not conducive to such norms. And so we unsurprisingly see, across the periods of *The Yale Report* and scientific management, the solidification of American education as a kind of segregative training camp. The work of critical pedagogues like Henry Giroux who read schools after Althusser as formative sites of cultural reproduction suggests that such nineteenth century educational trends didn't only change the landscape of education, but that of American culture more broadly. The rote and industrial leanings of such an education inhibited critical thought and encouraged youth to reiterate what they were taught; and what they were taught were Eurocentric forms of knowledge. Together with the already stratified racial politics of nineteenth century schooling that kept up the nation's founding white hegemony such an education deepened racial biases in the nation by foreclosing non-European forms of thinking and being, while at the same time reproducing unequal material conditions (that such slanted thought would only support). The rise of scientific management pedagogy further crippled any surviving critical capacities in normative educational frameworks and put student bodies to use to build a robust industrial economy. Schools became sites to foster and reproduce what Foucault might call a bio-politics of industry, where bodies were conditions to only support the industrial ideals (time off, in the latter emerging Fordist economy, only granted to enable subjects to consume the products of such labor). Schooling was and is still today caught up, irrevocably, in such a founding dynamics of power. Though there were many modes of schooling in the nineteenth century, such a history suggests that education emerged most normatively in the era as far from the democratic commitments it boasted, and rather, by the turn of the twentieth century, as training camps to fuel the American economy, as sites of capital reproduction.

Why does this history matter? It matters because it elucidates that nineteenth century American schooling normalized gender binaries, racial hierarchies, and stratified class and aptitudes—in short, it limited the distributions of cultural capital to stratify society in the interest of wealthy, white elites primarily by sorting the inheriting generation in ways that reiterated Eurocentric Western epistemologies and put them to work in the service of the American economy, the spoils of which were enjoyed primarily by such elite groups. But despite all this, many attempts were made in the nineteenth century and beyond to bring schooling back into the interest of the public good—to use it, as such early reformers like Dewey hoped, to make the American population more equitable—a necessary precursor for democracy. As Giroux (1984) argues in *Ideology, Culture, and the Process of Schooling*, schools aren't simply ideology machines, but sites of *contestation*, sites precisely where the struggle for the public good can be carried out. In this vein, reformers worked over the years to bring the voices of those students who didn't quite make the grade according to the norms of nineteenth century school design—to those students such a school design would have denied cultural capital, who would have been cast out from the mobility promised to them by the American Dream (I'm recalling here, groups like people of color [especially blacks and Native Americans], poor whites, women [who, though attending the same schools, received a different kind of education from young men, one that kept women in the home and confined her intellect to those things that supported masculine norms and agency], and non-cis gendered individuals). Though always at the margins of the US education system, such resistant pedagogies troubled nineteenth century school design norms and at times destabilized, if never overthrowing, the white hegemony in US culture that the education system worked determinedly to install.

Certainly, this history offers insights about the foundations of late modern American education that inspired my initial query into what it means to dwell in nineteenth century schools. I want to return now to one of my inciting questions: what does this history tell us about American education today? What politics and power structures does it reveal, deepen, or complicate? A quick glance around the late modern educational landscape reveals that out of all those norms formalized by nineteenth century school design, economy and rote learning remain the most definitive for schooling today, having survived—despite the best attempts of some reformers—counter-cultural struggles in education such as the open schools movement. More specifically, education remains today committed to sorting youth in ways that optimize their education for the market, that is, that prepare them for lives spent generating capital for the state and its directing corporations. As Giroux and Freire put it, schools have become "factories for the accumulation of capital".[2] Today, youth are encouraged at an early age to wed themselves to a career path which is then vetted and negotiated or approved with a number of authorities from teachers to guidance counselors at the K-12 level to admissions officers, professors, and career counselors once they reach higher education. Outside these more obvious sites of career-prep, K-12 today sorts the inheriting generation by encouraging teachers to use ability grouping and reminds students that their primary task is to be a productive worker by making vocational

[2] Henry A. Giroux and Paulo Freire, *Introduction to Education and the American Dream*, ed. Harvey Holtz. (Granby, MA: Bergin & Garvey, 1989), x.

learning labs and work placements primary as youth progress in their studies. And then there's recent push for public education to make students more "competitive" in the global economy, perhaps the nation's most legible attempt to use education to interpellate its children into the project of capital accumulation:[3] over the last couple of decades, pundits and politicians have popularized the idea that American education might best foster a better future ("better" synonymous in the neoliberal era with "profit") by supporting children's "*advancement*"—that is to say, by rearing brighter, highly inventive, and more ambitious generations able to hold their own in—or better yet, lead—late modernity's increasingly complex global markets.

This modus operandi of "advancement" perhaps first emerged most notably as a serious educational "value" with the Bush administration's 2001 *No Child Left Behind Act* (*NCLB*). Passed into law in 2002, *NCLB* infamously imposed state standards and evaluations ("standardized tests") to which it tied funding, under the argument that such a system would encourage schools to ensure that every student made the grade. The Act professedly emerged in response to over a decade of concern and largely failed attempts to fix the economic and racial gaps in achievement that *Nation At Risk* found in American education. The hope was that by implementing state standards, *NCLB* would make sure that every school offered students the same level of education – that no child would get "left behind" because they attended a school in a poorer zip code. In 2004, during the third presidential debate in Arizona, Bush mobilized this emerging norm of "advancement" into a discourse of global competitiveness by framing *NCLB*'s commitments as prerequisites for a well-functioning late modern economy: "in order to make sure people have jobs for the 21st century," he argued, "we've got to get it right in the education system, and we're beginning to close a minority achievement gap now. You see, we'll never

[3] Though K-12 does interpellate students into the project of capital accumulation in these ways, the sad truth is that it is today primarily occupied with warehousing, disciplining, and stratifying (with standardized testing) students, while the work of professionalizing them has moved to more legibly higher education. But entry into either prestigious colleges where, as in the era of the *Yale Report*, students are trained for elite professions or community colleges where students receive vocational training—in either case—all types of higher education frequently adjust their programming and pedagogy to what economy currently requires. Of late, the modus operandi has been "competitiveness", something that has trickled down to K-12 schools, where this economic preparation has materialized with the mandating of standardized testing.

be able to compete in the 21st century unless we have an education system that doesn't quit on children, an education system that raises standards, an education that makes sure there's excellence in every classroom".[4] With such rhetoric, standardization became the new norm in American education under the auspices that such state standards were assertedly designed to make youth more economically competitive global subjects—that these standards would only help, not hurt young Americans and the nation that would soon fall into their hands. Standardized tests became the vehicle by which to measure such achievement, and accordingly, over the last decade and a half, schooling has become deeply defined by the skill-and-drill test prep needed to meet such expectations.

Critics have since made clear that *NCLB* and other acts of "advancement" have not only come up short of their equalizing promises but have actually made worse those very disparities they were initially designed to redress. UMass educational theorist Kenneth Saltman, for example, argues that such [reforms] "can be fairly described as "failed"...[because] they [did] not increase standardized test scores, and no evidence for the success of turnarounds...exists".[5] Meanwhile, in *Expelling Hope*, social theorist Christopher Robbins succinctly summarizes that *NCLB*'s tying of funding to test scores under the auspices of "rewarding what works" has only worsened the achievement gap between those communities historically marked by background and poverty after which *Nation At Risk* so worried and those "white, middle-class" districts that had, by the time NCLB came around, already been performing better for decades. Such wealthy communities always have the educational advantage because they have more resources than poor communities (due to many factors such as a higher proportion of "homeowners" in wealthy areas than renters, the higher value of those homes yielding "a higher percentage of taxes on [such] propert[ies]"[6]). Ultimately, *NCLB* dried up any extant funding to already-struggling communities (mostly those "poor rural areas where family farms and industries have been devastated and poor urban areas where manufacturing has been eviscerated"[7]), because these schools just couldn't compete with those already-advantaged districts who could

[4] George Bush, quoted in Howard I. Chud. *Something Is Terribly Wrong*. (Indianapolis: Dog Ear Publishing, 2009), 109.

[5] Kenneth Saltman. *The Failure of Corporate School* Reform. (New York: Routledge, 2012), 74.

[6] Christopher Robbins. *Expelling Hope*. (Albany: SUNY Press, 2008), 67.

[7] Ibid., 66.

afford the best buildings, experienced educators, educational technologies, state of the art texts and materials, "rich programs in the arts, libraries, well-maintained campuses, and small classes" that enable these schools to successfully teach the "full curricula"[8]—districts to which *NCLB* would channel even more funding because their higher test scores were apparently "working".[9] NCLB's punitive system has encouraged many schools to, as Schept et al. detail, "push out 'problem' students who 'distract' others or whose scores would drive down…[their] aggregate scores".[10] Thus, those students who are in need of the most help were thrust even deeper into the margins of society. In this way, *NCLB* works as a sorting mechanism, foreclosing the futures of those youth who fail to immediately align with the high and constricting economical demands tests are assertedly geared to anticipate. Unable to prove themselves as normatively useful for the American economy, such students are cast out to the mercy of the worst reaches of the educational system where they learn little to prepare them for opportunities beyond dead-end minimum wage positions. Considering such conditions, there has been much criticism that the ways in which the questions on these tests are posed gear the evaluations to reward particular kinds of cultural capital and understandings. Accordingly, such tests can work as assimilative mechanisms, pressing students to take on a Eurocentric syntax to avoid losing any opportunities for social mobility. Taken to task, it certainly seems that *NCLB* and similar reforms not

[8] Diane Ravitch, *Reign of Error*. (New York: Vintage Books, 2013), 6.

[9] See, for example, Semuels article on such divisions in Connecticut schools: In Connecticut for example, "while students in higher-income towns such as Greenwich and Darien have easy access to guidance counsellors, school psychologists, personal laptops, and up-to-date textbooks, those in high-poverty areas like Bridgeport and New Britain don't. Such districts tend to have more students in need of extra help, and yet they have fewer guidance counsellors, tutors, and psychologists, lower-paid teachers, more dilapidated facilities and bigger class sizes than wealthier districts…Greenwich spends $6000 more per pupil per year than Bridgeport does, according to the State Department of Education" (Semuels, par. 1) This problem spreads across all states (par. 4). ++ "The No Child Left Behind Act (2001) extended zero tolerance policies beyond disciplinary infractions into the realm of actual educational performance. Indeed, the construction of an "at risk" and criminalized population is sutured to the narrow epistemology that promotes accountability through standardized testing via the neoliberal capitalist logics of accountability and individual responsibility. Due to pressure from *NCLB*, schools inevitably push out "problem" students who "distract" others or whose scores would drive down a given school's aggregate scores. Once a child drops out, he or she is eight times more likely to be incarcerated than youth who finish high school".

[10] Judah Schept et al., "Building, Staffing, and Insulating," *Social Justice* 41, 4 (2014): 99.

only divest students but whole communities, deepening the racially predicated urban and rural disparities that assertedly inspired such reforms in the first place. One of the most powerful arguments against these advancement reforms because of such ironically stratifying effects comes from their own architect, Diane Ravitch. Surveying the inequities *NCLB* deepened, Ravitch warns that.

> public education, established in America's towns and villages in the mid-19th century, born of advocacy and struggle, is now in jeopardy. This essential institution, responsible for producing a democratic-citizenry and tasked with providing equality of educational opportunity, is at risk. Under the cover of "choice" and "freedom," we may lose one of our society's greatest resources, our public school system.[11]

Here, Ravitch sounds the alarm that advancement reforms are destroying the public school system's ability to meet its founding goal of supporting America's public sphere. For Ravitch, such reforms have only perpetuated inequalities and injustices with narratives that strategically reek of false notions of choice. Because schooling does so little to progress changing class disparities, she asserts, it in fact supports the reproduction of these disparities.

Another important thing to note about this economically inspired shift to standardized testing is that such tests have understandably inspired many educators to teach using skill-and-drill pedagogy, because such tests demand little from students other than memorization. As a consequence, since *NCLB*, US pedagogy has swung back from those more radical and creative approaches to education popularized in the 60s and 70s to those rote styles of teaching and learning galvanized by *The Yale Report*. As I discuss in Chap. 4, such an approach to teaching curriculum only asks students to repeat what they're told, crippling any critical capacities and encouraging them to submit to and support authority—this obedient subjectivity, so characteristic of the era of scientific management, deeply strategic for a nation hell-bent on mobilizing its youth to support the bottom line. The end game of this now-common scheme of US education is that, as Ravitch succinctly put it in her infamous 2010 *Wall Street Journal* op-ed, our schools are "producing graduates who were drilled regularly on the basic skills but were often ignorant about almost everything else".[12] Extending Ravitch's worry, educational theorist Martha Nussbaum argues

[11] Diane Ravitch, *Reign of Error*. (New York: Vintage Books, 2013), 4–5.

[12] Diane Ravitch, "Why I Changed My Mind About School Reform." *The Wall Street Journal*, March 9, 2010.

that the rise of such rote pedagogy inhibits education's democratic potential. More specifically, Nussbaum locates the "imaginative, creative aspect, and the aspect of rigorous critical thought" so rapidly disappearing from US education as those "skills....needed to keep democracies alive".[13] "If this trend continues", she warns, "nations all over the world will soon be producing generations of useful machines, rather than complete citizens who can think for themselves, criticize tradition, and understand the significance of another person's sufferings and achievements"[14]—those facets of citizenship absolutely necessary for democracy. In a similar vein, Giroux (2011) worries after the ways in which such tests, in necessitating rote pedagogy, limit the autonomy of teachers, whose jobs now literally depend on their student's performance in these evaluations. For Giroux, one of the key requirements of truly democratic education is that teachers act as public intellectuals, teaching critical literacy and other important skills by responding thoughtfully to the complex and ever-changing needs of their students. By constraining teachers, *NCLB* and similar legislation "undermines the possibility of critical teaching and visionary goals for student learning",[15] and so democratic education itself. Such legacies of nineteenth century education thus reflect and are in part responsible for the broader democratic deficit in which the US currently finds itself.

Let's return for a moment to the nineteenth century norm of schooling as a site for capital accumulation; here I want to discuss an important and quite frightening new development from so deeply wedding school to industry. US education today has grown beyond what the nineteenth century could imagine as "economically predicated" education. Today, education *is* an economy. More specifically, as Saltman argues, the last three centuries have seen the rise of "corporate" school reform, which is to say the transformation of education from a public good into a market. As Saltman makes clear, more and more, school reform discourse has "champion[ed] private sector approaches to reform, including, especially, privatization, deregulation, and the importation of terms and assumptions from businesses".[16] School boards are being developed in consultation with management consulting firms who frequently recommend changes

[13] Martha Nussbaum. *Not For Profit.* (Princeton: Princeton University Press, 2010), 2.

[14] Ibid.

[15] Henry A. Giroux. *Education and the Crisis of Public Values.* (New York: Peter Lang, 2011), 2.

[16] Kenneth Saltman. *The Failure of Corporate School* Reform. (New York: Routledge, 2012), 1.

that favor the bottom line at the expense of a good education (e.g. replacing long-time teachers with less experienced hires they can snag for a song on short-term contracts with no pensions or insurance); school governance is being handed over to private groups (such as educational management organizations who, as Saltman details "extract profit by cutting teacher pay and educational resources while relying on high teacher turnover and labor precarity"[17]); principals are now "CEOs", framing their roles as managers, cost-cutters, and corporate liaisons (often tasked with attracting corporate presences to their schools) rather than educators and educational facilitators dedicated to the public good; and corporations are becoming a growing and celebrated presence in schools, now involved in everything from school lunches to curriculum (Saltman). We see corporate school reform perhaps most legibly in the rise of "privately managed charter schools [(which typically have no unions)], voucher schemes, and tax credit scholarships for private schooling".[18] As if these changes alone weren't enough to make clear that education itself is now considered an economy, take the corporate sector's more precise assertion that "education in the US [is] a roughly $600 billion per year 'industry',' ripe for takeover".[19] Such a juncture, Nussbaum warns, signals that we've arrived in a rather dystopian moment, one in which we value "education for profit-making" rather than, as the pioneers of the common school movement would have hoped, "for a more inclusive type of citizenship".[20]

To be sure, such a divestment in critical faculties and prioritizing of the bottom line stretches beyond curricula and into the physicality of the school building itself. As the education system has cemented its commitment to profit at the expense of meaningful and capacious education, jurisdictions have written off school architecture—except in the wealthiest areas as an unimportant, indeed luxurious, consideration in the recovery period. This is of course in part due to the fact that schools—especially in historically poor and black communities like West Philadelphia and South Chicago—are becoming corporatized and that those that have not yet been swept up by privitization are getting more vulnerable to such a takeover as they find themselves increasingly relegated to the margins of public funding, if not simply outright ignored. It is perhaps not surprising then

[17] Ibid.
[18] Ibid.
[19] Ibid., 2.
[20] Martha Nussbaum. *Not For Profit.* (Princeton: Princeton University Press, 2010), 7.

that, especially in poorer areas yielding immaterial tax revenues, extant schools have been left deteriorate at the expense of their learners' education, while any new schools have been built with razor thin budgets. In Rhode Island as in many states, the quality of public school construction over the past two decades has thus differed very sharply across postal codes. State-of-the-art schools have been built in wealthy communities, while poorer communities have had to make do with very low-cost constructions or virtually obsolete, unusable, but "available" facilities. In the early millennium, for example, Rhode Island municipalities tried to cope with unexpected enrollment increases by quickly erecting short-term (e.g. 20-year instead of 50-year) structures on the cheapest sites. Worryingly, such "affordable" sites were often toxic and would contaminate the school environment with hazardous vapors, by-products of Rhode Island's industrial past. Moreover, the lightning speed with which these schools were constructed was the product of very aggressive schedules designed to thwart any stakeholder input that might ramp up costs, a strategy that led to many short-sighted decisions in design. As a result, the architecture of such buildings is relatively thoughtless.

With schoolhouses now stripped to the bare minimum, school architecture has certainly been cast to the margins of school design discourse. Though it may go largely unnoticed today, school architecture, as this history of nineteenth century school design makes clear, is a language in itself, always conveying the failures, norms, and hopes of its culture. The language our schoolhouses speak is not one of words; the schoolhouse uses colors, textures, shapes, and symbols to convey its meaning (Lurie, 2014). The schoolhouse and its classrooms can be formal or informal, simple or complex, large or small, opened or closed, dark or bright, and, all these elements coming to a head, most importantly oppressive or liberating (Lurie, 2014). We must consider the ways in which school architecture, as a language, makes learners think, feel, and express in a multiplicity of ways (Lurie, 2014). It can be delightful, wondrous, serene, and inspiring and it can also be confusing, sad, depressing, hostile, and discouraging. To be sure, this language speaks more broadly to the ways in which public schoolhouses embody social, political, and cultural ideologies. Ultimately, they can even be symbolic of community values and the notion of the "common good" in its most positive sense. The way a community builds and maintains its public schoolhouses reflects its values and what hopes it has for its future. Further, public schoolhouses can also retain memory. Many children return to the schools their parents attended, making the past alive; in other words, the schoolhouse becomes a conversation across time and space (Goldberger, 2009). But today—rife with residual pastness and largely defined by unacceptable, dilapidated conditions—the language our schoolhouses speak is static and crumbling. If the above changes in curricula don't underscore our nation's contemporary negation of schooling as a site of nurturing and creation, this language, reflective of the horrifying new standards to which we hold school architecture, make it undeniably clear. Across the board, but especially in low-income areas, student well-being—a prerequisite to any kind of effective democratic education—has become second to finances in late modern school design, if considered at all. This static and crumbling language more broadly speaks to the nation's declining commitment to education as a public good, it suggests that we favor profit over the protection and fostering of the most vulnerable youth, over providing safe, clean, and inspiring spaces in which to let them think, experiment, love, and grow. In short, the popular abandonment of school architecture is only supporting the popular sense that schools should be sites of profit—and only profit. And so it seems to me that, true to the nineteenth and early twentieth century legacies this book lays out, late modern American school design remains committed to "improving society" by using rote learning and the dictates of scientific management to push its most struggling members, those who might most benefit from a critical, wide-reaching, and rigorous education more deeply into its margins. To be sure, such segregative consequences cannot signify "improvement" in the US; as an assertedly liberal democratic nation, our politics are necessarily always answerable to the equity democracy demands. How to tackle such a troubling conjuncture?

Considering this historicized politics of the present, I deeply worry about the consequences of trying to standardize education. But at the same time, I'm not convinced it's wise (or possible) to imagine school design without certain norms. Some degree of control in education—emerging from a consensus—seems prerequisite to working toward a better world. The question then becomes: what and whose curriculum is most worthy of shaping our schoolhouses? Is it a curriculum of social control, discipline, and scientific management? Or is it a student-centered and adaptive curriculum? My hope is that new controls for school architecture and curriculum will take the stratifying histories this book unpacks into account and, in response, will engage the theories of those resistant pedagogues I detail in the previous chapter who sought to hold American education to its democratic promise. Certainly, inspired by such pedagogies, much work has already been done in response to the problematics of the current conjuncture to create more suitable school designs. To be sure, whatever the answer is to such a debilitating approach to schooling, it must as this book has asserted throughout, consider *both* curriculum and school architecture. Much work has been done on what kinds of curricular reforms can bring education back to its democratic promise. Maintaining that schools *can* indeed be caring places and not just places of indoctrination to fuel the market, many scholars (see, e.g. Chomsky [2002], Giroux [2011], Nussbaum [2010]) have argued that we must begin to measure student success not simply by academics and career readiness, but by their ability to "come into presence" as Gert Biesta (2006, pp. 33–54) articulates and to be active participants in, active creators of, democratic life. Part of this, as many have argued, will require replacing conformist rote pedagogies with dialectical and inquiry-based ones that empower students and fuel their critical and creative capacities. Also, part of this, as I have argued, will require formal and non-formal spaces to support student dwelling. We need to incorporate into education curricula that destabilizes Western epistemologies and teaches empathy, change making, and systems thinking—those skills sorely negated by the current pedagogical imperatives—with multicultural perspectives, in other words, pedagogies that introduce students to a wide range of different and conflicting schemes of thought, contextualized within a globalized sensibility that takes into account the locally predicated differential place-based and critical pedagogies propagated by Dewey (1897), Orr (1992), Pinar (1995), and Lewicki (1997) in spaces that support such pedagogies. Such a democratic education, to recall Giroux, requires us to recognize and celebrate teachers as public intellectuals, to locate the teacher as a "valuable resource in teaching students how to take responsibility for their future, develop an unrelenting fidelity to justice, and hone their ability to discriminate between rigorous arguments and heavily charged opinions", in short, "an education…[that] enable[s] young people to develop the values, skills, and knowledge required for them to enter adult life as critical citizens capable of questioning "common sense," official knowledge, public opinion, and the dominant media".[21] This shift will not only require more rigorous and inventive forms of teacher education but also the removal of those policies, practices, and spaces that constrain the agency of students and teachers in the classroom.

[21] Henry A. Giroux, "On the Significance of the Chicago Teachers Strike." *Truthout*, September 13, 2010.

More directly responding to the disparities in race and wealth that standardized testing has deepened, Ravitch argues that more support must be given to schools in those communities defined by poverty and racial discrimination to level the playing field. In other words, Ravitch (2013) asserts that to eradicate achievement gaps, we must first eradicate gaps in opportunity, speak directly to the equitable, adequacy, and appropriateness of the schoolhouse form. Such a project, to be sure, must emerge from the perspective of social justice and recall the hopes of those movements across the last century that advocated for equal rights, the elimination of poverty and creation of basic income security, and adequate housing, and universal healthcare. Despite the importance of installing such policies, they remain largely unaccounted for in politics today. To address the deficit in schooling, we must create or mend those other public institutions outside the school to establish the equity democratic education demands. In addition to calling for such political revolutions, Ravitch (2013) also emphasizes the importance of redressing school design itself. Worrying after its dilapidating architecture, she asks reformers to move their attention away from closing public schools and opening market ones to fixing the segregation, overcrowded classrooms, and lack of resources *in* the public school itself. Not unrelatedly, she calls for education to drop standardized tests, no longer believing that they are adequate measures of educational success and fearing after their segregative consequences, evocative of those sorting techniques of the scientific management era. She rightly argues that such tests are not sufficient to measure the responsibility, cleverness, judgment, resourcefulness, and caring disposition required of a global democratic citizen. What we have to be aware of as researchers is if social efficiency is ever to be relevant, its tenants cannot be connected or driven by a cult that produces a specific subject, in a specific place, for a specific position in the job market and ignores the student's essence of being (dwelling). More concretely, it is impossible to maintain an educational system in which the very goal of education is to convert students into commodities; their cultural and economic currencies grounded in market logic. This is not an educational system but a training camp. This is a system that is hostile to humanity, that brutalizes the individual, and that turns its back on one of its essential core missions: to engage in a collective process that creates solid pillars for a democratic society. Schools can only truly engage in this mission if they respond equally to the needs of *everyone*. Ultimately, Ravitch (2013) insists we must get away from a system of schooling that reinforces social inequalities, perpetuates hopelessness, and undermines our public common good through an undo focus on commercialization. Her rhetoric is strong and polarizing, but so is our current educational landscape, defined as it is by a privileged few designing the best possible systems to secure the wealth and sovereignty of their own communities while making already-painful schooling more challenging for America's most vulnerable.

Ravitch (2013) is certainly not wrong when she asks reformers to respond to the contemporary problematics not only of curriculum, but also of the static and crumbling conditions of our schoolhouses. While many educational reform theories offer some enormously helpful interventions to better orient schools in the interest of the social, Ravitch (2013) is one of the only to consider—albeit briefly—the formative role school architecture plays in the educational relation (Tyack, 1990) (with the exception perhaps, of recent work done comparing prison and school architecture in discussing the school-to-prison pipeline). To be sure, there have been moments when school architecture has received attention over the years—the infamous schools of *The Yale Report* and scientific management eras stand as key examples, as do the open schools of the 60s. But of late, even some of our most transformative educators fail to consider school architecture. The fact of the matter is that with the exception of the more innovative schools constructed in wealthier communities who have the time to advocate for facilities and the capital to patron them, our culture still doesn't give school design much clout. We tend to consider it a kind of afterthought, a low priority on a list more immediately concerned with test scores and profit. In short, due to a combination of cost-cutting imperatives and our own oversight we've largely relegated K-12 schoolhouses to the "children's table" of educational and architectural history. Segregated and abstracted from the more lauded and serious "grown-up" table, the children's table—a metaphor I borrow from Anna Mae Duane—is a marginal site. If we really want to make our schools more answerable to the dreams we have for our futures, we can't just locate that possibility in curriculum alone. We must also take school architecture seriously as a key part of the educational relation. This book has thus tried to rearrange the seating arrangement by bringing school architecture out of the margins of school design. Such a reorientation crucially, as Duane puts it, "chang[es] the term of inquiry and forc[es] a different set of questions"[22]

[22] Anna Duane, introduction to *The Children's Table*, ed. Annette Ruth Appell (Athens, GA: University of Georgia Press, 2013), 1.

in the field of education that understands the formative work of schooling as defined by the ideo-spatial school design nexus, as always implicated in *both* architecture and curricula. Without considering school design as such, our reforms will continue to be fatally limited: residual pastness will prevail and trouble new redressive pedagogies. Those schools designed with the directives of *The Yale Report* or standardized testing or the much-criticized priority of security in response to school shootings now too numerous to count, limit those critical pedagogies crucial for democracy. Accordingly, in remediating school design, it's important to take seriously architecture and to create designs that might support more democratic pedagogy—architecture that offers students opportunities to be thoughtful, discerning, and creative, that empowers teachers as public intellectuals and enables them to be responsive to the unique and diverse needs of an ever-shifting student body.

Here we might pause for a moment and reflect on this quote by the famous architect Sullivan, in which he emphasizes the formative power of architecture and the need to be deeply reflective about what our buildings might do:

> Throughout this stream of human life, and thought, and activity, men have ever felt the need to build; and from the need arose the power to build. So, as they thought, they built; for, strange as it may seem, they could build in no other way. As they built, they made, used, and left behind them records of their thinking. Then, as through the years new men came with changed thoughts, so arose new buildings in consonance with the change of thought – the building always the expression of the thinking. Whatever the character of the thinking, just so was the character of the building. (1968, p. 228)

Just as it's possible for architecture to constrict, it can also encourage more capacious ways of thinking and being—if we go into it with such an intention. In other words, what Sullivan suggests is that with the right consciousness we can theorize a democratic schoolhouse design. There are countless foundations upon which such a design might rest, but first, some basics: working to fulfill its responsibility to provide students with a proper learning environment, the public school must provide an environment that nurtures its students' well-being and "coming into presence" (Biesta, 2006). At the very minimum, this means that the school must be a place where students are safe (which, it's important to note, does not mean a prison-like site that is highly securitized, the like of which dominate the educational landscape today); a place that is clean, warm, and dry; a place with adequate ventilation, acceptable air quality; a place with excellent acoustics and lighting; a place that is appropriately equipped for the tasks demanded by society's educational goals; and a place that supports their being. While these conditions may sound obvious, the current state of many schools, as documented by the *State of Rhode Island Schoolhouses* (RIDE, 2017) makes clear that these standards must be emphasized.

In moving beyond such basic requirements for schoolhouse architecture, it is important to first acknowledge that whatever controls we hope to set out with a design, the schoolhouse's form (like its prescribed curriculum) can never absolutely determine the movements of those who dwell within it. The history I sketch in this book makes clear that controls yield more complicated spatial social configurations than we can ever anticipate. Though we often understand controls as objective mechanisms, they're so much more complicated: their formative impact is deeply dependent on broader social configurations, on contemporary politics, and, at a more focused level, on how builders and teachers respond to and enact them. In working to make education more democratic, we have to recognize that any controls we set out will never hold eternally, will never offer any guarantees. It's not just about establishing controls with the expectation that they will be absolutely definitive. Instead, it's about establishing a constantly critical and reflexive relationship with education and being ever-responsive to the ways in which power structures in education and society change over time. Part of this work must involve acknowledging that controls set out with democratic intentions are not always "good" or might not always work in the ways we intend them to. As I've stated many times, this history of school design suggests that exclusion, if not abjectification, is the necessary product of any normalizing school design. While I'm not convinced schooling can ever jettison its normalizing function (its founding legitimation is, after all, to teach), I do think its inevitably abjectifying consequences demand that we more carefully consider what kinds of ways of thinking and being our future school designs might nurture and which ones they shut down. Because this formative work of such emerging schemes of education, as I suggest in the opening pages of this book, derives at least in part from that of the broader history of US school design, taking the democratic claims of late modern American education to task will require reformers to take seriously this history of US school design and to be ever open to critical insights and interventions about the ways in which education is working in the service of or against democracy. In other words, the school design nexus we must work to create is one that, as democratic, is always self-critical. As an architect, I must emphasize that one part of this is to make any controls we do set out as amenable to such critical insights and interventions as possible. As such, it's important to make school architecture more responsive, capable of resisting the limiting work of residual pastness. It is necessary for future architects, planners, and educators to approach school design with a consciousness of a building's inherited philosophies (either that it already has, if it's being built, or that it will eventually have, if it's under construction) in order to design education architecture more democratically and supportive of student coming into being. The deeper point here is that a democratic system of education can only emerge if we are always taking to task and responsive to feedback about any controls we set out. And so, at a less basic but no less crucial level, schoolhouse design must remain flexible, able, in other words, to perpetually respond to the needs of diverse populations as they change over time and to the recent findings in pedagogical theory. Here, I mean more specifically giving students and teachers the ability to easily move furniture and walls to best suit the lesson at hand; access to a wide array of technologies; various kinds of seating; and many different spaces of learning (e.g. covered verandas, window seats, atriums, etc.). While these flexible schoolhouses remain rare in the US today, they have taken off in other countries like Finland, which celebrates "more flexible and informal open-plan layouts" that are designed to give students and teachers the ability to easily move furniture and walls to best suit the lesson at hand; access to a wide array of technologies; portable panels (some magnetic, some mesh, corkboard, blackboard, digital screens, and whiteboard) that can even be set into windows to facilitate learning when, how, and where its most needed; and various kinds of seating, some of which can act as "learning nests" where students can explore a topic together, perhaps with a teacher acting, in the discovery-based style derivative of Freirian pedagogy, a "guide-by-side". During my own tenure with the Rhode Island Department of Education, I had the incredible opportunity to bring some of these techniques home: in 2014, I worked with an inspiring building team to design and build a more flexible (and net-zero environmental impact mission driven) schoolhouse in Newport,

RI, Paul Crowley MET Centre (see Fig. 5.1). The project was designed and administered by the Department's School Construction Program, with strong staff, student, and community input.

The ultimate goal of the design was to stimulate student curiosity, free movement, and creativity by leaving the design of the school "open" (i.e. exposing the ductwork, the electrics, etc.), to inspire students to be conscious of their space and to think about the knowledge behind such processes and by offering many different spaces in which to explore knowledge with such as covered verandas, multiuse rooms with moveable furniture, and community gardens (in short, we tried to bring the classroom out of the "classroom", to make the school at large and the areas beyond it into a myriad of learning environments). After Giroux, such flexible designs will crucially empower teachers as public intellectuals and inspire student dwelling by designing classrooms that aren't constricted by residual pastness and the prevailing curriculum, but instead supportive of countless possibilities. Such classrooms also empower students to take charge of their own learning by enabling them to follow their curiosities and work how and on what they want over the course of their study.

Fig. 5.1 Photograph of the Paul Crowley East Bay MET School in Newport, RI. (William Marchetti Photographer, 2014)

But for such a design to really be able to respond to democratic deficits, we must open the schoolhouse construction process up to more pluralistic voices, to listening to all stakeholders in our children's education. In other words, to counter the centuries of marginalization this book makes clear, we must give space in school design to the voices of teachers (historically classroom teacher's voices have been spatially limited to within the classroom's four walls), to the parents of minority youth and those youth struggling in an education system that just doesn't meet their needs, and to youth themselves. We must get back to the students, the core elements of education, and strive to better understand and respect their lived experiences. Today, not enough attention is given to understand what our diverse citizenry demands of public education. Design teams still largely fail to be more participatory, and, distracted with the economic drivers our neoliberal society demands, have little time to address this slant. The makeup of the Rhode Island public school building committees, for example, is primarily limited to school administrators and city or town officials and does not include teachers or students (RIDE School Construction Regulations, 2007). By more carefully approaching school design in these ways, we can build facilities that create the opportunity for equitable, transformative and meaningful learning.

While this book does not have room to more fully theorize the ways in which schooling might become more democratic and foster greater student awaking of their presence, I hope the centuries-old problematics it outlines and the brief responses to contemporary schooling it previews encourages other thinkers to take on school reform with an eye for the historicized politics of its present. We must work to open education up against the marginalizing legacy of nineteenth century school design to more diverse student bodies, giving previously silenced subjects a voice. By redressing the structural conditions that create inequities in our school systems, implementing more critical pedagogies, and making schoolhouse architecture adequate and responsive, school design might work to decenter those troubling nineteenth century norms, from whiteness to capital, that largely continue to define it today; might be reoriented to meet its democratic promise. As sentient beings with a spiritual soul, our children are all worthy of dwelling in schools that support their well-being, which celebrate their humanity, nurture their dignity, awaken their presence, and provide countless opportunities for their futures. We must demand this and no less.

References

Biesta, G. J. J. (2006). *Beyond Learning: Democratic Education for a Human Future*. Boulder, CO: Paradigm Publishers.

Chomsky, N. (2002). *Chomsky on Democracy and Education*. New York: Routledge.

Chud, H. I. (2009). *Something Is Terribly Wrong: The Sad Truth About Education in America*. Indianapolis, IN: Dog Ear Publishing.

Duane, A. (2013). *Introduction to The Children's Table*. Athens, GA: University of Georgia Press.

Giroux, H. A. (1984). *Ideology, Culture, and the Process of Schooling*. Philadelphia, PA: Temple University Press.

Giroux, H. A. (2010, September 13). On the Significance of the Chicago Teachers Strike. *Truthout*. www.truthout.org. Accessed 13 June 2016.

Giroux, H. A. (2011). *Education and the Crisis of Public Values*. New York: Peter Lang.

Giroux, H. A., & Freire, P. (1989). *Introduction to Education & The American Dream*. Granby, MA: Bergin & Garvey.

Goldberger, P. (2009). *Why Architecture Matters*. New Haven: Yale University Press.

Lurie, A. (2014). *The Language of Houses*. New York: Delphinium Books.

Nussbaum, M. (2010). *Not for Profit*. Princeton: Princeton University Press.

Ravitch, D. (2010, March 9). Why I Changed My Mind About School Reform. *The Wall Street Journal*. www.wsj.com. Accessed 13 May 2017.

Ravitch, D. (2013). *Reign of Error*. New York: Alfred A. Knopf.

Rhode Island Department of Education. (2007). RIDE 1.00 School Construction Regulations. *Rhode Island Department of Education*. Retrieved from http://www.ride.ri.gov/

Rhode Island Department of Education School Building Authority. (2017). *State of Rhode Island Schoolhouses*. Providence, RI: Jacobs Engineering.

Robbins, C. (2008). *Expelling Hope*. Albany, NY: SUNY Press.

Saltman, K. (2012). *The Failure of Corporate School Reform*. New York: Palgrave.

Schept, J., Wall, T., & Brisman, A. (2014). Building, Staffing, and Insulating: An Architecture of Criminological Complicity in the School-to-Prison Pipeline. *Social Justice, 41*(4 (138)), 96–115.

Sullivan, L. (1968). *Kindergarten Charts and Other Writings*. Chicago: Courier.

Tyack, D., & Cuban, L. (1995). *Tinkering Toward Utopia*. Cambridge, MA: Harvard University Press.

Tyack, D. B. (1990). *The One Best System*. Cambridge, MA: Harvard University Press.

Appendix: Chronological Inventory Chart of Public Schoolhouses in RI from 1870s to 1920s

These charts include architectural information on various schoolhouse designs obtained from the Rhode Island Board of Education's archives. These charts will include information on year built, school name, list of major program spaces, square footage, costs, and architects, where available.

© The Author(s) 2018

J. da Silva, *School(house) Design and Curriculum in Nineteenth Century America*, https://doi.org/10.1007/978-3-319-78586-8

Year	*School name*	*Program spaces*	*Square footage*	*Cost*	*Architects*
1875	**Newport**-Rogers High School Building	4 classrooms, 1 library & lecture room, 1 Chemical lab, 1 **chapel**, toilet, apparatus, recitation, lunch counter, boiler rooms	3180	$30,000	
	Bristol-Byfield School Building			$45,000	
1876	**Providence**-Jackson Avenue School House	4 classrooms, recitation, coat and boiler rooms		$20,220.06	
	Providence-Point Street Grammar School	12 classrooms, 1 hall, 1 teacher's room	11,332	$115,000	
1877	**Providence**-Doyle Avenue School-House	10 classrooms, 1 hall	7056	$52,920	
	Woonsocket-High and Grammar Schools	4 classrooms, 3 teacher's rooms, 1 Chemical lab, toilet, study, recitation, lunch counter, boiler rooms	5862	$40,000	
1878	**Providence**-Oxford Street Grammar School	10 classrooms, 3 reception rooms, 1 ante-room & bell room	8928	$50,000	Mr. Clifton A. Hall
	Providence-Candace Street Grammar School	8 classrooms, 2 recitation rooms	6048	$45,000	E. L. Angell of Providence
1879	**Cumberland**-Berkeley School-House	4 classrooms, 8 coat rooms	2046	$8094	
	Providence-Providence High School	4 classrooms, 1 hall & library, chemical and physical labs, 1 drawing room, coat, play, toilet, boiler, storage, and store rooms	19,608	$216,974.63	
1880	**Providence**-State Normal School	6 classrooms, 1 dressing room, 1 study hall, 1 committee & lecture room, 1 retiring room	4256		
	Woonsocket-Fairmount School House	2 rooms (total)	4075		
	Woonsocket-Constitution Hill School House	4 rooms (total)	7587		

	Woonsocket-Bernon District School House	1 rooms (total)	1800		
1881					
1882					
1883					
1884	**Cranston**-Auburn School House	2 recitation rooms, 2 closet rooms	2240		
1885	**Pawtucket**-Broadway School-House	4 rooms (total)		$10,196.20	
	Providence-Elmwood Grammar School-House	4 classroom, recitation rooms, Principal's & 4 teacher's rooms	26,607	$10,698.80	
	Richmond-Arcadia School House	(#'s of rooms not specified)			
1886					
1887	**Warwick**-Pawtuxet School House	4 classrooms	1890	$6000	
	Warwick-Phenix School House	4 classrooms	2479	$12,000	
	Woonsocket-Jencksville School House Lincoln	(#'s of rooms not specified) 1 loft, boiler room	2240	$5600	
1888	**Newport**-Lenthal School House	4 classrooms, 2 porches, coat rooms	7496	$50,238	
	Pawtucket-Middle Street School House	4 classrooms		$22,000	
	Pawtucket-Garden Street School House	*not specified		$25,000	
1889					
1890	**Pawtucket**-Bridge Avenue School House	~Not specified~		$12,000	
	Pawtucket-Hancock Street School House	~Not specified~		$25,000	
1891	**Cranston**-Arlington School House	4 classrooms, 8 coat rooms	3264		Edgar B. Peck of Providence

(*continued*)

(continued)

Year	*School name*	*Program spaces*	*Square footage*	*Cost*	*Architects*
	Cranston-Edgewood School House	4 classrooms, basement play room	3276	$11,000	Messrs. William R. Walker & Son
	Cumberland-Lonsdale School House	4 recitation room, 8 dressing rooms and 3 reception rooms		$20,000	
1892	**Providence**-Academy Avenue Grammar School	12 classrooms, 1 hall, coat and ante-rooms, boiler and toilet rooms		$54,214.14	Frederic E. Field of Providence
	Providence-Charles Street Grammar School	8 classrooms, 1 principal's office, 1 teacher's room, toilet, coat, and storage rooms		$36,138.83	Read & Hoppin of Providence
	Providence-Veazie Street Primary school	6 classrooms, 1 recitation room, coat, storage, and ante-rooms		$15,011.95	Frederic E. Field of Providence
	Providence-Meader Street Primary School	4 classrooms, 2 recitation rooms, balconies, play, coal, and cold air rooms		$10,922.59	George W. Cady of Providence
1893	**Pawtucket**-Grove Street School	6 classrooms, 2 recitation rooms, 1 teacher's room, toilet, coal, coat, and storage	8265	$35,000	W. R. Walker & Son of Providence
	Pawtucket-Auburn Grammar School	6 classrooms, 1 teacher's room, toilet, coat, play, coal, and storage		$23,082	Edgar B. Peck of Providence
	Central Falls-Garfield Street School	6 classrooms, 1 teacher's room, toilet, air, janitor, supply, and furnace rooms	7125	$34,000	Albert H. Humes of Central Falls

1894	**Providence**-Manual Training High School	6 classrooms, chemical, and physical labs, 1 museum & office, 1 library & hall, engine, coat, boiler, project, janitor, electrical, store, draughting, and toilet rooms		$22,000	
	East Providence-A. P. Hoyt Grammar School	8 classrooms, toilets	5372	$21,000	
1895					
1896	**Westerly**-Spruce Street Primary School	4 classrooms, 1 teacher's room, toilets	4200	$11,451.08	Wilson & Webber, 49 Mason Building of Boston, MA
	Johnston-Concord School	4 classrooms, 1 hall, 2 play room, coat, coal, recitation, janitor, and toilet rooms	5250	$27535.17	D. Howard Thornton of Ohneyville
	Providence-Courtland St. Primary School	4 classrooms, 4 wardrobes, coat, coal, and toilet rooms		$22,000	Martin & Hall of Providence
	Woonsocket-Park Avenue School House	4 classrooms, 2 recitation rooms, coal, and toilet rooms	2304	$7000	
1897	**Newport**-Townsend Industrial School	1 hall & office, numerous vocational classrooms, coat, coal, storage, and toilet rooms	5265	$12,440	
	Bristol-Walley School	8 classrooms, porch, fuel, play, toilet, and coat rooms	6764	$25,000	W. R. Walker & Son of Providence
	Woonsocket-Kendrick Avenue School House	6 classrooms, 1 teacher's & supply room, coat, and toilet rooms	5175	$23,000	

(*continued*)

(continued)

Year	*School name*	*Program spaces*	*Square footage*	*Cost*	*Architects*
1898	**Pawtucket**-Pawtucket High School	10 classrooms, 1 hall, 1 gymnasium, physical & chemical labs, 1 principal office, 2 teacher's rooms, janitor, drawing, apparatus, boiler, recitation, waiting, toilet, and ante-rooms	11,792	$80,000	
	Pawtucket-Kindergarten Cottage	2 exercise rooms, coat, and toilet rooms	1564	$6300	
	Newport-Henry R. A. Carey School	8 classrooms, 1 teacher's room, coat, and toilet rooms	6888	$36,000	
	East Providence-Ellis Primary School	2 classrooms, 2 recitation, 4 coat rooms, 1 toilet room	4200	$5,850.71	
1899	**Cranston**-Eden Park School House	4 classrooms, 2 recitation rooms, coat, supply, and toilet rooms	5525	$15,000	Angell and Swift of Providence
	Providence-Wayland Park School House	4 classrooms, coal, coat, and toilet rooms		$9000	Edwin T. Banning of Providence
1900	**Cranston**-Highland Park Grammar School	6 classrooms, 1 hall, 4 recitation rooms, 4 teacher's rooms, 1 principal's office, toilets, and coat		$19,464	Edwin T. Banning
	Newport-Coggeshall School	8 classrooms, 1 hall, coat, and toilet rooms	4089		
1901					
1902					
1903	**Warren**-Joyce Street School	8 classrooms, 1 elevator & porch, 1 principal office, store, coal, supply, teacher's and toilet rooms	4173	$25,000	Albert H. Humes of Pawtucket

	Burrillville-Harrisville School	8 classrooms, 1 hall, 2 teacher's rooms, coat, storage, porch, toilet, and ante-rooms		$20,000	W. R. Walker & Son of Providence
	Warwick-Crompton School	6 classrooms, teacher's and principal's rooms, play, porch, bicycle, coal, and toilet rooms		$23,311	Angell and Swift of Providence
1903	**Bristol**-Oliver School	6 classrooms, 2 teacher's rooms, boiler, recreation, toilet, storage, fresh air, and porch rooms		$25,000	W. R. Walker & Son of Providence
1904	**Warwick**-Central School	2 classroom, porch, wardrobe & lavatory		$4900	Colwell & Gould of Providence
	Westerly-Westerly High School	4 classrooms, 2 commercial study rooms, drawing and science rooms, toilet, bicycle, coat, recreation, lunch, athletic, and boiler rooms	9313	$55,000	Loring & Phipps of Boston, MA
1905	**Cranston**-Cranston High School	9 classrooms, 3 office rooms, 1 library, commercial, stenography, type writing room, Chemical & physical laboratories, locker, lunch, toilet, gymnasium, lunch counter, boiler rooms, 5 entrances	8300	$50,000	Banning & Thornton of Providence
	Hopkinton-Ashaway School	6 classrooms, 1 hall, 2 recreation rooms, toilet, bicycle, boiler, play rooms	4356	$19,000	W. R. Walker & Son of Providence
	Pawtucket-Darlington School	3 entrances, 11 classrooms, 1 hall, recitation, reference, boiler, coal, electric switchboard, toilet, office rooms		$55,503.92	C. N. Monahan of Pawtucket

(*continued*)

(continued)

Year	*School name*	*Program spaces*	*Square footage*	*Cost*	*Architects*
1905	**Pawtucket**-South Woodlawn School	4 unfinished, 12 classrooms, 2 store rooms, 2 teacher's rooms, 1 principal's room, 1 hall toilet, closet,		$57,189.31	W. R. Walker & Son of Providence
	Barrington-Drownville School	4 class rooms, 2 teacher's rooms, open cellar, boiler, toilet, porch rooms	3584	$1916	W. R. Walker & Son of Providence
	Cumberland-Clark Street School	4 rooms, alcove (toilet)		$13,000	W. R. Walker & Son of Providence
1906	**Warwick**-Warwick High School	6 classrooms, 1 commercial room, 2 manual training rooms, 2 teacher's rooms, 1 photographic, reception, stenography, principal's and typewriting rooms, chemical and physical labs, library, gymnasium, locker, lunch counter, toilet, and boiler rooms	1920	$75,000	Banning & Thornton of Providence
	Providence-Lexington Avenue Grammar school	12 classrooms, 1 hall, 1 library, 2 teacher's rooms, 1 principal's room, 1 janitor room, boiler, toilet, coal, recreation rooms	1920	$85,000	Martin & Hall of Providence
	Providence-Regent Avenue Primary School	11 classrooms, 1 hall, 1 teacher's & principal's & fire & office room, toilet, play, coat, supply rooms	1920	$71,000	Fred E. Field of Providence
1906	**Central Falls**-West Side Grammar School	8 classrooms, 1 janitors & principal's & teacher's room, 1 recreation room, heater, fuel, toilet, and wardrobe rooms	1920	$38,000	Robert C. N. Monahan of Pawtucket

	South Kingstown-Matnuck School	2 classrooms, 1 exercise room	1920	$4600	F. J. Sawtelle, Providence
1907	**Newport**-Rogers High school (improvement)	12 classrooms, 2 teacher's rooms, 1 principal's & recreation room, 1 gymnasium & library, toilet, office, and storage rooms		$151,280	
	Warwick-(Westcott) Warwick High School	6 classrooms, 1 commercial room, 1 principal's & reception office, 2 teacher's & manual training rooms, chemical, physical, stenography, and photographic labs, library, locker, boiler, and lunch counter rooms		$75,000	Banning & Thornton of Providence
	Barrington-Hampden Meadow School	2 classrooms, 2 entrances, 1 bicycle & play room, teacher's closets,	4067	$5363	Richard C. Sanders of Providence
	East Providence-Brightridge Primary School	2 classrooms, boiler room		$4828	Stone, Carpenter, and Sheldon, Providence
1908					
1909	**Exeter**-RI School For The Feeble-Minded	boys dormitory, farm house, administration		$29,460.72	
	Wickford-North Kingstown High School	4 classrooms, 3 recitation rooms, 1 chemical lab, 1 hall & principal's office & teacher's room, 2 recreation rooms, toilet, storage,	6,790	$30,000	William R. Walker & Son of Providence
	Providence-Temple Street School	12 classrooms, 1 hall & principal's office & teacher's room, boiler, toilet, storage, janitor	11,552	$91,000	Martin and Hall of Providence

(*continued*)

(continued)

Year	*School name*	*Program spaces*	*Square footage*	*Cost*	*Architects*
	Cranston-Auburn School	8 classrooms, 1 teacher's room & principal's office, 1 recreation, coat & boiler room		$28,748	Angell and Swift of Providence
	Cranston-Edgewood School	5 classrooms, 3 extra rooms, 1 hall		$31,369.04	Banning & Thornton of Providence
	Cranston-Thornton School	6 classrooms		$21,642.91	Banning & Thornton of Providence
	Cranston-Elmwood Avenue School	2 classrooms, 1 teacher's room & janitors room		$10,150.89	Angell and Swift of Providence
	Warwick-Pontiac School	6 classrooms, 1 hall & 2 teacher's rooms		$22,000	William R. Walker & Son of Providence
	Lincoln-Albion School	4 classrooms, 2 teacher's rooms principal's office, toilet, boiler, & play		$9,000	Robert C. N. Monahan of Pawtucket
1909	**Middletown**-Witherbee School	1 classroom, 2 coat rooms		$3500	Kerr and Beeson of Newport
1910	**Bristol**-Colt Memorial High School	4 classrooms, 2 teacher's rooms, 1 hall & library, 1 biological, physical, and chemical lab, 1 principal's office & typewriting, and drawing room, 1 lecture room, lunch, furnace, and toilet rooms		$250,000	Cooper and Bailey of Boston

	Pawtucket-Prospect Street School	13 classrooms, 2 kindergarten rooms, 1 hall, principal's office & teacher's room, storage, porches, boiler, bicycle, toilet, loft, and recreation	$65,000	William R. Walker & Son of Providence
	Providence-Veazie Street Grammar School	12 classrooms, 1 hall & library, 1 principal's office, 2 play, and teacher's rooms, shower, janitor, boiler, and toilet rooms	$86,000	Clarke, Howe and Homer of Providence
	Warren-Child Street School	4 classrooms, 2 halls, 1 principal's, and teacher's room, toilet and coat rooms	$12,000	Robert C. N. Monahan of Pawtucket
	Smithfield-Esmond School	2 classrooms & hall, coat rooms	$13,000	Martin and Hall of Providence
	Portsmouth-Newtown School	3 classrooms, coat rooms	$6,000	John A. Coggeshall, Portsmouth
1911	**East Providence**-East Providence High School	8 classrooms, 1 hall & commercial, 1 library & gymnasium, 1 typewriting room, 1 teacher's office & principal's room, physical and chemical labs, boiler, training, shower, locker, and toilet rooms	$79,000	Banning and Thornton of Providence
	Newport-Mumford School	8 classrooms, 2 teacher's rooms, 1 recreation room, coat, play, toilet, boiler, store rooms	$45,000	Darlington and Slade of Newport
	South Kingstown-Wakefield Grammar School	8 classrooms, 1 teacher's & committee room, toilet, play, and coat rooms	$29,000	Clarke, Howe and Homer of Providence

(*continued*)

(continued)

Year	*School name*	*Program spaces*	*Square footage*	*Cost*	*Architects*
	Woonsocket-Pothier School	6 classrooms, 1 recreation room, 1 office, furnace, firing, play, toilet, and coat rooms	4050	$28,000	Fontaine & Kinnicutt of Woonsocket
	Burrillville-Oakland School	2 classrooms, 2 play rooms, toilet, and heater rooms		$3500	Walter L. Collins of Milford, MA
	Tiverton-Lincoln School	2 classrooms, 2 play rooms, 1 library	2736	$7000	Walter L. Collins of Milford, MA
	Warwick-Lincoln Park School	2 classrooms, 2 wardrobe rooms, 2 teacher's, and supply rooms		$8000	Angell and Swift of Providence
1912	**Wakefield**-South Kingstown High School	5 classrooms, 3 unfinished rooms, 2 recitation room, 1 hall & teacher's room. 1 principal's office & store room, Chemical and Physical labs, boiler, toilet, locker, coal, heater, & coats		$42,500	Clarke, Howe and Homer of Providence
	Providence-Branch Avenue Primary School	10 classrooms, 2 recreation rooms, principal's, teacher's, coat, toilet, play, bath and store rooms	8928	$64,278	Martin and Hall of Providence
	Johnston-Lincoln School	4 classrooms, 2 play rooms, toilet, teacher's, and coats rooms		$7100	Frank F. Potter of Providence
1913					
1914	**East Providence**-Rumford Grammar School	6 classrooms, 1 principal's office, 1 teacher's room, 1 hall, library, store, toilet, play, coat, recreation,	6016	$40,000	Leslie P. Langworthy and Son of Providence

	South Kingston-West Kingston School	2 classrooms, supply and play rooms	1944	$8500	Angell and Swift of Providence
	Warwick-Greenwood School	2 classrooms, 2 coat closets & play rooms	1881	$6100	Frank F. Potter of Providence
	Westerly-Portable School-House	2 classrooms	1800	$1250	American Portable House Co of Seattle, WA
	Tiverton-Commodore Perry School	1 classroom, 1 teacher's room		$3000	Joseph Darling, Fall River, MA
1914	**Glocester**-Clarkville School	1 classroom, 1 alcove (toilet)		$728.23	
1915	**Lincoln**-Manville Grammar School	8 classrooms, 2 teacher's rooms, 2 play rooms, toilet, boiler, store, and coats		$20,000	Charles H. Learned, Lonsdale
	North Providence-Greystone School	4 classrooms, teacher's, store, principal's, toilet, coat, boiler, and play rooms		$11,500	Burritt S. D. Martin of Providence
	Warwick-Bayside School	4 classrooms, 1 hall, play, teacher's, principal, coat, toilet, boiler, and store rooms		$12,500	T. J. H. Peirce of Providence
	North Kingstown-Slocum School	1 classroom		$2,262.91	William R. Walker & Son of Providence
1916	**Woonsocket**-Woonsocket High School	9 classrooms, 4 recreation rooms, 1 principal's & office, 1 library, hall, gym, chemical, physical, biological labs, drawing, and typewriting rooms, lecture, cooking, play, coat, lunch, toilet, locker, bank and boiler rooms	11,534		Walter F. Fortaine

(*continued*)

(continued)

Year	*School name*	*Program spaces*	*Square footage*	*Cost*	*Architects*
	West Warwick-Natick Grammar School	8 classrooms, 4 entrances, 2 play rooms, 2 coat rooms per classroom, 1 principal office, 1 teacher's, & toilet rooms		$42,000	
1917	**Warwick**-Hillsgrove School	6 classrooms, 1 hall, 1 teacher's room, 1 principal's office, 1 play room, manual training, toilet, boiler, and storage rooms	3741	$21,035.75	
	Lincoln-Saylesville School	6 classrooms, play, toilet, and coat rooms		$25,000	
	Portsmouth-Quaker Hill School	2 classrooms, 2 coat rooms, 2 recreation rooms, toilet rooms	1922	$9722.19	
	Johnston-Simmonsville School	2 classrooms,			
	Providence-Bridgham School	30 rooms (total), 1 hall, toilets, class, office, play, boiler, coat, and storage rooms			Hoppin & Field of Providence
	North Providence-Vincent Avenue School	Portable Schoolhouse 2 class rooms			
1918	**Newport**-John Clarke School	9 classrooms, 1 principal office, 1 teacher's room, 1 sewing & cooking & wood working & manual training room, boiler, coat, play, and toilet rooms			
1918	**Providence**-John Howland School	10 classrooms, 1 hall, 1 sewing & cooking & wood working & manual training room, 1 principal's office & teacher's room, boiler, coat, play, and toilet rooms	13,500		
	Warren-Warren Grammar School	8 classrooms, boiler, coat, play, and toilet rooms			Burritt S. D. Martin of Providence

	Pawtucket-James C. Potter School	10 classrooms, 1 principal office, 1 teacher's room, 1 kitchen, sewing, cooking & lunch room,	13,824		
	Providence-Laurel Hill Avenue School	11 classrooms, 1 hall & balcony, 1 sewing & cooking & wood working & manual training room, 1 principal's office & teacher's room, boiler, coat, play, rest and toilet rooms	12,450		
	Woonsocket-McFee School	8 classrooms, 2 teacher's rooms & principal office, boiler, coat, stock, play, and toilet rooms			Walter F. Fontaine
	Pawtucket-Abbott Street School	13 classrooms, 1 principal's office, 1 teacher's room, boiler, coat, play, storage, janitor, and toilet rooms	11,997		
1918	**Warwick**-Buttonwoods School	3 classrooms, 1 teacher's rest room, boiler, coat, recreation and toilet rooms	3240	$13,427.94	
	Providence-George J. West School	3 classrooms, 1 hall, cooking room, boiler, coat, play, and toilet rooms	12,000		Murphy, Hindle & Wright
	Warwick-Spring Green School	2 classrooms, 1 teacher's & Principal's & rest rooms, boiler, coat, recreation, and toilet	3564	$11,933.73	
1919	**Warwick**-Cowesett School(should be under 1918)	2 classrooms, 1 hall, 1 teacher's room, boiler, coat, recreation, and toilet rooms	3960	$18,375.42	
	Pawtucket-Nathanael Greene School	20 classrooms, 1 teacher's & rest room, 1 auditorium & library, 2 dinning room, 1 principal's office, 1 kitchen & lunch room, toilet, boiler, and storage rooms			Robert C. Monahan of Pawtucket
	East Providence-Tristam Burges School	4 classrooms, 1 teacher's room, 1 library & rest room	4675	$26,500	

(*continued*)

(continued)

Year	*School name*	*Program spaces*	*Square footage*	*Cost*	*Architects*
	Barrington-Leander R. Peck School	1 hall, 1 teacher's & rest room, 1 principal's office, 1 kitchen & lunch room, toilet, boiler, play, and storage rooms			
1919	**Providence**-Esek Hopkins School	28 classrooms, 3 teacher's rooms, 1 hall, 1 principal's, 1 kitchen & lunch room, rest, toilet, janitor, boiler, coat, play, & storage rooms	12,600		William R. Walker & Son of Providence
	Middletown-Berkeley School	3 rooms (total)	5040	$12,494.69	
	Bristol-John Post Reynolds School	11 classrooms, 1 hall, 1 teacher's & superintendent's room, 1 principal's office, toilet, boiler, play, rest and storage rooms	11,868		Clarke & Howe of Providence
	Tiverton-Eliza H. L. Barker School	4 classrooms, toilet rooms	3850		
1920	**North Smithfield**-Union Village School(Should be under 1919)	4 classrooms, 1 principal's office, 1 teacher's room, recreation, boiler and toilet rooms			William R. Walker & Son of Providence
	Woonsocket-Fifth Avenue School	8 classrooms, 1 hall, 1 teacher's & rest room, 1 principal's office, toilet, boiler, play, and storage rooms		$60,000	Walter F. Fontaine
	Burrillville-Burrillville High School	6 classrooms, 1 hall, physical and chemical labs, toilet, boiler, janitor, and storage rooms		$63,000	Thomas S. McLaughlin of Providence

1920	**Charlestown**-Pawcatuck Valley School	4 classrooms			
1921	**Barrington**-Maple Avenue School	4 classrooms, 1 teacher's room, recreation, boiler, and toilet rooms			Wm. Walker & Son
	Warren-Windmill Hill School	2 classrooms	3000		
1922	**Lincoln**-Lincoln Memorial School	2 classrooms, toilet, boiler, janitor, and storage rooms		$72,000	John O'Malley
	Johnston-Thornton School	10 classrooms, 1 teacher's room, 1 principal's office, toilet, boiler, janitor, and storage rooms			Walker Company

Index[1]

A
Abjecting, ix
Accommodationist, 158
Achievement, 13, 54, 55, 141, 159, 174, 175, 183
Afrocentrist, 158, 159
Alcott Plan, 39
American, ix, x, xiii, 1, 2, 4, 5, 9, 10, 12, 13, 17, 18, 21, 21n2, 24, 26, 26n6, 27, 30, 34, 41–43, 45, 51, 53, 55, 63, 68–70, 75, 89, 107, 119, 120, 124, 127, 129, 133, 148, 150–152, 154, 156–158, 162, 167, 168, 170–174, 173n2, 176, 181, 187
Ancient languages, 31, 33
Architects, 3, 6, 9, 13, 28, 35, 40, 40n13, 60, 63, 70, 83, 103, 138, 150, 187
Architecture, ix, x, xiii, xiv, 1, 2, 2n1, 4–6, 8, 10, 12, 17, 18, 20–22, 25, 26n6, 28, 29, 34–37, 34n9, 40–42, 42n15, 49, 50, 52, 63, 68–70, 76, 81, 82, 84–88, 104n7, 107, 114, 119–121, 133–141, 145, 149–153, 155, 156, 162, 168, 170, 179–181, 183–186, 189
Assimilation, xii, 118, 156
Assimilative process, 118

B
Banking education, 78, 152
Banking model, 134, 144, 152, 161
Being, ix, xi, xv, 1, 9, 11, 12, 17, 25, 39, 51, 53, 60, 70, 76, 84, 86, 118, 123, 125, 126, 129–131, 133, 134, 138, 140, 142, 152, 154, 156, 162, 172, 178, 181, 183, 185, 186, 189
Black Nationalist, 158
Blue-collar, 124
Broad, 31, 32, 41, 63, 69, 78, 105, 129, 138, 168

[1] Note: Page numbers followed by 'n' refer to notes.

© The Author(s) 2018

J. da Silva, *School(house) Design and Curriculum in Nineteenth Century America*, https://doi.org/10.1007/978-3-319-78586-8

C
Child study, 46, 47, 171
Circular, 18, 159
Civil society, 118–121, 125, 126, 154, 155
Class, ix, xi, xiii, 1, 3, 4, 6, 11, 13, 32n8, 36, 39, 49, 51, 52, 80, 83, 85, 86, 108, 111, 121, 123–126, 128, 132, 136, 137, 144, 150, 153–157, 161, 162, 171, 172, 175, 176n9, 177
Classical, 21, 22, 30
Colonial, 9, 18, 22, 24, 26–28, 75, 77, 87, 126, 128
Colonialism, 10, 158, 159, 171
Come into presence, 134, 182
Committee of Fifteen, 45, 46, 170
Committee of Ten, 45, 46, 46n17, 82, 170
Commodity, 138
Common, xiv, 2, 13, 27, 29, 32, 35–37, 37n11, 41, 48, 51, 52, 55, 60, 61, 66, 67, 77, 78n2, 81, 84, 86, 94, 95, 99, 100, 107, 109, 120, 121, 123, 126, 133, 134, 136, 137, 144, 145, 149, 151, 152, 160, 162, 167, 170, 177, 179, 180, 182, 184
Common schools, 27, 35, 37, 41, 43, 78, 81, 95, 107, 144, 170
Constructs, 11, 122, 126
Continuity, 8, 48
Cook County Normal School, 53
Correspondence principle, 125
Critical thinking, 49, 69
Crow Island School, 63
Cultural capital, 52, 59, 123, 126, 132, 138, 144, 172, 176
Cultural movements, 9
Cultural reproduction, 142, 171
Currere, 162
Curriculum, ix, 2, 2n2, 5, 6, 8–13, 17, 25, 31, 33, 34, 36, 38n12, 44–49, 47n18, 52, 56–58, 61, 63, 66–68, 79, 82, 85, 87, 92n6, 99, 104, 111, 114, 119, 120, 122, 125, 127, 129, 131–134, 137, 142, 151, 153–159, 161, 168, 170, 177, 179, 181, 184, 186, 188

D
Deep, 31, 32, 41, 69, 78, 105, 138, 168
Delight, 138
Democratic, x, xiv, 1, 10, 12, 13, 20, 26, 43, 50, 59, 67, 121, 154, 159, 160, 162, 168, 171, 177, 178, 181, 183, 185, 186, 189
Developmentalists, 5, 10, 44, 46, 47, 60, 131
Disciplinary pedagogies, 69
Discipline and Punish, 141, 154
Discourse, 2, 53n20, 105n7, 121, 132, 134, 140, 142, 149, 160, 170, 174, 178, 180
Discursive, 120, 121, 124, 128, 133, 140, 142, 155
Disparities, 4, 35, 118, 171, 175, 177, 183
District, 3, 7, 37, 108
Diverse, xv, 5, 13, 24, 35, 50, 52, 56, 121, 128, 134, 171, 185, 187, 189
Dominant ideologies, 4, 135
Dwell/dwelling, ix, x, 2, 6, 8, 13, 17, 20, 24, 60, 68, 70, 118, 119, 127, 133–136, 139, 142, 155, 156, 173, 182, 183, 186, 188, 189

E
Educational specification, 7
Educators, 6–8, 12, 13, 35, 40, 41, 44, 47, 53, 56, 58, 60, 68, 69, 131, 161, 171, 176, 177, 179, 184, 187
Efficiency factor, 103

Enlightenment, ix, 9–11, 18, 27, 28, 35, 52, 69, 78, 105n7, 128, 140, 168, 170
Epicenter, 23, 43, 76, 154, 171
Epistemological, 6, 11, 13, 18, 18n1, 21n2, 126, 138, 152
Epistemologies, 11, 12, 18, 27, 69, 142, 152, 156, 158, 159, 161, 176n9
Essence of being, 134
Eurocentric, 11, 156, 168, 172, 176

F
Facher, 37
Feminists, 162
Firmness, 138
Formative, x, 2, 3, 6, 8, 11, 68, 70, 75, 81, 105n7, 114, 117, 119, 120, 127, 134, 136, 137, 140, 149, 150, 155–157, 161, 167, 172, 184–186
Freedom, 18, 22, 26, 46, 75, 87, 130, 134, 156, 177
Free play, 47, 51
Functionalist, 42, 158

G
Gender, 3, 4, 6, 39, 41, 51, 59, 63, 94, 98, 100, 137, 155–157, 172
Gothic, 22, 24, 42, 77, 86, 94, 104, 137, 138
Governance, 4, 20, 80, 137, 140, 170, 179
Grammar, 11, 40, 41, 44, 97, 100, 103, 104
Gross National Product (GNP), 58, 132, 149

H
Habitus, 123, 126, 132
Harmonious intelligence, 37n11
Harmonious society, 54
Hegemony, 9, 12, 18, 69, 121, 123, 129, 131, 136, 138, 152–155, 157, 159, 161, 162, 172, 173
Herbartians, 44, 53
Hidden curriculum, 125
Hotspot, 10
Humanism, 5, 18, 133, 139
Humanistic, 6, 41, 47, 52, 128–130, 137–140
Humanists, 5, 44, 46, 129, 131
Hysterical, 156

I
Ideological, xiii, 9–11, 21, 119, 122, 125, 127, 130, 136, 153, 157, 161
Ideological state apparatuses (ISA), 122
Ideologies, 5–7, 10, 11, 43, 92n6, 94, 95, 99, 101, 104, 128, 129, 133, 136, 138, 139, 153–156, 159, 162, 180
Ideology and Ideological Apparatuses, 122
Ideo-spatial nexus of school design, 9, 157
Indigenous, 9, 18, 20, 21, 69
Individual, x, 8, 20, 21, 36, 50, 52, 55, 56, 58, 124, 128, 134, 148, 155, 156, 176n9, 183
Industrial revolution, 9, 10, 27, 29, 44, 76
Inequities, 4, 13, 52, 118, 120, 126, 157, 177, 189
Interaction, 8
Intermediate, 37, 84

L
Laboratory school, 8, 49
Labour, 22, 70, 172
Lancaster system, 29

Learning, xi, 1, 2, 2n2, 7, 8, 12, 24, 29, 36, 41, 45, 47, 49, 53, 57, 63, 68, 80, 86, 107, 128, 129, 133, 141, 152, 158, 159, 161, 173, 177, 181, 185, 187–189
Learning experience, 7
Lecturing, 25
Liberal, 31–33, 40, 69, 78, 81, 119, 129, 151, 158, 159, 168, 181
Liberalist/liberalism, 9, 28, 69
Liberatory, 10, 12, 69, 168, 170
Life adjustment, 10, 67, 68
Linearities, 18

M
Mechanisms of control, 141
Medieval, 22
Merit, 59
Meritocracy, 155
Mind (as muscle), 33, 41
Mixed, 37
Modernity, 9, 17
Monitorial, 29, 36, 84, 143
Monitorial school, 29

N
Nation At Risk, 174, 175
Native Americans, 18, 20–22, 24, 25, 75, 131, 173
No Child Left Behind Act (NCLB), 174, 175, 176n9, 177
Normal, 37, 81, 107, 133, 143–145, 148–154, 162
Normative, xv, 11, 12, 18, 122, 135, 142, 155, 156, 172
Norms, ix, xiv, 2, 9–12, 22, 27, 59, 68–70, 81, 85, 86, 103, 105, 105n7, 107, 111, 114, 118, 120–122, 124–126, 130, 133, 134, 136–138, 140, 142, 150–154, 156–158, 160, 161, 167, 168, 171, 173, 180, 181, 189

O
Ontology, 6, 133
Oppressive, 13, 122, 154, 157, 161, 180
Organic, 42, 138
Orientations, 5, 158–161
Other, 122n1, 139, 140, 153, 156, 157
Othering, 12

P
Panoptic, 140, 142
Panopticon, 142
Patriarchal, 12, 13, 137, 150, 154–156, 162
Pedagogies, ix, xi, xii, 9–11, 13, 25, 33, 34n9, 37, 37n11, 41, 44, 45, 47, 50, 52, 55, 59, 60, 68, 69, 78, 81, 82, 89, 99, 100, 114, 118, 120, 127, 130, 131, 136, 137, 141, 144, 151, 153, 155, 158, 159, 162, 168, 173, 181, 185, 189
Philadelphia Plan, 41
Pluralist, 18
Power, xiv, 2, 3, 7, 8, 11, 17, 21n2, 45, 51, 55, 80, 104n7, 105, 117, 121, 122, 125, 126, 137, 139, 141, 149, 152–154, 156, 158, 161, 170, 171, 173, 185, 186
Power dynamics, 126, 140, 142
Primary, 7, 18, 26, 34, 37, 49, 50, 57, 66, 70, 75, 79, 80, 82, 84, 84n4, 108, 123, 127, 135, 142, 143, 145, 168, 173
Prussian, 40
Public high, 30, 37
Public realm, 119–121, 127
Puritan, 9, 22, 24n4, 34, 76

Q
Quincy Plan, 40, 41, 46, 83, 92, 95, 99, 100, 103

R
Race, 3, 4, 6, 51, 155–160, 183
Reasonable, 12, 69, 156
Recitation, 11, 25, 34, 36, 39, 60, 69, 82, 86, 100, 108, 136, 141, 144, 145, 158, 168
Reconceptualist, 161
Reconstructionist, 158
Religious freedom, 23, 75, 87
Religious intolerance, 22
Repressive state apparatuses (RSA), 122
Reproduce of the relations of production, 122
Republican, 26
Residual pastness, 5, 10, 92, 92n6, 101, 133, 136, 138, 181, 185, 187, 188
Resistant, 12
Resistant pedagogues, 12, 181
Rote, 9, 11, 12, 53, 69, 78, 131, 141, 144, 151, 152, 168, 172, 173, 177, 181, 182

S
Savage, 153, 156
Schoolhouse, xiv, 2–6, 2n1, 8–11, 13, 24, 25, 25n5, 27, 30, 34–36, 34n9, 38, 40, 41, 47n18, 49, 50, 61, 63, 76, 77, 82, 87, 88, 99, 103, 104, 114, 119, 120, 127, 133, 134, 137, 140, 150, 152, 156, 180, 183, 185, 186, 189
Schooling, ix, x, 1, 2, 2n1, 6, 9–13, 25–27, 29, 35, 39, 43, 46, 50, 51, 56, 57, 61, 68, 77, 78, 78n2, 82, 84, 88, 117, 119–122, 125, 126, 131, 133, 134, 136, 141, 143–145, 148–151, 153, 156–159, 162, 167, 168, 170–173, 175, 177, 178, 181–183, 185, 186, 189
Schoolmaster, 24, 25, 77
Scientific management, x, 6, 9–11, 44, 50, 52, 54–57, 60, 66, 68–70, 77, 81, 82, 87, 88, 95, 99, 101, 103, 104, 111, 114, 119, 120, 124, 127, 131, 132, 134, 136, 144, 145, 148–151, 153–155, 158, 161, 168, 170, 171, 177, 181, 183, 184
Secondary, xiii, 7, 21n2, 24, 37, 67, 82, 88
Segregative racial dynamics, 157
Silenced voices, 12
Simultaneous, 36
Skill-and-drill, 12, 151, 175, 177
Social constructions, 6
Social control, 4, 43, 54, 55, 70, 81, 83, 127, 181
Social Darwinism, 50
Social efficiency, 5, 10, 44, 52, 54, 55, 60, 66–68, 70, 76, 83, 89, 101, 103, 111, 131, 153, 154, 171, 183
Social efficiency educators, 5, 10, 54, 60, 83, 89, 131
Socialization, 118, 122, 124, 127
Social justice, 51n19, 118, 128, 131, 139, 183
Social meliorists, 5, 10, 44, 50, 52, 60, 171
Social production, 119, 152
Social reconstructionists, 5, 44, 50
Social (re)production, 117, 120, 143, 154
Social will formations, 120, 121, 127, 132, 144
Solid, 31, 32, 41, 69, 78, 80, 82, 85, 93, 105, 138, 168, 183
Spaces, ix, xi, xiv, 2n1, 7, 8, 11, 13, 18, 20, 21, 23n3, 25, 34, 37, 39–41, 50, 57, 60, 75, 78, 80, 82, 83, 86–89, 87n5, 91, 95, 100, 103, 104, 107, 108, 113, 118, 119, 121, 124, 127, 130, 139, 142, 145, 150, 154, 181, 182, 187–189

Spatiality, ix, 13, 105n7, 139, 140, 155
Spatial school design nexus, 119, 135, 136, 185
Standardized testing, 12
State Normal School, 11, 107–109, 143–145, 148, 149, 151
State, economic, and cultural, 119, 121
Structuring Sociality, 11
Student, ix, xiv, 8–11, 13, 25, 29, 32, 33, 39–41, 48–50, 54, 55, 57, 58, 60, 67–70, 77, 80, 82, 85, 89, 111, 114, 117–119, 122, 125, 127, 129, 131, 134, 135, 139, 141–143, 152–155, 157, 160, 170–172, 174, 178, 181, 183, 185, 187–189
Subject, 2n2, 6, 9, 18, 22, 25, 31, 32, 45, 47, 48, 56, 60, 69, 82, 109, 117, 123, 126, 128, 129, 133, 135, 138, 141–143, 149, 152, 154, 156, 183
Subjectivity, xiii, xiv, 12, 13, 152, 177
Subject matter, 45, 48, 49
Supplementary, 37

T

Taylorism, 66
Teacher training, 45, 142–144, 151, 153
Teaching, xi, 2n2, 8, 35, 46, 47, 49, 53, 57, 63, 68, 69, 78, 107–109, 125, 134, 137, 143, 150–152, 159, 177, 182
Traditionalist, 9, 12, 25, 43, 45, 70, 77–79, 81, 82, 86, 88, 95, 99, 100, 104, 114, 129, 132, 144, 145, 149, 151–154, 156, 161, 168, 170
Transcendental, 42
Truth, 11, 48, 105n7, 129, 140–142, 152, 174n3
Typology, 25

U

Unreasonable, 156

V

Vocational education, 132, 144, 151, 154, 170

W

Ways of knowing, 11
Western epistemologies, 12, 133, 153, 154, 172, 182
Western hegemony, 6
Western philosophy, 21
Western thought, 21, 129
Western ways of thinking, 12
Wetu, 9, 18, 20
What knowledge, 5, 128, 142
White, xi, xiii, 10, 12, 13, 35n10, 37, 54, 69, 84, 108, 109, 121, 124, 126, 128–130, 132, 136, 137, 150, 152, 154–159, 162, 170–172, 175
White-collar, 124
White male, 12, 109
Whose knowledge, 5, 128
Written system of architecture, 139

Y

Yale Report, 6, 9–11, 24n4, 31–34, 34n9, 37, 41, 43, 45, 48, 55, 60, 69, 70, 78, 79, 81, 82, 84, 85, 87n5, 94, 99, 100, 104–107, 114, 119, 120, 127, 129–132, 134, 136, 138, 141, 143–145, 151–153, 168, 170, 171, 174n3, 177, 184

The manufacturer's authorised representative in the EU is Springer
Nature Customer Service Centre GmbH, Europaplatz 3, 69115 Heidelberg,
Germany. If you have any concerns regarding our products, please
contact ProductSafety@springernature.com

Printed and bound by CPI Group (UK) Ltd, Croydon, CR0 4YY
05/10/2026
02228128-0003